'Being sustainable is an ever-evolving concept as expectations about economic growth, investment risk and the role of companies in society are influenced by new and complex considerations. Business leaders are being pulled in all directions. The research distilled by Paolo Taticchi and Melina Corvaglia-Charrey in this book can only be helpful.'
**Silvia Pavoni, Editor in Chief, *The Banker* and Founder and former Editor of *Sustainable Views*, both part of the Financial Times Group**

'In a world where the challenges we face are complex and urgent, *How to Be Sustainable* offers a much-needed blueprint for real, actionable change. Paolo Taticchi and Melina Corvaglia-Charrey provide a compelling guide for businesses and leaders who are serious about moving beyond words to create lasting impact. With insights from top sustainability leaders and practical strategies, this book is an invaluable resource for anyone looking to lead with purpose and shape a sustainable future. A must-read for today's leaders and tomorrow's changemakers.'
**Jan Mühlfeit, former Chairman Europe, Microsoft Corporation**

'The nature of the risks a company faces in the competitive market battlefield continues to change. Understanding this evolution is a crucial step in selecting the risks worth taking and the way to manage them properly. It is also important to choose those risks that need to be avoided. A sustainable strategy is about projecting a company's success over a longer period of time and choosing the right risks. This book is a great manual for achieving this goal. A sustainable company is a company that knows and consciously manages the proper risk portfolio.'
**Francesco Starace, Partner at EQT Group and SBTi Chair**

# How to Be Sustainable

*Business strategies for leading change*

Paolo Taticchi
Melina Corvaglia-Charrey

KoganPage

First published in Great Britain and the United States in 2025 by Kogan Page Limited

**Kogan Page**
Kogan Page Ltd, 2nd Floor, 45 Gee Street, London EC1V 3RS, United Kingdom
Kogan Page Inc, 8 W 38th Street, Suite 90, New York, NY 10018, USA
www.koganpage.com

**EU Representative (GPSR)**
Authorised Rep Compliance Ltd, Ground Floor, 71 Lower Baggot Street, Dublin D02 P593, Ireland
www.arccompliance.com

Kogan Page books are printed on paper from sustainable forests.

**ISBNs**
Hardback    978 1 3986 1854 1
Paperback   978 1 3986 1852 7
Ebook       978 1 3986 1853 4

**British Library Cataloguing-in-Publication Data**
A CIP record for this book is available from the British Library.

**Library of Congress Control Number**
2024050241

Typeset by Hong Kong FIVE Workshop
Print production managed by Jellyfish
Printed and bound by CPI Group (UK) Ltd, Croydon, CR0 4YY

*To my incredible wife, Manuela, whose unwavering support and love are my greatest treasures. And to my cherished sons, William, Derek and Jackson, who light up my world. I love you to the moon and back.*
*Paolo*

*For my loving mother, Maria, and in memory of my father, Quintino, whose love and support I cherish. And to Fabien and our nature-loving daughters, Chloé and Amélie – my northern stars who guide and inspire me every day.*
*Melina*

# CONTENTS

# ABOUT THE AUTHORS

## Paolo Taticchi

Paolo Taticchi is Professor in Strategy and Sustainability and School Deputy Director (MBA, Global Engagement, Executive Education) at UCL School of Management. He also serves as the Co-Director of the UCL Centre for Sustainable Business.

Highly active in executive education, Paolo has trained thousands of managers and executives from Fortune Global 500 companies and is a sought-after speaker, frequently invited to deliver keynotes at prestigious academic, governmental and industry events. His research on corporate sustainability and performance measurement is internationally recognized. Paolo's latest books, *Disruption* and *Sustainable Transformation Strategy*, were both published in 2023. Paolo is also the host of the *#InLoveWithBusiness* podcast channel. This channel is dedicated to exploring the fascinating world of business, where passion meets profession.

Paolo has significant consultancy experience in strategy and sustainability, assisting companies and governments across several countries. Paolo has received numerous awards for the impact of his work, and his projects, quotes and opinions have been featured over 350 times in international media outlets.

From 2021 to 2023, Italy's leading business daily, *Sole 24 Ore*, named Paolo the most influential Italian under 40. In 2024, he received the prestigious Stefan A Riesenfeld Memorial Award from Berkeley Law in recognition of his significant contributions to sustainable business practices.

Learn more about Paolo's work at paolotaticchi.com

## Melina Corvaglia-Charrey

Melina is a Researcher at UCL School of Management, where she works on various projects focused on business strategy and sustainability, including developing case studies and white papers. Melina is also a consultant supporting organizations with their sustainability reporting, marketing and communications. In collaboration with Professor Paolo Taticchi and Melissa Demartini, Melina co-authored a book titled *Sustainable Transformation Strategy*, published in May 2023. In 2024, Melina co-hosted a podcast series with Professor Paolo Taticchi titled *Chief Sustainability Heroes*. Leaning on her marketing and sustainability experience, Melina was also a Sustainable Content Marketing Strategist for a UK-based consulting agency specializing in the sports and sustainability field. Passionate about the role sport can play in driving sustainability forward, Melina served as a member and volunteer with Sport and Sustainability International, a not-for-profit organization that is focused on accelerating sustainability in and through sport. Previously, Melina worked in the Media Sponsorship and Marketing field for more than 15 years in Canada, where she collaborated with various Fortune 500 companies and brands to develop strategic partnership marketing initiatives, including several programmes that garnered awards from the Sponsorship Marketing Council of Canada. A mother of two young girls, Melina is motivated to collaborate with organizations and individuals who are committed to creating a better world for future generations.

# ACKNOWLEDGEMENTS

This book was made possible thanks to the invaluable contributions and support of many colleagues, industry leaders, friends and family.

In particular, we would like to thank each fearless sustainability leader (aka chief sustainability hero) we interviewed for their commitment to driving sustainable transformation in business and imparting their wealth of knowledge and passion to us and our readers.

We would also like to thank our respected academic and industry colleagues for sharing their expertise and contributing to this work: Jan Dauman, Allegra Fortunato, Adam Kingl, Sunny Lee, Andreas Rasche, Riccardo Angelini Rota and Giuseppe Stigliano.

We are incredibly grateful to the amazing team at Kogan Page whose guidance and support helped bring this book to life. A special thanks to our editor Chris Cudmore whose thoughtful feedback and notes enhanced this book for our readers. We would also like to thank Matt James, who we worked with at the onset of this project, for believing in our vision for this book and for his helpful advice from the start.

We thank the *#InLoveWithBusiness* and *#ChiefSustainabilityHeroes* podcast production team, namely Catrina Beatrice Daly and Pietro Rosignoli, for their valuable support.

We would also like to thank our loving family and friends, near and far, for their ongoing love and support.

Lastly, we would like to thank our readers for joining us on this exciting journey of sustainable transformation in business – and beyond.

# CONTRIBUTORS
*Biographies of the inspiring sustainability leaders interviewed for this book*

## Magali Anderson, Board Member, Chief Sustainability and Innovation Officer

Magali Anderson is a global sustainability leader and advocate, having started her career as a field engineer on offshore oil rigs in Nigeria. She has spent 27 years working in the oil and gas industry, living across four continents, managing large teams, P&L and transversal functional roles. She is a non-executive director for Anglo-American and Capitals Coalition. Magali's raison d'être is to transform businesses for the better. In 2016, Magali joined Holcim as Group Head of Health & Safety, before becoming Chief Sustainability Officer in 2019 and adding innovation to her remit in 2021. During her Holcim tenure, Magali was a member of the advisory boards of industry organizations: Business for Nature, the MIT Climate and Sustainability Consortium, the World Green Building Council and the 50L Home Coalition on water efficiency; and co-chair of the 2050 net-zero work for the Global Cement and Concrete Association. Prior to joining Holcim, Magali spent the majority of her career with SLB, where she started as a field engineer and progressed to Country CEO Angola, Head of Europe, and worked across roles such as VP in Marketing and Sales, VP Shared Services, and VP Maintenance. Magali ended her career at SLB in Shanghai, where she was overseeing a high-technology manufacturing centre with 800 employees. In 2022, Magali was awarded Edie Sustainability Leader of the Year and IRF Personality of the Year. She is a mentor of startups at Creative Destruction Lab and works tirelessly to promote women in the industry.

## Peter Bragg, Canon EMEA Sustainability and Government Affairs Director

Peter Bragg is the EMEA Sustainability and Government Affairs Director at Canon. An internationally experienced senior sustainability and environmental leader, Peter has a wealth of experience in developing organizational strategies, driving transformational change and delivering successful business outcomes in sustainability and corporate social responsibility programmes across a range of sectors in the UK, Europe and Australia. He previously worked as Director of Environment & Sustainability at Jacobs, a professional services firm. Prior to that he held senior environment and sustainability roles, including at Sydney Trains, Eurostar and Network Rail.

## David Costa, Chief Sustainability Business Officer at NTT DATA Inc. Global

David Costa is the Chief Sustainability Business Officer for NTT DATA Inc. Global. David brings over 27 years of experience in the management and IT consulting industry, showcasing a blend of creativity, emotional intelligence and fortitude to deliver. His passion for people and commitment to inspiring teams sets him apart as a leader who drives growth and profitability while fostering a culture of trust and high-standard teamwork. NTT DATA works to improve clients' business performance, through transformation, technology and business consulting. In addition to his role at NTT DATA Inc. Global, David consults and advises universities and charities in a voluntary capacity. He also serves as an unpaid non-executive member of the Board of Directors of Maanch (UK), a group that provides SaaS and advisory solutions around ESG and sustainability data to investors, asset managers, corporates and donor-advised funds.

## Michelle Davies, Global Head of Sustainability at EY Law

Michelle Davies is the Global Head of Sustainability at EY Law. With over 20 years of experience working solely in sustainability, she specializes in helping clients operationalize sustainability so that they can better manage or avoid risk and importantly access value. In her role at EY, Michelle and her team advise clients on how to protect and drive value across contractual frameworks, M&A and corporate transactions, disputes and reputation management, regulatory compliance, carbon credit strategies, decarbonization planning and solutions, due diligence protocols, tech design and utilization, governance structures and infusing sustainability into legal operations. Michelle sits on many industry bodies including the Policy Committee of the Renewable Energy Association, Chair of the Climate Change Committee

Advisory Group, Chair of the REA Finance Steering Group, and the Climate Bond Initiative Advisory Board, to name a few. She has also received industry recognition for her work including being listed as a leader in renewables by The Lawyer Hot 100 lawyers, being named Solar Woman of the Year for MENA by the Middle East Solar Industry Association (MESIA), Women Powering Smart Energy Leader, being invited to the UK Government's POWERful Women Group, and named for the last three years as being one of the top 100 people in global wind power and one of the top women in global wind power by A Word About Wind. Michelle is qualified as a solicitor in England and Wales and as an attorney in New York.

## Giulia Genuardi, Managing Director at Enel Foundation, former Head of Sustainability at Enel Group

Giulia Genuardi is Managing Director of Enel Foundation, after having served as Enel Group's Head of Sustainability. She joined the Enel Group in 2003 as part of the internal auditing team, covering a wide range of roles. From 2008 to 2013, she was Secretary to the Enel SpA Supervision Council pursuant to Legislative Decree 231/01 and from 2011 to 2013 she was Compliance Officer ex Legislative Decree 231/01 in various Enel companies. From 2013 to 2024 she led sustainability activities at Enel Groups, responsible for embedding environmental, social and governance (ESG) issues into business management and financial instruments through the definition of the sustainability strategy and management of sustainability projects. She has been a board member at Enel Americas (Chile), energy company in four South American countries. Starting from 2019, she was a member of various working groups at EFRAG (European Financial Reporting Advisory Group) in Belgium and in May 2022 she was appointed member of the EFRAG Sustainability Reporting Technical Expert Group. In September 2020, she was named member of the Global Sustainability Standards Board at GRI (Global Reporting Initiative), in 2023 member of the OIC (Organismo Italiano Contabilità) Committee for sustainability standards and in 2024 member of the EU Sustainable Finance Platform. She is active in external advisory councils, working groups and steering committees (i.e. Global Compact, WBCSD, Ambrosetti, CSR Europe) on matters related to sustainability (i.e. climate change, human rights, diversity, nature). She graduated in Economics from the University of Palermo (Italy), received a master's degree in Administration, Finance and Control from Luiss

Management, and has attended education courses at IESE Business School and Bocconi. She is Professor of Corporate Social Responsibility – master's degree in Marketing and Digital Communication at LUMSA, Libera Università degli Studi Maria Ss. Assunta (Italy).

## Sam Israelit, Partner and Chief Sustainability Officer at Bain & Company

Sam Israelit is Partner and Chief Sustainability Officer at Bain & Company and is based in San Francisco. In his role, Sam works with clients in the retail, consumer products and technology industries to help them transform their operations and achieve their performance goals. His focus is on managing the end-to-end supply chain and optimizing manufacturing and distribution processes. As Bain's Chief Sustainability Officer, Sam leads Bain's Carbon Net-Negative programme, driving efforts to measure and reduce Bain's carbon footprint, source its carbon offset investments, and manage its public ESG reporting. He is also a leader in the Environment Pillar in Bain's global Social Impact Practice, working on issues related to climate change, responsible production, and land and ocean conservation. His work focuses on natural climate solutions, especially related to reforestation, sustainable agriculture and blue carbon.

## Sean Jones, Chief Sustainability Officer at Microsoft Germany

Sean Jones is the Chief Sustainability Officer at Microsoft Germany. He was appointed to the role in 2023. With a rich background spanning over 25 years in consumer goods, chemicals and digital transformation consulting, Sean is a UC Berkeley-trained chemical engineer and an INSEAD MBA holder. His journey through the sustainability landscape has significantly contributed to integrating sustainability practices within business models.

## Klaus Kunz, Head of Development at PI Industries, and Founder and Managing Director at Ephrin

Klaus Kunz is Head of Development at PI Industries and Founder and Managing Director at Ephrin, a sustainability consulting company.

Previously, Klaus held the role of VP Head of ESG Strategy at Bayer. A veteran in the field of sustainability, Klaus's tenure at Bayer spans over two decades, steering Bayer's strategic directions in sustainability, research and development on a global scale. His roles have encompassed leadership positions in research, R&D project management, regulatory and public/governmental affairs, sustainability and business stewardship. He was also responsible for stewarding the company's ESG strategy, for non-financial and sustainability reporting and engaging stakeholders on ESG and sustainability-related matters. Integrating sustainability into business has been at the core of Klaus's work for many years. Klaus holds a PhD in Organic Chemistry and an MBA and serves as a senior external advisor for Climate & Company. He is also a member of the advisory board of the Policy Liaison Group on ESG (UK), the advisory council of the Minor Use Foundation and other international initiatives. He is passionate about driving innovation, positive change and cross-cultural collaborations.

## Montse Montaner, former Chief Sustainability Officer at Novartis

Montse served as the first Chief Sustainability Officer at Novartis. She is a visionary and strategically driven transformational leader with more than three decades of international experience across large pharma companies delivering excellence in quality and manufacturing operations management and sustainability. Her strong business acumen and deep operational understanding make her very effective in defining how quality and sustainability can become a business accelerator to deliver and make a positive impact into the organization. Prior to her appointment as Chief Sustainability Officer at Novartis, Montse held the role of Chief Quality Officer, leading quality organization from research to commercial. Since joining Novartis in 2007, she has held different roles in Novartis and Sandoz, including VP Quality Technical Operations, Third Party and CMO Quality Head and Novartis Quality Management Systems & Control Operations Head. Prior to Novartis, Montse worked for more than 15 years at Sanofi where she held different leadership positions locally and globally across the corporation. Montse has received several accolades for her work, including being named a Top 100 Women in Sustainability (Ranking #1 in Pharma and #46 cross-sector), as well as being recognized in *Sustainability Magazine*'s Top 100 Leaders Programme.

## Elisa Moscolin, Executive Vice President for Sustainability and Foundation at Sage Group plc

Elisa Moscolin is a sustainability professional with a track record of driving this agenda in global blue-chip organizations. She advises boards and executive teams on sustainability strategy and execution. She has worked in the ICT and Financial Services sectors. Elisa is currently Executive Vice President for Sustainability and Foundation at Sage Group plc.; Sage is a global market leader for technology for small and medium businesses and Elisa is leading its sustainability agenda. Prior to that, Elisa was Head of Sustainability & ESG at Santander where she led the transformation from old-fashioned CSR to sustainability. During her time at Santander, Elisa turned around all legacy programmes, worked with the board and executive team to agree on the bank's ESG vision and ambition, designed a new ESG strategy, built a diverse and high-performing team, designed a sound governance and operating model, established an active dialogue with top investors and enhanced the bank's ESG credentials. Elisa was also responsible for the bank's Foundation, which she restructured by working closely with its board of trustees to enhance its governance, reputation and impact. Before Santander, Elisa worked for Vodafone Group in global and local roles in Italy, the UK and Kenya. In Kenya she worked with Safaricom, a subsidiary of Vodafone, which developed M-Pesa, the iconic mobile-based money transfer and banking platform that has greatly improved financial inclusion in the country. She is an alumna of Cambridge Institute for Sustainability Leadership and holds a master's degree in International Studies and Diplomacy. Elisa's professional ambition is to contribute to shifting the business community toward more ethical and responsible business practices.

## Garrett Quinn, Group Chief Sustainability Officer at Smurfit Westrock

Garrett Quinn has been the Group Chief Sustainability Officer at Smurfit Westrock (formerly Smurfit Kappa) since July 2021. He joined Smurfit Westrock in 2000 and has held several roles in operations across the Group in Argentina, France and Ireland before moving to the UK where he managed a number of corrugated box plants. In 2016, he took up the role of Head of Investor Relations for the Group, a position he held until 2021. Garrett holds a bachelor's degree in commerce from University College Dublin and completed his postgraduate studies with the Cambridge Institute of Sustainability Leadership. He was appointed as Director to the Smurfit Kappa Foundation in May 2022. Garrett is also the company representative to the World Business Council for Sustainable Development (WBCSD), The Conference Board (Europe) and the Consumer Goods Forum.

## Jeffrey Whitford, Vice President of Sustainability and Social Business Innovation at Merck Life Science

Jeffrey Whitford is the Vice President of Sustainability and Social Business Innovation at Merck Life Science. In this role, Jeffrey serves as a strategic partner to the Life Science Business, aiming to accelerate, embed and amplify sustainability principles and impact throughout its operations. With his profound experience and unwavering dedication to sustainability, Jeffrey provides insightful perspectives on integrating sustainable practices fundamentally within businesses, driving environmental responsibility, new business models, innovation and economic growth. Ragan & PR Daily's 2022 CSR/ESG Professional of the Year, Jeffrey was included in Fast Company's 2020 list of the Most Creative People in Business, selected as PRNEWS CSR & Nonprofit Awards' CSR Professional of the Year in 2020, and named to Assent Compliance's Top 100 Corporate Social Responsibility Influence Leaders in 2019. Most recently, under his leadership, the company was recognized as a Best Workplace for Innovators by Fast Company and received a Sustainability Excellence Award from the World Sustainability Awards. Jeffrey also serves a board member of MyGreenLab and the Advisory Board of the ACS Green Chemistry Institute.

## Charlotte Wolff-Bye, Chief Sustainability Officer at Petronas

Charlotte Wolff-Bye is the Chief Sustainability Officer at Petronas. She is an award-winning business leader at the forefront of the sustainability movement. Since joining Petronas in 2021, she has turned the company's net-zero carbon emission aspiration into management plans to drive decarbonization and social progress. Previously, Charlotte worked for Norwegian energy company Equinor as Vice President Sustainability, and she was also the company's representative on the Oil and Gas

Climate Initiative (OGCI), the World Bank's Global Gas Flaring Reduction Imitative (GGFR) and the World Business Council for Sustainable Development (WBCSD). Charlotte's earlier experiences include working in the steel, mining and telecommunications sectors. She is the recipient of Devex's leadership award for her contribution to international development and was ranked as one of the world's Top 100 Chief Sustainability Officers. She also serves on the Board of Trustees of WCMC, Cambridge, UK.

# Introduction

The industrial revolutions that characterized the last two centuries marked a significant era of transformation in society and business that saw economies shift from ones rooted in agriculture to those driven by automation, manufacturing, energy and the internet. This era signalled an exciting period that showcased what is possible when human ingenuity, creativity and innovation are channelled towards common ambitions and goals. Businesses thrived – giving rise to many of the modern-day comforts we enjoy today, such as transport, communication and digital services.

And while business was booming, it became clear over the past century that society was developing in an unsustainable way, and business and industrial models needed to evolve. Recognizing the need for the world to change course, in 1987 the United Nations (UN) defined sustainable development as 'meeting the needs of the present without compromising the ability for future generations to meet their own needs.'[1] Driven by the urgent need to address environmental degradation, ensure equitable and ethical economic growth and social inclusion, manage the pressures of population growth and urbanization, and harness technological innovations responsibly – sustainable development became a key topic in society.

Given the pivotal role businesses have played in shaping society and our modern world – by harnessing the same human ingenuity, creativity and innovation that fuelled the Industrial Revolution – businesses can undoubtedly make a significant impact in addressing today's global challenges. The need for bold and steadfast leadership has never been greater for businesses to address these challenges. And while over 90 per cent of business leaders recognize the importance of sustainability, only 60 per cent have a strategy in place.[2] Many of these strategies are inefficient, ineffective or simply don't go far enough to address the various global challenges we are facing.

With this book we invite you to join us on a journey into the evolving and dynamic world of sustainability leadership. As our planet faces unprecedented environmental and social challenges, the role of the Chief Sustainability Officer (CSO) has become increasingly important for business, society and the planet. This book invites you to explore the multifaceted nature of the CSO position, delving deep into the experiences, strategies and insights of some of the most influential sustainability leaders across various industries.

In preparation for this book, we interviewed Chief Sustainability Officers from various sectors to gain a deeper understanding of the challenges as well as the rewards that come with the task of leading sustainable transformation in business. Through our discussions, we also set out to better understand the current corporate sustainability landscape – both in terms of how far this field has evolved over the years and how far it still needs to go.

Our conversations with sustainability leaders formed the basis of a podcast series we created in parallel to writing this book, which is aptly titled *Chief Sustainability Heroes* (see Podcast links). Featured in both the podcast series and this book are the following guests:

- Magali Anderson, Board Member, Chief Sustainability and Innovation Officer
- Peter Bragg, EMEA Sustainability and Government Affairs Director at Canon
- David Costa, Chief Sustainability Business Officer at NTT DATA Inc. Global
- Michelle Davies, Global Head of Sustainability at EY Law
- Giulia Genuardi, former Head of Sustainability Planning, Performance Management and Human Rights at Enel, and current Managing Director at Enel Foundation
- Sam Israelit, Partner and Chief Sustainability Officer at Bain & Company;
- Sean Jones, Chief Sustainability Officer at Microsoft Germany
- Klaus Kunz, Head of Development at PI Industries, and Founder and Managing Director at Ephrin
- Montse Montaner, former Chief Sustainability Officer at Novartis
- Elisa Moscolin, Executive Vice President for Sustainability and Foundation at Sage
- Garrett Quinn, Group Chief Sustainability Officer at Smurfit Westrock

- Jeffrey Whitford, Vice President of Sustainability and Social Business Innovation at Merck Life Science
- Charlotte Wolff-Bye, Chief Sustainability Officer at Petronas

This book summarizes the many insightful, stimulating and even surprising accounts and examples of sustainable business practices that emerged from our discussions, as well as key insights stemming from our research and work in this field. In the chapters ahead, you will discover the multitude of responsibilities that define the CSO role. From steering companies towards greener practices to advocating for social justice, the scope of a CSO's work is vast and ever-changing. Through in-depth interviews and real-world examples, we explore how these leaders navigate the complexities of sustainability, balancing economic imperatives with sustainability-focused considerations.

Expect to gain a comprehensive understanding of the strategic imperatives that drive sustainability forward in business. Learn how CSOs integrate environmental, social and governance (ESG) factors into the core operations of their organizations, transforming challenges into opportunities for innovation and growth. You'll see how they leverage data to inform decisions, manage risks and measure progress towards ambitious sustainability goals. These leaders are not only visionaries but also pragmatic thinkers who understand the necessity of grounding their strategies in robust, actionable data.

The journey also highlights the power of collaboration. You'll read about how CSOs build partnerships within and outside their organizations, engaging with suppliers, customers and regulatory bodies to exchange knowledge and gain a better understanding of key issues affecting their stakeholders. The stories of initiatives like Canon's Young People Programme and Merck Life Science's Curiosity Cube Mobile Lab will illustrate the collective efforts and zest required to drive meaningful change. The industry-leading examples shared in this book will show you that true sustainability requires a network of committed partners working towards a common goal. They also shed light on the inspiring programmes aimed at future generations. By engaging the next generation of leaders in business and communities, CSOs are not just shaping the present but also nurturing the innovators of tomorrow. These initiatives highlight the importance of educational outreach and community engagement in creating a sustainable future. You'll be moved by the dedication of these leaders to instil a sense of environmental stewardship in young minds, ensuring that the fruit of their work endures. You will also be inspired by efforts CSOs make to engage employees on sustainability. To fulfil their ambitious sustainability goals and targets, organizations must foster a sustainability culture by engaging their employees on this journey.

As you delve into each chapter, you will be inspired by the resilience and adaptability of these leaders. The concept of 'better practices' over 'best practices' will resonate as a guiding principle, encouraging a mindset of continuous improvement and innovation. Through their stories, you'll see how sustainability is not a destination but a continuous journey – one that requires unwavering commitment and a passion for positive impact. These narratives will reveal the personal and professional growth accompanying the pursuit of sustainability, offering a deeper understanding of the challenges and rewards inherent in this path.

With this book we aim to inspire current and future leaders to embrace sustainability as an integral part of their organizational strategy. Whether you are a seasoned professional, an aspiring CSO, or simply passionate about making a difference, this book offers valuable insights and practical guidance to help you on your sustainability journey. The lessons learned from these leaders can serve as a roadmap for integrating sustainability into your own practices, providing you with the tools and knowledge needed to effect meaningful change.

As we embark on this journey, you will meet individuals who have dedicated their careers to driving change. From different industries and backgrounds, they bring unique perspectives to the table, showcasing the diverse ways in which sustainability can be approached. You'll encounter leaders who have revolutionized their industries, turning sustainability from a mere compliance issue into a core strategic priority. Their experiences highlight the versatility and creativity required to succeed in this field, offering a broad spectrum of strategies and solutions that you can adapt and implement in your own context.

You'll also read about the challenges they face, from managing complex supply chains to overcoming internal and external barriers, and how they turn these obstacles into opportunities. Their insights will demonstrate that while the path to sustainability is fraught with challenges, it is also filled with opportunities for innovation, growth and positive impact. By learning from their experiences, you can anticipate and navigate the challenges in your own journey towards sustainability.

Throughout the book, we emphasize the importance of adopting a holistic approach to sustainability. This means considering not only environmental impacts but also social and economic dimensions. You'll see how successful CSOs balance these often-competing priorities, crafting strategies that promote overall well-being and long-term success. Their holistic approach ensures that their organizations' sustainability-focused initiatives are not just effective but also equitable and inclusive, benefiting all stakeholders – today and in the future.

This book also provides practical tools and frameworks that you can use to develop and implement your own sustainability strategies. From setting measurable goals to engaging stakeholders, these tools will help you translate vision into action. The practical guidance offered here is designed to empower you, giving you the confidence and knowledge needed to drive sustainability within your organization – and beyond.

Join us as we explore the transformative power of sustainability leadership. We invite you to approach this book with an open mind and a readiness to be inspired. The insights and examples shared here are not just about the challenges that come with leading sustainability in business – but also about the successes and rewards gained along the way. They are a testament to the dedication, resilience and innovation of CSOs who are paving the way towards a more sustainable future. Let this book ignite your passion and inspire you to contribute to a more sustainable and equitable future. Together, we can create a world where business success goes hand in hand with social and environmental stewardship.

## Notes

1 United Nations, Sustainability, www.un.org/en/academic-impact/sustainability (archived at https://perma.cc/5MZ9-LPNV) (archived at https://perma.cc/ Y3LM-YH4G)

2 Amdani, Yusuf (2023) Can sustainable practices generate business? *Forbes*, 11 August, www.forbes.com/sites/forbesbooksauthors/2023/08/11/ can-sustainable-practices-generate-business/ (archived at https://perma.cc/ W6WW-XEND)

# 1

# Transforming tomorrow

*The evolution and impact of sustainable transformation*

Sustainability is no longer a choice but a necessity for modern businesses. Integrating sustainability into core business strategies enhances competitive positioning and ensures long-term profitability and compliance with emerging regulations. This chapter delves into the intricacies of building a competitive advantage through sustainability, drawing insights from research led by the authors of this book and practical case studies.

## From CSR to modern corporate sustainability

Corporate sustainability has undergone a significant transformation over the decades, evolving from a peripheral concern into a central strategic priority. Understanding this evolution is crucial for grasping the current landscape and the imperative for businesses to integrate sustainability into their core operations. This section explores the key milestones and shifts in corporate sustainability practices from the mid-20th century to the present day.

The concept of corporate social responsibility (CSR) emerged in the 1950s, primarily focusing on ethical behaviour towards society. Howard Bowen's seminal work, *Social Responsibilities of the Businessman* (1953), is often cited as the starting point of modern CSR. Bowen, exploring the intersection between business ethics and social responsibility, argued that businesses should consider a plurality of stakeholders, not just shareholders, and CSR should be integrated into strategic planning and decision-making. This pivotal thinking laid the groundwork for the idea that businesses should go beyond profit maximization to consider their broader social and ethical responsibilities.

In his 1963 book *A Business and Its Beliefs*, Thomas Watson Jr, then Chairman of IBM, eloquently captured the shifting corporate landscape, stating, 'More and more there seems to be entering into relationships between government and labour, a fourth force – the force of the public... ultimately, we are all accountable to it. We exist at its tolerance. We are bound by its laws. In planning for the future of our own particular interest, we must recognize the rights and requirements of the public and the millions of individuals that make it up.'

By the 1970s, CSR had gained widespread recognition. Archie Carroll's pyramid of CSR, introduced in 1979, provided a framework for understanding corporate responsibilities in four layers: economic, legal, ethical and philanthropic. This period saw businesses beginning to formalize their social responsibilities, often through philanthropic activities and community engagement. This quickly became widespread in corporate America. Until that moment, philanthropy, which had been on the rise for more than a century, was an activity performed by individuals (e.g. big industrial entrepreneurs of the likes of John D Rockefeller donated more than half a billion dollars to religious, educational and scientific activities).[1]

However, this era also sparked a significant debate over the role of businesses in society, particularly highlighted by economist Milton Friedman's views on CSR. The 1976 Nobel Memorial Prize in Economic Sciences recipient, in his influential 1970 article 'The social responsibility of business is to increase its profits', argued that the primary responsibility of a business is to its shareholders and that engaging in social or environmental efforts beyond what is legally required was essentially a misallocation of resources. Building on the concepts of agency theory, Friedman asserted that managers are agents of the shareholders and therefore must operate the business following their desires, which typically involve maximizing profits within the bounds of the law and ethical custom. Friedman's perspective emphasized that businesses should not take on the role of social agents, a responsibility he believed belonged to individuals and government institutions.

Friedman's view, often perceived as controversial, has been largely misinterpreted. His shareholder-centric view of business was shaped by the fact that at the time shareholders were mainly interested in profit, and there was less pressure from society for businesses to be responsible and to impact positively on a range of social matters. As we'll discuss later, the world – and business with it – has evolved significantly since then.

Despite Friedman's critiques, many businesses continued to embrace CSR in the 1970s and 1980s, driven by a combination of ethical motivations and strategic considerations. They recognized that CSR initiatives, focused on developing programmes and initiatives with the aim of creating a positive social impact, were key to enhancing corporate reputation.

The predominant philanthropic approach, where part of revenue/profit was reinvested to create some social good, however, quickly led CSR to be completely disconnected from real business, strategy and decision-making. Bowen's seminal vision didn't materialize, with CSR in the 1970s and 1980s substantially becoming a marketing and communication topic.

The 1990s marked a significant shift with the introduction of the triple bottom line (TBL) by John Elkington in 1994. TBL expanded the notion of corporate performance to include social and environmental dimensions alongside economic ones. This approach argued that businesses should simultaneously focus on 'people, planet and profit' (also known as the 3Ps) to achieve true sustainability. The concept emphasized that financial success should not come at the expense of social equity and environmental health. During this period, companies began to adopt more comprehensive sustainability practices, integrating them into their core strategies and operations.

However, new ideas weren't the only thing driving change in the 1990s. The spread of media and investigative journalism (later supported and accelerated by the internet and social media) increased the exposure of business activities and pushed corporations to become more transparent.

The first big corporate scandals in the 1990s highlighted all the shortcomings of philanthropy-based CSR approaches. In our view, there was one scandal in particular that changed everything forever: the scandal of Nike in 1996. The famous article published in 1996 in *Life Magazine* by Sydney H Schanberg brought to the public's attention the topic of child labour, and more generally, unethical labour practices.[2]

In the 1990s, the Pakistani city of Sialkot, about 70 miles from Lahore, was the hub of the nation's soccer ball industry, producing about 35 million balls a year. In factories located in the region, adults prepared soccer ball components that were then loaded onto trucks to be farmed out to the villages, where the most crucial process – the stitching – was performed by children.

Further investigations highlighted the use of child labour and instances of slavery and physical abuse, sparking widespread criticism and boycotts. The scandal significantly damaged Nike's reputation, and Nike's stock price collapsed by 58 per cent in 19 months.[3] This shock began Nike's deep interest in the social impact of their business and has since landed them at the top of the Dow Jones Sustainability Index (DJSI).

In the aftermath of this scandal, corporations started recognizing that environmental and social issues can lead to major reputational problems, and these can quickly lead to financial problems. Suddenly, the topic of sustainability became connected to the topic of risk, and the need for new approaches not based on philanthropy or marketing became evident. CSR began shifting in the early 2000s, leaning towards environmental responsibility and sustainable business practices.

The early 2000s saw the integration of environmental, social and governance (ESG) factors into investment and business decision-making processes. The launch of the United Nations' Principles for Responsible Investment (PRI) in 2006 encouraged investors to incorporate ESG factors into their investment strategies. This period witnessed the rise of sustainable finance, with increasing numbers of investors recognizing the financial materiality of ESG issues. Companies like Unilever, IKEA and Enel Group started to lead by example, embedding sustainability deeply into their business models and supply chains.

The 2010s marked the mainstreaming of sustainability, with significant advancements in both awareness and implementation. Sustainability became a key driver of innovation, transforming products, processes and business models. Within this decade, sustainability began to shift from having a PR focus to being more integrated into core business strategies. Companies like Tesla, with its focus on electric vehicles and renewable energy, demonstrated that sustainability could be a source of competitive advantage and innovation. This decade also saw the establishment of ambitious global frameworks, such as the United Nations Sustainable Development Goals (SDGs) in 2015, which provided a universal blueprint for achieving a sustainable future.

This current decade, which has been coined the decade of action, is characterized by an unprecedented focus on ESG, driven by heightened regulatory scrutiny, stakeholder expectations, and the tangible impacts of climate change. Companies are now under immense pressure to demonstrate their sustainability credentials with regulators, investors, consumers and employees demanding greater transparency and accountability.

In a previous book published by one of the authors of this book, Taticchi and Demartini researched the building blocks of modern corporate sustainability intending to forge a new definition.[4] What emerged from that exercise is that modern corporate sustainability builds on four key concepts:

- The first concept is purpose. Purpose is a powerful force for change, and today there is evidence that purpose-led companies have greater financial performance and purpose-led brands have the potential to establish stronger customer relationships, which increase customer loyalty and sales.[5] A purpose-driven strategy can help companies explore new opportunities and reshape their value propositions.

- The second concept is creating shared value.[6] This means rethinking business models so that economic value is created jointly with societal value. This calls for considering all stakeholders instead of only shareholders and moving away from CSR-based approaches, which focus primarily on reputation with limited connection to business, and more towards approaches where sustainability is fully integrated into business strategy.

- The third concept is power-sharing and ESG-based decision-making.[7] In order to create value and enable change for all stakeholders, companies need to give a real voice not only to shareholders, but also to employees and other parties who represent the interests of the environment and society more broadly. ESG criteria should be integrated at all levels of decision-making, and ESG performance needs to be disclosed in a transparent way.

- The fourth concept is the objective of enhancing competitiveness.[8] If sustainability is correctly integrated into business strategies, it results in higher levels of competitiveness and profit. Having a sustainability plan doesn't mean having a sustainability strategy. A sustainability strategy involves the development of a commercial mindset at the base of sustainable transformation, with the goal of exploring marketing opportunities and enhancing competitiveness.

Building on the pillars above, the definition proposed reads as follows:

> Corporate sustainability is an integral approach to business aimed at enhancing competitive positioning and profitability through the sustained creation of shared value, co-creation practices with stakeholders and the integration of ESG factors in decision-making (Taticchi and Demartini, 2021).[9]

Dr Jan Dauman, ESG and impact investing expert, shared with us his definition of sustainability, as well as his perspective on the key challenges and opportunities business leaders are facing as they navigate the many dimensions of sustainability and impact investing.

'I like to define sustainability as the anticipated, planned, managed and measured response to changes in the business environment. Defined this way, it is of course nothing new. Successful businesses have implemented sustainability principles for decades. What is new are the accelerating changes, complexity and uncertainty in that environment, creating new challenges and demanding new and innovative responses. One central challenge, as part of a holistic response, is to identify the full range of stakeholders and understand their changing interests, values and expectations, including, importantly, large institutional investors who have recognized that, as part of their fiduciary duty to their investors, they need to act on long-term societal challenges, starting with climate change but now expanding to a wide range of social and governance issues.

'A lot of people in the sustainability/ESG "industry" are trying to develop measurement tools that will allow them to evaluate and compare companies' sustainability performance. In my experience, every company is very different, with its own unique culture and unique balance of stakeholder interests and priorities and so such comparisons are often misleading and sometimes invalid. And multinationals have the added challenge of evaluating material sustainability issues and stakeholder priorities in different countries, each with its own culture, values, social priorities and political structure. A key answer to all this complexity is to create a sustainability culture in which every director, manager and employee applies sustainability criteria to every decision and action and has the permission and flexibility, within a defined process, to change course when circumstances change.'

## The business case for sustainable transformation

The research and consulting experiences of the authors suggest five drivers of the business case for sustainable transformation, as summarized in Figure 1.1.

These drivers are not equal for all companies, but very often it is a combination of them that builds the business case for change and for investments. Indeed, it is important to note that the two drivers related to the management of 'market risks' and 'market opportunities' are the most strategic drivers of the business case for sustainable transformation. The following paragraphs review these drivers, articulating the value of sustainability for business.

FIGURE 1.1    The drivers of the business case for sustainable transformation

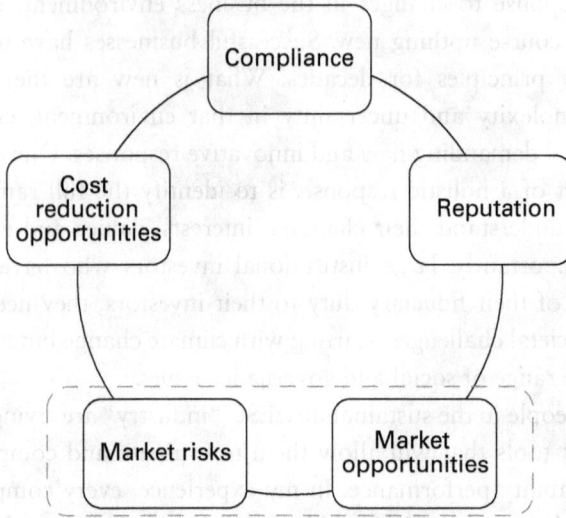

## Compliance

Compliance is a crucial driver of sustainable transformation because it creates a framework of standards and regulations that organizations must adhere to, ensuring that their operations and reporting practices align with environmental, social and governance (ESG) criteria. These regulations compel businesses to adopt practices that reduce their environmental footprint, enhance social equity and improve governance structures. By complying with these standards, companies are often forced to innovate and implement sustainable practices, such as reducing emissions, conserving resources and promoting fair labour practices. Compliance not only helps companies mitigate risks associated with non-compliance, such as legal penalties and reputational damage, but it also helps to foster a culture of responsibility and long-term thinking within organizations. Therefore, in addition to ensuring businesses meet legal requirements, compliance drives them towards innovation and efficiency, contributing to a broader transition towards a sustainable economy.

With the increasing complexity of ESG regulations, a comprehensive approach to compliance is crucial. This ensures efficient risk management and reporting, helping companies stay ahead of regulatory changes. According to the PRI Association, close to 1,000 ESG-related regulations have been issued for the investment industry alone.[10] Additionally, the '2023

State of the Corporate Law Department' report produced by Thomson Reuters identified ESG and the fluctuations in regulatory requirements as a top concern among managers worldwide.[11]

Adding complexity is the fact that ESG legislation can differ significantly from country to country, making it difficult for multinational companies to develop a uniform approach to ESG compliance. This increases costs, as companies need to develop or acquire specialized knowledge and processes tailored to each jurisdiction. It also increases the risk of unintentional non-compliance and could create situations of competitive disadvantage for companies operating in regions with more stringent ESG regulations than those operating in regions with less rigorous standards. Different standards in Europe and the US, where anti-ESG legislation has emerged in several states, make it very difficult for investors and asset managers to operate. This issue is well narrated in the *Who killed the ESG party* movie, published in July 2024 by the *Financial Times*, which highlighted the fact that a number of organizations, including the world's largest asset manager Blackrock, are moving away from the use of ESG language to prevent problems.

## Reputation

One of the benefits gained by companies that actively engage in sustainable practices is an enhanced reputation. A strong reputation can attract better talent, foster customer loyalty, and create a favourable image among investors and regulators. Several factors explain the link between ESG performance and corporate reputation. Strong ESG performance builds trust with stakeholders, including customers, investors, employees and the community. Moreover, in competitive marketplaces, companies can try to develop a sustainable brand to differentiate themselves or to build a competitive advantage in industry. For instance, brands like Patagonia and Unilever are celebrated for their commitment to sustainability, which bolsters their market positions and customer loyalty. Companies that consistently meet or exceed regulatory requirements are also less likely to face legal issues, fines and sanctions that very often are at the base of negative corporate reputation. Positive ESG performance generates favourable media coverage and public perception too. Stories of companies implementing innovative sustainable practices, contributing to social causes, or achieving governance milestones can enhance their public image. Conversely, poor ESG performance can lead to negative media attention, damaging a company's reputation.

A comprehensive study that we recommend reading on this is the '2024 Global RepTrak 100 Report' which highlights the importance of ESG and business conduct for corporate reputation.[12] In this study, business conduct is analysed through three factors that consider a company's fairness, ethicality and its openness and transparency:

> These elements are foundational to a company's ability to cultivate and enhance its credibility among stakeholders. Strong performance in these areas signals to the public that a company is committed to high standards of operational integrity – actively building a distinguished corporate identity that equally resonates positively with stakeholder expectations.

## Cost-reduction opportunities

Sustainable transformation offers significant cost reduction opportunities through more efficient operations and the adoption of circular models. Sustainable operations focus on reducing waste, conserving energy and optimizing resource use, which directly translates to lower operational costs. For instance, energy-efficient technologies and practices can significantly cut utility expenses, while waste reduction initiatives can decrease the costs associated with disposal and raw material procurement. Companies can also streamline their supply chains by prioritizing local sourcing and reducing transportation distances, thereby saving on logistics and fuel costs. However, some argue that the term 'sustainable operations' is old wine in a new bottle – and they are probably right! What we refer to as 'sustainable operations' today is what we used to refer to as 'optimization of operations', which led to the development of well-known manufacturing models like the Toyota production system (TPS), and lean manufacturing, which is now applied to services too, that are sustainable in their DNA and offer tangible operational and financial benefits. The TPS, for example, is a manufacturing philosophy developed by Toyota that aims to eliminate waste and achieve the best possible efficiency. The philosophy is based on two pillars: *jikoda* and *just-in-time*. The first pillar of *jikoda*, which translates to 'automation with a human touch', refers to the process of work stopping immediately when abnormalities are detected.[13] This ensures quality control and improved productivity. The second pillar of *just-in-time* refers to a continuous production flow that minimizes waste, ensuring the company is making only what is needed, when it is needed, in the amount that is needed.

Adopting circular models amplifies these benefits by promoting the reuse, recycling and repurposing of materials, thereby minimizing waste and reducing the need for new raw materials. Circular models encourage the design of products for longevity, reparability and recyclability, which can lower production costs and create new revenue streams from secondary markets. For example, a company can refurbish and resell returned products, turning what would have been waste into a profitable venture. This has led to the development of entirely new marketplaces enabling sharing, reuse and repairs. One notable example is Poshmark, a social commerce marketplace where users can buy and sell new and second-hand fashion, home goods and electronics. The platform has over 80 million users, with over 200 million available listings and revenue in 2021 that exceeded $320 million.

## Market risks

Companies that fail to engage with ESG topics and sustainable transformation face significant market risks that can adversely affect their long-term viability and competitiveness. As discussed earlier in this chapter, one of the primary risks is non-compliance and reputational damage. In an era where consumers, investors and other stakeholders are increasingly prioritizing sustainability and ethical practices, companies perceived as neglecting ESG responsibilities may suffer from negative publicity and public backlash. This can lead to a loss of customer trust and loyalty, which is difficult to regain and can result in declining sales and market share, as we saw happen to Nike in the 1990s. In the case of non-compliance behaviours, this can lead to major fines, too. This is something that Volkswagen learned the hard way when they were caught hiding excessive levels of toxic diesel emissions in 2015. In 2020, Volkswagen said its diesel cheating scandal had cost it 31.3 billion euros in fines and settlements alone.[14]

Additionally, poor ESG performance can attract activism from non-governmental organizations (NGOs) and other advocacy groups, further tarnishing a company's public image and leading to boycotts or divestments.

Investors are also increasingly using ESG criteria to guide their investment decisions. Companies with poor ESG ratings may find it difficult to attract investment, leading to higher capital costs or limited access to financing. Furthermore, as supply chains become more transparent, businesses with unsustainable practices might face disruptions from suppliers or partners who prioritize ESG standards, potentially leading to operational inefficiencies and increased costs. These market risks underline the importance of integrating ESG considerations into business strategies to ensure long-term resilience and success.

## Market opportunities

Engaging with ESG and sustainable transformation opens numerous market opportunities for companies, starting with the ability to describe their products and services as sustainable. Try to search for something on Amazon today, and try again by adding the word 'sustainable' in front of what you searched. You'll find something!

By incorporating sustainability into product design, companies can meet the growing demand from environmentally conscious consumers who prefer products with lower environmental impact. This differentiation not only attracts new customers but also allows for premium pricing, enhancing profitability. Companies that innovate to meet these demands can capture significant market share and drive growth. For example, Tesla's focus on electric vehicles has positioned it as a market leader in sustainable transportation, creating vast opportunities and reshaping the automotive industry.

The 2023 Sustainable Market Share Index™ published by NYU Stern Center for Sustainable Business found that products marketed as sustainable are responsible for nearly a third of the growth in consumer packaged goods from 2013 to 2023, despite representing less than one-fifth of the market share.[15]

Moreover, a strong sustainable brand can significantly boost market competitiveness. Companies known for their commitment to ESG principles often enjoy higher customer loyalty, improved brand reputation, and increased market share as consumers and businesses alike seek partners who align with their values.

Sustainable transformation also unlocks opportunities in the realm of sustainable finance. Global ESG assets surpassed $30 trillion in 2022 and are on track to surpass $40 trillion by 2030 – over 25 per cent of projected $140 trillion assets under management (AUM) according to Bloomberg Intelligence.[16] Investors are increasingly favouring companies with robust ESG practices, as they are seen as lower risk and more resilient in the long term. Access to green bonds, sustainability-linked loans and other forms of sustainable finance can provide favourable financing terms and attract a broader base of investors. Research produced by McKinsey in 2023 found that 85 per cent of the chief investment officers they surveyed state that ESG is an important factor in their investment decisions, and they are prepared to pay a premium for companies that show a clear link between their ESG efforts and financial performance.[17]

Additionally, a strong ESG profile can enhance opportunities in supplier selection and tender processes. Many organizations now require their suppliers to meet specific ESG criteria, and those that excel in sustainability are more likely to win contracts and partnerships. Finally, focusing on ESG encourages innovation, driving companies to develop new products, services and business models that address environmental and social challenges. This innovation can lead to new revenue streams, increased market relevance and a competitive edge in a rapidly evolving marketplace.

## The business case: timing and strategic approach

During this decade of action, timing is crucial for businesses transitioning to sustainable practices. Companies that proactively integrate sustainability into their strategies can gain a competitive advantage, while late adopters may face significant disadvantages. The risk of businesses being left behind is a key theme underscored in Paolo Taticchi's TEDx Talk, which he delivered in 2021, titled 'Business Strategy and Sustainability: Change to survive and thrive'.[18] During his talk, Paolo emphasized the need for sustainable transformation in business, stating, 'We are presently aware that our planet is at risk, and the type of capitalism we have built over the last century is no longer working for society today. Simply put: the ways in which we used to approach business are no longer sustainable.'

In every market/industry today it is possible to recognize companies that developed a 'first mover approach' in sustainable transformation, companies that are 'following' and companies that are not engaged yet with the process of sustainable transformation – 'late transformers'. If we analyse these different timings associated to sustainable transformation, and we put them in the context of the most strategic drivers of the business case – the management of ESG risks and the exploration of ESG opportunities – it becomes evident that first movers seek to develop a competitive advantage through sustainable transformation, while late transformers may end up in a situation of competitive disadvantage. Late-transforming companies will be particularly exposed to ESG risks and unable to explore market opportunities, which will be won first by first movers and followers.

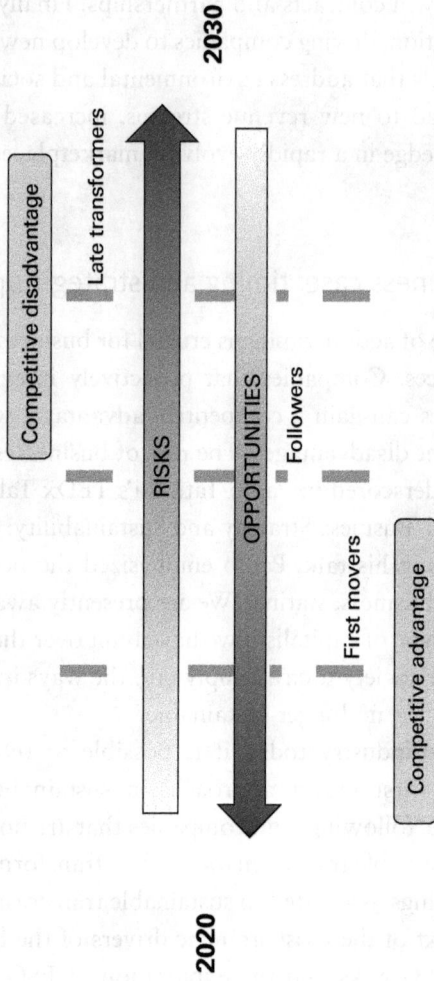

FIGURE 1.2  Sustainable transformation: timing and impact on competitive advantage

The timing of sustainable transformation is also linked to the company's corporate sustainability maturity and approach, and to what extent this is strategic. Today, it is possible to identify four different corporate approaches related to sustainable transformation:

- **Compliance-driven**: these are companies that follow legislation and limit their approach to do the minimum in relation to ESG. These companies might have formal sustainability plans in place and sustainability reports, but normally lack a comprehensive sustainability strategy and often address only a subset of ESG topics.

- **Best practice-driven**: these are companies that go beyond compliance to align to what they perceive is an emerging best practice. An example of this is companies that voluntarily produce sustainability reports, not because they are driven by a genuine sense of transparency or strategy – but simply because others do it. Very often these organizations lack comprehensive sustainability plans.

- **Differentiation-driven**: these are companies that have clear sustainability strategies that are well integrated into their competitive strategies. These firms very often seek to differentiate products, services and business models through sustainability, and therefore have developed a commercial mindset for sustainable transformation. In these organizations, sustainability is a driver of innovation.

- **Competitive advantage-driven**: these are companies that go beyond differentiation, and seek to build a competitive advantage in industry through sustainability. In this category we often find sustainability leaders. There are companies that have comprehensive sustainability strategies fully integrated into their competitive strategies.

Companies in the first two categories tend to have an operational approach to sustainability and very often a reactive behaviour in relation to ESG topics. On the other hand, companies in the last two categories tend to have a strategic approach to sustainability and proactive behaviour in relation to ESG topics.

Of course, different corporate approaches impact companies' ESG performance. To assess qualitatively the profile of organizations, we propose here a classification scheme which builds on the concepts proposed by Taticchi and Formentini (2016).[19]

Using several criteria, three levels of maturity are identified, namely: 'traditionalists', 'practitioners' and 'leaders' as reported in Table 1.1.

FIGURE 1.3    Different corporate approaches to sustainable transformation

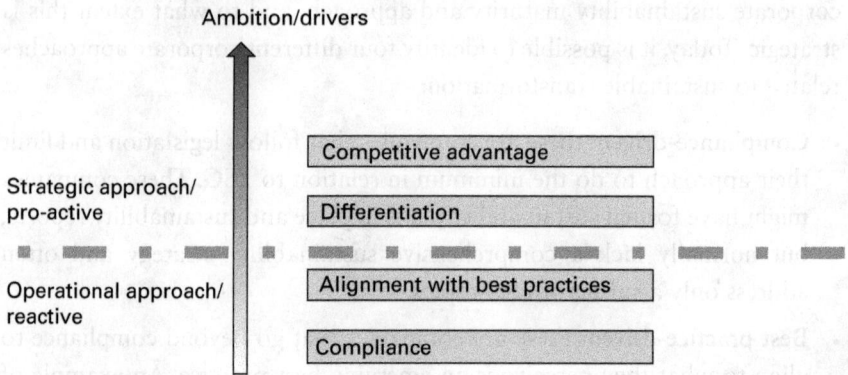

Ambition/drivers

Strategic approach/
pro-active

Operational approach/
reactive

- Competitive advantage
- Differentiation
- Alignment with best practices
- Compliance

© Paolo Taticchi, 2021

TABLE 1.1    Sustainability maturity model

|  | Traditionalist | Practitioner | Leader |
|---|---|---|---|
| **Stakeholder focus** | Primarily focused on shareholders' interests | Considers key stakeholders selectively | Holistically engages all relevant stakeholders |
| **Triple bottom line focus** | Economic sustainability is the primary focus | Environmental and social aspects considered but secondary | Fully integrated economic, social, and environmental sustainability |
| **Sustainability approach** | CSR or marketing-driven; focuses on compliance and responsibility | Primarily aimed at reducing risks and managing negative impacts | Proactively focuses on creating positive impact and embedding sustainability into core strategy |
| **Sustainability agenda** | Limited sustainability initiatives, often ad-hoc | Several sustainability initiatives aligned with business goals | A fully integrated sustainability agenda aligned with long-term goals |
| **Integration with business strategy** | Sustainability is siloed and not part of the business strategy | Sustainability partially integrated into business functions | Sustainability fully embedded into the core business strategy and various business functions |

TABLE 1.1    *continued*

|  | Traditionalist | Practitioner | Leader |
| --- | --- | --- | --- |
| **Level of action** | Focused on internal corporate sustainability | Includes some supply chain sustainability initiatives | Covers both corporate and comprehensive supply chain sustainability |
| **Approach to innovation** | Innovation focused on business performance, rarely linked to sustainability | Sustainability considered occasionally in innovation | Innovation driven by sustainability objectives |
| **Governance for sustainability** | No dedicated governance for sustainability | Basic governance structures, often reactive | Fully developed governance structures ensuring sustainability oversight at the highest levels |
| **Sustainable leadership** | Leadership not engaged in sustainability | Leadership sporadically involved in sustainability | Leadership actively champions sustainability initiatives |
| **Capabilities for sustainability** | No internal sustainability expertise | Limited capabilities, often relying on external expertise | Advanced internal capabilities with integration of external partners when necessary |

In summary, building a competitive advantage through sustainability is not only about compliance and risk management but also about seizing market opportunities and fostering innovation. Companies that integrate sustainability into their core strategies can achieve long-term success, enhance their reputation and create value for all stakeholders. As demonstrated by the insights and cases presented in this chapter, the time to act is now, and the benefits are substantial. By embracing sustainability, businesses can navigate the challenges of the modern world and emerge stronger, more resilient and more competitive.

KEY TAKEAWAYS

- **Evolution of corporate sustainability**: Corporate sustainability has evolved significantly from the early days of CSR, which focused on ethical behaviour and philanthropy, to the modern approach that integrates environmental, social and governance (ESG) factors into core business strategies. This evolution highlights the growing recognition that sustainability is essential for long-term business success and resilience.

- **Drivers of the business case for sustainability**: The business case for sustainable transformation is driven by several factors including compliance with regulations, reputation enhancement, cost-reduction opportunities, managing market risks and exploring market opportunities. These drivers collectively build a compelling case for businesses to invest in sustainable practices.

- **Timing of sustainable transformation**: Timing is crucial in the journey towards sustainable transformation. Early adopters gain a competitive edge by proactively integrating sustainability into their strategies, while late transformers face significant risks and missed opportunities. Companies must act decisively in this decade of action to capitalize on the benefits of sustainable practices.

- **Different corporate approaches to sustainability**: Companies exhibit varied approaches to sustainability, ranging from compliance-driven (meeting minimum legal requirements) to best practice-driven (aligning with emerging standards), differentiation-driven (integrating sustainability to stand out in the market), and competitive advantage-driven (using sustainability to build industry leadership). These approaches reflect the maturity and strategic integration of sustainability within the organization.

- **Sustainability maturity model**: The proposed maturity model categorizes companies as traditionalists, practitioners and leaders based on their level of formalization of sustainability strategy, sustainability planning, comprehensiveness of the triple bottom line approach and focus on the value chain, among other criteria. This model helps organizations assess their current state and identify areas for improvement in their sustainability journey.

# Notes

**1** Thomas (2023) A brief history of corporate social responsibility (CSR), www.thomasnet.com/linsights/history-of-corporate-social-responsibility/ (archived at https://perma.cc/7LVQ-VSRG)

**2** Schanberg, Sydney H (1996) Six cents an hour, *Life Magazine*

**3** Expert 360 (2024) Nike's mistakes 20 years ago created $87B of market value. What can we learn from them? 28 March, https://expert360.com/articles/learn-from-mistakes-nike (archived at https://perma.cc/9NJ4-HSU5)

**4** Taticchi, P and Demartini, M (2021) *Corporate Sustainability in Practice*, Springer International Publishing

**5** Buche, I, Dharnaraj, C and Malnight, T W (2019) Put purpose at the core of your strategy, *Harvard Business Review*, September to October, https://hbr.org/2019/09/put-purpose-at-the-core-of-your-strategy (archived at https://perma.cc/HLG9-FSWR)

**6** Porter, M E and Kramer, M R (2011) Creating shared value, *Harvard Business Review*, 1–17, January to February

**7** Battiliana, J and Casciaro, T (2021) Power sharing can change corporations for the better, *Harvard Business Review*, 13 May

**8** Lubin, D A and Esty, D C (2010) The sustainability imperative, *Harvard Business Review*, May

**9** Taticchi, P and Demartini, M (2021) *Corporate Sustainability in Practice*, Springer International Publishing

**10** Boston Consulting Group (2022) ESG compliance in an era of tighter regulation, 20 September, www.bcg.com/publications/2022/navigating-esg-compliance-in-an-era-of-tighter-regulation (archived at https://perma.cc/9QC9-E9F5)

**11** Thomson Reuters (2023) ESG insights from the '2023 State of the Corporate Law Department report', www.thomsonreuters.com/en-us/posts/esg/corporate-legal-esg-insights/ (archived at https://perma.cc/Q5SW-VSLV)

**12** RepTrack (2024) The 2024 Global RepTrak 100 Report, www.reptrak.com/globalreptrak/#2zzmhhdAPWprMriaiKHNlc (archived at https://perma.cc/52GX-767Z)

**13** Toyota, https://global.toyota/en/company/vision-and-philosophy/production-system/ (archived at https://perma.cc/F5MH-9WNP)

**14** Reuters (2020) Volkswagen says diesel scandal has cost it 31.3 billion euros, 17 March, www.reuters.com/article/business/volkswagen-says-diesel-scandal-has-cost-it-313-billion-euros-idUSKBN2141JA/ (archived at https://perma.cc/8JA4-PR7K)

**15**  NYU Stern Center for Sustainable Business (2023), The 2023 Sustainable Market Share Index™, www.stern.nyu.edu/experience-stern/about/departments-centers-initiatives/centers-of-research/center-sustainable-business/research/csb-sustainable-market-share-index (archived at https://perma.cc/CQD6-4RJN)

**16**  Bloomberg Intelligence (2024) Global ESG assets predicted to hit $40 trillion by 2030, despite challenging environment, forecasts Bloomberg Intelligence, 8 February, www.bloomberg.com/company/press/global-esg-assets-predicted-to-hit-40-trillion-by-2030-despite-challenging-environment-forecasts-bloomberg-intelligence/ (archived at https://perma.cc/3CP7-C6EH)

**17**  McKinsey & Company (2023) Investors want to hear from companies about the value of sustainability, www.mckinsey.com/capabilities/strategy-and-corporate-finance/our-insights/investors-want-to-hear-from-companies-about-the-value-of-sustainability (archived at https://perma.cc/W3TV-GVPP)

**18**  Taticchi, P (2021) Business strategy and sustainability: Change to survive and thrive, Tedx Talk, November, www.ted.com/talks/paolo_taticchi_business_strategy_sustainability_change_to_survive_and_thrive?subtitle=en (archived at https://perma.cc/VW66-BGWR)

**19**  Formentini, M and Taticchi, P (2016) Corporate sustainability approaches and governance mechanisms in sustainable supply chain management, *Journal of Cleaner Production*, 112, pp. 1920–1933

# 2

# Defining the role of the Chief Sustainability Officer

Given that the field of sustainability is multidimensional – covering environmental, social, governance and economic spheres – the CSO role itself can have many different meanings and profiles. An article published by the *Harvard Business Review* in 2023 shed light on the fact that despite sustainability gaining traction in corporate agendas, there is still a lack of clarity about CSOs' key tasks and responsibilities. Part of the reason for this is that compared to other more traditional functions, which have been established and have existed for much longer, such as finance, human resources or marketing, the role of CSO is still relatively new. Additionally, the role is often defined based on the priorities and mandates of a company, as well as by reporting lines. For example, if a CSO reports into the CFO, their focus may be more on investor relations or reporting; if they report into the COO, it could be more of an efficiency function.[1] Given the many different functions and responsibilities that are often applied to the role, it is not surprising there is a lack of clarity around the job specifications of a CSO.

## The role of CSO defined by CSOs

To help bring some clarity and a common understanding about the role and the core tasks and responsibilities, we asked the CSOs we met with to define the role based on their own experiences and journeys. Being an influencer, a spider in a net, and conductor of a big orchestra were just some of the words and phrases used by those doing the job to describe the role. Although each response differed slightly, they all shared a common theme, which is that

CSOs are responsible for shepherding many areas of an organization towards a common vision and goal. Looking at a business through a sustainability lens, the CSO's primary objective is to ensure a company is operating responsibly and working towards improving its sustainability performance, in line with the sustainability strategy and objectives the company has set out to achieve.

Jeffrey Whitford, Vice President of Sustainability and Social Business Innovation at Merck Life Science, describes the role of CSO as being twofold: an advocate and an influencer. Central to the role of CSO is your ability to build partnerships with stakeholders across an organization, both internally and externally, and as Jeffrey points out this requires being an advocate and influencer, among many other attributes. He says:

'I can't really do command and control, right? Go do this, go do that. That's not how this works. My role and the success of me in this role is my ability to build partnerships within our organization and with external stakeholders, and to help them understand why this is going to be beneficial for them. Why does it matter? Why is it important? Why can it change the outlook or trajectory for whoever that individual is or what they're doing? And I think if I can be a successful influencer in that – and I don't mean like social media influencing – I mean really influencing the people that we take along on this journey.

'So, how I think about the conversations and the framing about how a choice affects more things and why is that beneficial? Because what we recognize is that people don't necessarily think of sustainability as the lens that they're using when they make decisions. And so, our ability to change that and embed that into the business has really been a core part of what I'm focused on doing. And so, I think my role is influencing people to think differently about what the future is, what our impact can be.'

Fostering relationships and building a strong network internally across an organization, as well as externally across your industry is a critical part of a CSO's role. Closely linked to this is being able to communicate essential topics in ways that are relatable to different stakeholders while addressing the needs and interests of those stakeholders.

Peter Bragg, EMEA Sustainability and Government Affairs Director at Canon, shares Jeffrey's view that a CSO can be described as, among other titles, a *Chief Influencer*. Peter explained that a central part of the CSO role is to collaborate with other functions of an organization – whether it's finance, HR or production – with the focus of engaging each business area on the topic of sustainability. In Peter's view, networking and collaborating with key stakeholders and decision-makers across an organization is vital in this role.

'Defining the role is actually quite hard,' he says. 'I think it partly depends on your type of business. It is probably one of the broadest roles in a company in terms of the many different business areas you intersect with and collaborate with. I guess, really, you could define the role as Chief Change Maker or Chief Influencer. You can add to this Chief Knowledge Demystifier. Sustainability is always the kind of phrase that most people understand a little bit, but it has become so broad now that it is the CSO's responsibility to try and translate as well.'

A report published by Deloitte and the Institute of International Finance emphasized the point that a CSO needs to act as a translator or interpreter of sorts, describing the role as being the 'sense-maker in chief' of an organization.[2] Given the extent and complexity of sustainability topics, CSOs indeed play a pivotal role in interpreting and distilling information that can help key stakeholders, especially leadership teams, make informed business decisions that consider both the risks and opportunities linked to sustainability.

When asked to define the role of CSO, Klaus Kunz, Founder and Managing Director at Ephrin, offers a more visual interpretation of the role, likening it to a *spider in a net*. Reflecting on the role and how it has evolved over the years, Klaus explains that one of the biggest differences he observed is how the role has shifted from a PR function to one that is much more closely linked to the core business.

'It's really a spider in the net. And I think there's also changing tasks. It's depending a little bit on where you are in the journey. Five years ago, the big task was to get sustainability as a topic out of this public relations corner where it was in many corporations over many years. You know, sustainability is the 'nice to do' things when you have done your job, then you can do some sustainability things. And that was the task five years ago. I mean, really hammer it into the business with the big support of the board. It's not possible if the board is not backing this agenda. When I was at Bayer, it was really a board decision for the company to really strive towards becoming an impact generator. These were extremely important messages. And then you needed to craft some landmark commitments and start the execution. Setting big commitments is the starting point, then you need to evolve those plans further. Once the commitments are set you then need to keep track, even in quarters or in years when there's more pressure on economic performance, to make absolutely clear and sure that the investments into those commitments are not to be debated. In this role you need to insist on execution all the time, and spread the word.'

Klaus's spider in the net metaphor is a fitting description given the many different areas of a business that a CSO needs to interact with, as well as the widespread network of stakeholders that a CSO needs to engage on this journey.

Leaning on her more than 15 years working in the sustainability field, Elisa Moscolin, Executive Vice President of Sustainability and Foundation at Sage, describes the role very simply as being *a tough gig.*

'I think about Chief Sustainability Officers as activists in suits,' she says. 'They are trying to rewire how companies operate with the ambition that they can rewire markets and deliver a more sustainable world. This means that the CSO's role is a tough gig. Many people approach me with a bit of a naive view of the work I do. Some believe it is all about doing good and possibly imagine me spending my days in nature or with charities. Instead, I spend my days in meetings, analysing spreadsheets, and creating PowerPoints to try to drive massive transformation across big, complex organizations that are not necessarily set up or incentivized by markets to be sustainable. CSOs are also likely to have an agenda that is disproportionately big to the size of their team and the resources they typically have. They are dealing with a field that's relatively immature, but with a very urgent need for action. They need to drive a cultural and market shift while not always sitting in the rooms where decisions are being made. It is just recently that CSOs made it to the C-suite, and even today, many leadership teams are not the actual subject matter experts but rather someone who has "adopted" the sustainability team into their function. Another interesting aspect of the role is that most of the time, boards and management are not very close to the topics the CSO is talking about. These were not on the agenda while they were doing their MBAs or rising through the ranks – so the CSO has a double job to do: drive change and educate. Don't get me wrong, I am incredibly passionate about the job I do, and I think CSO is the best role you could have, but it is not frustration free.'

Elisa points to climate change as one example of an urgent topic that needs addressing, but the practice is still relatively immature. As a consequence, Elisa explains that organizations' understanding of this topic is also a work in progress. As a result, CSOs are faced with many conflicting priorities, and it is their role not only to drive strategy execution but also to educate and influence key stakeholders on these issues. Similar to the sentiments shared by Jeffrey Whitford, who described the role as being an influencer of sorts, Elisa underscored the need for CSOs to use soft power to really influence and get things done. She noted that the role also requires steadfast leadership. As Elisa explains, the CSO's ultimate goal is to win hearts and minds, not least the hearts and minds of the CEOs and boards who are driving the corporate agenda. Garnering support from the top is key for a CSO to ensure sustainability is integrated into the core business strategy. To make the role all the more interesting, Elisa points out there is no template and it is the CSO's job to navigate and assess the best way forward.

'As a Chief Sustainability Officer, you often have to do things that have not been done before, and that companies are not used to doing. Therefore, CSOs often have to deal with ambiguity and come up with solutions, templates and methodologies that challenge the status quo. Sometimes I think of a CSO as being the composer and conductor of a big orchestra. You compose the symphony and then have to get everyone to play from the same music sheet. You really have to rely on the expertise and interpretation of each musician for it all to come together and sound good.'

Elisa's description of the role speaks to the many challenges CSOs face, be it a limit of resources, or having to gain the support of various stake-holders, the tasks are tall and plentiful. Remaining resilient, perseverant and unwavering in the face of these challenges is what makes the role challenging – but also rewarding.

> 'Sometimes I think of a CSO as being the composer and conductor of a big orchestra. You compose the symphony and then have to get everyone to play from the same music sheet. You really have to rely on the expertise and interpretation of each musician for it all to come together and sound good.'
>
> **Elisa Moscolin, Executive Vice President of Sustainability and Foundation at Sage**

## How the Chief Sustainability Officer role has evolved

According to an article published by the *Harvard Business Review*, the role of CSO has evolved fairly rapidly over the years. Traditionally, CSOs took on more of a PR function, whereby their focus was to develop narratives that would promote a company's corporate sustainability initiatives to various stakeholders. The CSO's function was positioned far from the core business strategy or from the executive team. Fortunately, the role has evolved over the years and so, too, has its position in organizational structures, with more CSOs reporting directly into CFOs and CEOs, rather than operating on the sidelines.[3] We consider this an important milestone for the professionals in this field.

Elisa Moscolin experienced this evolution first hand. When asked about how the sustainability field has evolved over the course of her career, Elisa shared a story that aptly illustrates just how much the field, and the CSO role, has changed over the years.

'I always tell the story about how my first job was on the ground floor next to the bins and the storage office. During the past 15 years, I have seen the practice rising through the floors and ranks of organizations, in recognition of the strategic importance it has for business success and longer-term viability. This awareness of its strategic importance is what has brought it on top of boards' and executive teams' agendas. This climb through the corporate ladder started decades ago, before I was even born, so I'm really glad that I've had the pleasure of experiencing this change over the past decade. And my hope is that to some extent, my peers and I have contributed to driving this change within organizations and we will keep sustainability really at the top of the board and executive team's agendas, because I think it is really about a strategy and about long-term business success.'

Elisa's story struck a familiar tone with many of the CSOs we interviewed. Not only has the topic of sustainability traditionally been approached separately from core business strategies; more than that, it was simply not top of mind of the executives leading the corporate agenda.

Leaning on years of researching, teaching and consulting in this field, Paolo Taticchi, Professor of Strategy and Sustainability and co-author of this book, shares his thoughts on the various factors that led to this shift over the past decade.

'Firstly, how companies approach sustainability has changed due to increased pressure from various stakeholders, not least employees and customers. Traditionally, corporations have operated to meet the interests of shareholders. Over the last decade, we have seen a shift whereby more companies are considering the interests of all stakeholders. This shift has led companies to assess their impact on people and the planet. Finally, companies are much more aware of the risk to reputation, which can negatively impact an organization's bottom line. All of these factors combined are pushing businesses towards taking sustainability more seriously and towards adopting a triple-bottom-line approach to business – which considers people, planet and profits. This explains why organizations today need capable CSOs.'

As we've learnt through our discussions with CSOs, the evolution of corporate sustainability is often mirrored and seen in the evolving role and profile of CSOs.

While the CSO role has made great strides over the past decade in reaching the C-suite level of many organizations, too many companies still do not take the topic of sustainability seriously. A study published by PwC in 2022 underscores this point. The study looked at the role of CSOs at 1,640 listed companies and found that only one third of the companies had a formal CSO role, and approximately half of all the CSOs were two or more hierarchy levels below the C-suite, and therefore had little decision-making influence.[4] The research showed that even for the companies where CSOs were in place, in many cases their focus was on initiatives related to CSR (corporate social responsibility) or addressing specific health, environmental or safety issues.

Montse Montaner, a sustainability leader who has worked in the pharmaceutical industry for more than 30 years, has seen the role of sustainability evolve significantly over the course of her career. In her view, the role of CSO is very much linked to the maturity level of the organization.

'I think the role is very much linked to how the companies are seeing sustainability. And this is what I refer to as a maturity level. So, if you see that you need to be just compliant with regulations, then it's one type of profile that you're looking at for a CSO. But that does not exactly help you to change the operating model, or to change the business itself, right? So, that's why you need to add this business acumen, and very strong financial background. So, this tells you how the company evolves. If the role is very much reporting, you are still in the early stages of the maturity of sustainability. If you see that the role is much more embedded into the overall sustainability across all the business and operations, to really enable the company to make products and services sustainable, and also impact in the way that the consumer will change the criteria on decisions as a result of whether that product is or is not sustainable, then it's a different maturity, and then it's a different level of skills that you need. You need skills that are much more on the dimension of business operations. So that tells you how the companies are evolving. And it's fascinating to see how companies are evolving from one year to another year and also how the Chief Sustainability Officer is supported with different people in the organization. The person themself evolves differently as part of the different needs that company has as part of their journey.'

During our discussion, Montse highlighted another key factor that often shapes the role of a CSO, which is the industry they are working within, and more specifically the maturity of that industry. She pointed to the healthcare and life-science sector as an example of an industry that is highly regulated. As a result, pharmaceutical and life-science companies are very conscious of regulations and compliance. Therefore, a lot of focus is placed on this area. Even within this sector, however, there are varying degrees of maturity between organizations. Montse explained that companies that are further along on their journeys are already in a position where they can supply medicines to the marketplace that are more sustainable. Other companies that are just beginning to engage with sustainability are more focused on understanding the regulations and the implications for their businesses. There are other factors companies need to consider as well, such as having a positive societal impact. Many pharmaceutical companies that produce generic medicines are still in an early stage of maturity, yet the role they can play in making a positive social impact is immense, given the fact that they are able to make medicines much more accessible to more people. By adopting more sustainable practices, they can have a significant positive societal impact, as well as environmental.

## Key tasks and responsibilities of a Chief Sustainability Officer

Given the multidimensional nature of sustainability, CSOs are responsible for a wide range of tasks that require collaborating with many different areas of a business. In a study published by the *Harvard Business Review* in 2023, the authors looked at the key tasks a CSO is responsible for within an organization. During an executive workshop with a German manufacturer, the authors of the study used a spider graph to illustrate eight key tasks of a CSO. The eight tasks outlined in the study included: ensuring regulatory compliance; ESG monitoring and reporting; overseeing the portfolio of sustainability projects; managing stakeholder relationships; building organizational capabilities; fostering cultural change, scouting and experimenting; embedding sustainability into processes and decision-making. As part of the study, the key tasks of the company's CSO were mapped out in a *pre-workshop* exercise. The pre-workshop graph revealed that the CSO's focus leant mostly towards tasks related to compliance, reporting and overseeing the implementation of projects. What the graph also revealed was that many areas of the CSO's function were left uncovered. The authors then provided a graph to show the *desired* CSO positioning for the company, which showed a more balanced approach that covered all eight tasks more equally.[5] It is clear from this study the desired positioning for a CSO is to adopt a holistic approach that encompasses all eight tasks. Taking a balanced approach that considers environmental, social and governance aspects, and doesn't place too much emphasis on any one area, is the ideal positioning that will set CSOs and organizations up for long-term success. In addition to the tasks outlined in this study, we believe it is essential for CSOs to also have financial acumen and change management skills in order to effectively lead sustainable transformation across their organizations. Furthermore, as we've gleaned from our discussions with CSOs, to succeed in their role CSOs need to take a balanced approach that leans on a mix of hard skills and soft skills. Hard skills typically refer to technical skills that are job-specific, such as ensuring regulatory compliance, while soft skills refer to personality traits such as communication, teamwork and collaboration, which are so vital to this role. CSOs who are able to hone both sets of skills are well-positioned to drive sustainability forward alongside their teams and colleagues.

While this example is based on one organization, it sheds light on the fact that a CSO's role is not stationary, and in many ways the CSO's positioning in a company is determined by the organization's own position and approach to sustainability. Through this lens, the role is in many ways defined by the sustainability maturity of the company. This view aligns with the perspectives shared by sustainability leaders Montse Montaner and Klaus Kunz, who stated that a CSO's role and focus will depend largely on where a company is on its sustainability journey. For companies that are just beginning their journey of sustainable transformation, their focus may be on compliance and reporting, and in turn this is where the CSO will spend much of their time and effort. With the increase of regulations mandating companies to be more transparent with their environmental, social and governance impact, such as the European Union CSRD (Corporate Sustainability Reporting Directive), many companies are focused on improving their disclosure efforts in accordance with new regulations.

For companies who may be further along on their journeys, those CSOs are likely to be adopting a more holistic approach to sustainability that goes beyond compliance and reporting – taking into consideration how sustainability can be embedded across all areas of the business. One example of how a CSO can go beyond compliance and turn their attention towards initiatives that can help a company advance its progress and performance is by convincing the executive team to link executive remuneration to ESG performance metrics. This kind of initiative has proven to be effective in ensuring a company's sustainability agenda is being embedded into an organization's business and decision-making processes. It also ensures the company's objectives are being communicated and supported throughout the organization. This type of initiative also demonstrates how sustainability functions have evolved from being PR-focused, to ones that drive major transformational change.

CSOs who are approaching their role in a holistic way are responsible for many areas and functions, including regulatory and compliance, HR (hiring, recruiting and training), reporting, measurement and tracking, development and implementation of ESG strategies and initiatives, R&D and innovation, digital transformation, fostering a sustainability-focused culture and building relationships with internal and external stakeholders.

While the list of responsibilities is long, not everything falls on the shoulders of the CSO. To address sustainability issues in each of these areas, the CSO needs to work in close collaboration with every division of a company – legal, HR, finance, marketing and communications, operations, IT, procurement and so on. To be effective in their role, the CSO also needs to be working closely with the executive team or board. Furthermore, CSOs need to be supported by a specialized team. The size and scope of a sustainability team will largely depend on the size and resources of an organization, as well as the organization's maturity when it comes to sustainable transformation.

What is clear from our conversations and research that delves into the role of CSO is that CSOs wear many hats. Magali Anderson, sustainability and innovation leader in the building material industry, describes the role as a being a *Jill or Jack of all trades* whose primary focus is to change a business for better.

'I think the role of the Chief Sustainability Officer is truly to change a business. Let's change the model in such a way that we make more money when we produce less, so everyone is happy, as less $CO_2$ means more profit. So how do we make more with less? It sounds a bit basic, but it's all about creating a circular economy. When we speak about circular economy, it's about designing things differently, in order to reach the same function with less product. For example going from an ownership model to a leasing one. And so, for me, the Chief Sustainability Officer is a Jill (or Jack) of all trades – they are someone who needs to understand business, understand markets, and understand how to change all of that. But they also need to understand the technology side, because they are going to work with a lot of technology people who are going to help them on that journey, and they will need to speak their language.'

While CSOs indeed need to be Jills or Jacks of all trades as Magali points out, it is important to keep in mind they do not need to be experts of every trade. For this reason, as we've learnt through our discussions, it is important for CSOs to be supported and surrounded by a team of experts. In an ideal structure, the CSO is surrounded by a team of specialists where each member specializes in a specific area of sustainability, such as compliance and regulations or reporting. Within this team structure, members impart expertise and exchange knowledge with their colleagues daily. As a result, each member learns from one another, and everyone's knowledge base is continuously elevated and enhanced – including the CSO. Moreover, many sustainability teams today leverage the expertise of external consulting firms to quickly access knowledge not available in-house. Finding the right balance between in-house expertise and consulting support can be challenging, based on the interactions we had with our guests.

## Building a support network and culture driven by sustainability

Beyond the technical tasks and responsibilities that come with the role of CSO, there is also the human side. Leading an organization's sustainability strategy is no easy feat, especially when faced with many barriers or challenges, such as limited resources. Elisa Moscolin put this perfectly when she described the role as being *a tough gig*. Being resilient, focused and remaining optimistic are all essential qualities that a CSO needs to bring to the role. Building relationships and a strong network within an organization, as well as externally with various stakeholders, is also vital for a CSO to thrive in their role. Establishing a strong network with CSOs from other companies and industries has also proven incredibly helpful and valuable for many of the CSOs we spoke with. Attending industry events and engaging with sustainability leaders from different companies, sectors and regions enables a CSO to stay abreast of new and emerging issues and regulations that impact all organizations. This sharing of knowledge and industry-leading practices also allows CSOs to approach and see topics through different lenses and perspectives.

Equally important to establishing a strong support network is building a culture where sustainability is embedded into an organization's business approach, its values and its day-to-day operations. A CSO alone cannot achieve a company's sustainability goals. Successful CSOs are supported by executive teams that understand the importance of sustainability and the positive impacts a sound sustainability strategy can have on the business. The CSO also needs to be surrounded by a team of experts who can help steward a company's strategy forward, and by engaged employees who are actively contributing to and advancing an organization's performance and progress. Supported by a sustainability-focused leadership team, a strong network of co-advocates and influencers, and a culture that embraces sustainability and innovation, CSOs will be well-positioned to meet any challenge they encounter on this journey.

At its core, the role of Chief Sustainability Officer can be defined as being the chief steward of an organization's sustainability strategy. The primary focus of a CSO is to help a company improve its sustainability performance and steer it towards achieving its environmental, social and governance goals. Furthermore, by collaborating and networking with various industry partners and stakeholders, CSOs play a pivotal role in influencing change beyond their organizations.

---

KEY TAKEAWAYS

- **Multidimensional role**: The role of a Chief Sustainability Officer (CSO) is multifaceted, covering environmental, social, governance and economic aspects. The specific tasks and responsibilities can vary significantly based on a company's priorities and reporting lines.

- **Influence and advocacy**: A CSO acts as an influencer and advocate within the organization, building partnerships and fostering relationships with stakeholders to integrate sustainability into the business strategy. Effective communication and advocacy are crucial for promoting sustainability initiatives.

- **Network and collaboration**: Establishing a strong internal and external network is essential. CSOs need to collaborate with various business functions such as finance, HR and production, as well as engage with external stakeholders and industry peers to drive sustainability efforts.

- **Evolving role**: The role of the CSO has evolved from being primarily a PR function to becoming integral to the core business strategy. Today, CSOs are often part of the executive team, reflecting the growing importance of sustainability in corporate agendas.

- **Challenges and resilience**: The role is challenging, requiring resilience and perseverance. CSOs often face limited resources and conflicting priorities but must remain focused and optimistic. They also need to navigate ambiguity and develop innovative solutions to drive sustainable transformation.

- **Balanced approach**: A successful CSO adopts a holistic approach that considers environmental, social and economic factors. A CSO also needs to take a balanced approach that combines both hard (or technical) skills and soft (or people-focused) skills. This balanced approach ensures long-term sustainability and business success.

# Notes

1   Farri, E, Cervini, P and Rosani, G (2023) The 8 responsibilities of Chief Sustainability Officers, *Harvard Business Review*, 2 March, https://hbr.org/2023/03/the-8-responsibilities-of-chief-sustainability-officers (archived at https://perma.cc/T44T-R6M8)

2   Deloitte and the Institute of International Finance (2021) The future of the Chief Sustainability Officer sense-maker in chief, February, www.deloitte.com/an/en/Industries/financial-services/perspectives/the-future-of-the-chief-sustainability-officer.html (archived at https://perma.cc/T45Q-3GZZ)

3   Eccles, R G and Taylor, A (2023) The evolving role of Chief Sustainability Officers, *Harvard Business Review*, July to August, https://hbr.org/2023/07/the-evolving-role-of-chief-sustainability-officers (archived at https://perma.cc/Q56N-Z45T)

4   Strategy& (2022) Empowered Chief Sustainability Officers: The key to remaining credible and competitive, www.strategyand.pwc.com/de/en/functions/sustainability-strategy/cso-2022.html (archived at https://perma.cc/PC3B-ZK6T)

5   Farri, E, Cervini, P and Rosani, G (2023) The 8 responsibilities of Chief Sustainability Officers, *Harvard Business Review*, 2 March, https://hbr.org/2023/03/the-8-responsibilities-of-chief-sustainability-officers (archived at https://perma.cc/T44T-R6M8)

# 3

# What compels people to pursue a job in sustainability

As we discussed in Chapter 2, the role of a CSO can be described as a tough gig. It is true that doing the right thing is not always synonymous with doing the easy thing. Rather, it requires resilience to remove barriers, courage to stay the course, and stamina to not lose sight of the long-term goals when faced with the occasional setbacks.

Given the many challenges CSOs face in their roles, we wanted to gain a better understanding of what compels people to pursue a job in sustainability. In other words, we wanted to better understand *why* sustainability leaders do what they do. During our discussions with CSOs we asked what inspired them to pursue a career in sustainability. In this chapter, we also explore the significance and impacts of purposeful leadership on organizations – and why leading with purpose is good for society, the planet and business.

## Sources of inspiration for a career in sustainability

Our discussions with CSOs taught us that corporate sustainability, as a vocation, isn't just about business. It is also a personal matter inspired by an appreciation for our natural world, the goodness of humanity, and an unremitting desire to create a better world for future generations.

This is certainly the case for Charlotte Wolff-Bye, Chief Sustainability Officer at Petronas. Charlotte credits her lifelong love of nature and business as being her primary sources of inspiration for pursuing a career in sustainability. Growing up in beautiful Finland, Charlotte learnt early on that when you grow up surrounded by nature you really learn to appreciate it. Growing up close to nature also allows you to see it change over time, and as Charlotte points out, that change can be worrisome.

'When you grow up in the Nordics, you're always close to nature. And when you see nature changing, it's worrying. I was a young child when Chernobyl happened and that point, I became very aware of what the human impact on nature can be. In my family, around the dinner table we used to talk about world affairs and everything that comes with it. So my interest in societal matters started early on, along with a very close connection to nature. And at the same time, my family is a family of entrepreneurs. I strongly believe in the positive power of business. I think business can be a positive force for society, but unchecked, it's not always the case. I wanted to be part of that journey where you do business that does good.'

With its vast coastlines, deep boreal forests and northern mountain ranges, it's no surprise Finland has been a source of inspiration for Charlotte, shaping her views of the world and her vision for a better future. What also served as a source for inspiration for Charlotte was being brought up in a family of entrepreneurs.

Altogether, it is Charlotte's love of nature combined with her appreciation for the positive role business can play in society that served as sources of inspiration that motivated her to pursue a career in sustainability, and specifically to the role of CSO – a role that she sees as being pivotal in protecting the planet for generations to come.

Similar to Charlotte, when asked about what inspired him to pursue a career in sustainability, Klaus Kunz reflected on his own personal experience growing up as being the place where his drive to create a better world started to take shape. For Klaus the question was in some ways a philosophical one that required thoughtful reflection and introspection.

Growing up as a child of East German refugees, Klaus appreciated more than most perhaps the importance of creating a better world for future generations.

'How do you become a leader in ESG or in sustainability? If you allow me to share my personal journey, it goes very far back; because, if you want to work in this space of sustainability and ESG, you need to be open to dream a bit bigger. And I'm a child of refugees, my parents were refugees from East Germany to West Germany. So basically, I was growing up in a family separated by a wall. And we had a dream – and it was really a dream. Today, people say my dream is to go on TV or whatever. But we had a dream, and the dream was that the wall could come down. And it was something which you could only imagine in a dream to really happen. It was so surreal or unrealistic to ever happen. I was 17 and I'm forever grateful that I was old enough to fully embrace that my dream came true. And the wall came down. It was an unbelievable situation for my family. And it made me believe that unbelievable, positive things are possible. You don't know when it comes, but it may come. And when it comes, you need to be ready to go. You can't let these opportunities go off the table. So that is basically a little personal background of why I am where I am today.'

Like so many other families living in Germany at the time, the wall represented a physical barrier that divided not only a city and a nation – it divided families, communities and ideological beliefs as well. Despite the distress and struggles the wall presented, as Klaus explained, it also inspired him to dream big. And dreaming big is exactly what Klaus believes is needed to succeed as a CSO.

Inspired by this moment in history – which taught him not to let opportunities pass him by – Klaus later went on to study chemistry. Klaus shared that in his family there was one hard and fast rule they all had to follow, and that was to not follow the path of the majority simply because it is the easiest path to take. Staying true to this rule, which Klaus points out was perhaps a testament to being a child of East German refugees, he chose a path that was probably least taken. In addition to studying chemistry, Klaus also went on to study economics in parallel, completing a PhD and MBA at the same time. Soon after completing his studies, Klaus began to work for Bayer as a researcher. As Klaus points out, he never intended to follow a career path that would lead to corporate sustainability. Yet, his unique set of skills and experience, that combine science and business, are precisely the kind of skills that make for a strong corporate sustainability leader. Leaning on both his science and business education, Klaus is able to consider and assess sustainability issues and impacts through a science as well as a business lens. By looking at sustainability through this dual lens, he is able to consider the impacts an organization has on the planet, society and the business. For instance, Klaus's experience working in research broadened his awareness around the different and sometimes controversial perspectives the public has towards a company's environmental impact. Looking at these issues through a business lens, Klaus recognizes that the public's perception is real, and rather than avoiding controversial topics he emphasized the need for companies to engage and be part of the conversation. Passionate about the roles of science and business in driving sustainable transformation and contributing to the global sustainability agenda, Klaus credits his combined experience in research and business for paving the way to his career in sustainability.

What inspired Montse Montaner, former Chief Sustainability Officer at Novartis, to pursue a career in sustainability was, very simply, her desire to improve people's lives. For this reason, she studied pharmaceuticals and went on to work in the pharmaceutical industry for more than 30 years. Initially her work focused on the healthcare system, operations and product development functions. It was around 2020, when Montse was the Chief Quality Officer at Novartis, that she decided to shift her focus towards sustainability. Following a lengthy and successful career in the pharma and healthcare sector, Montse pointed to her children as being the source of inspiration behind her decision to switch her focus towards improving planetary health.

'Being close to my children, I see how they needed to live in the future. And when we look at the challenges the planet is facing, I really felt in my heart that I needed to do something different, personally. And I also knew that we could make a positive difference as a company, in the way that we can really improve planetary health. Because we know there is a very close correlation between human health and planetary health. And we are already seeing that as a result of climate change. For example, there are new infectious diseases, there are new respiratory diseases. So, I knew we needed to do something different. And then came this wonderful opportunity at Novartis to be the company's first Chief Sustainability Officer. And with that came the opportunity to be a change agent or a catalyst to really help the company make a more positive impact on society.'

Taking inspiration from her children, through her work as a sustainability leader, Montse remains steadfastly committed to creating a better world for her children, as well as for future generations.

## Being inspired by the corporate purpose

For David Costa, Chief Sustainability and Business Officer at NTT DATA, what inspired and attracted him to the role of CSO was the very thing that would likely deter many people away – driving change at scale. When you consider the many dimensions that sustainability covers, and the associated global targets, it is true – the task is colossal.

In addition to being drawn to the challenge, David was equally motivated by the opportunities the challenge presented. An ardent believer in the impactful role business can play to drive positive change, David recognizes that incremental improvements alone cannot meet these challenges. Instead, the task requires a significant and accelerated transformation that can only be achieved through bold actions.

'I don't believe that this is going to be solved with incremental change. Achieving our objective will require a big transformation. One of the things I did before accepting the role was to align with the top management of the company. There are three topics that are relevant. The first topic is that whoever takes the role needs to report to the CEO of the company. The second: we need to have a very capable and subject-matter-expert team. Top talent! And the third was to have the right empowerment and investment capacity. And I got the answers – sustainability now reports to the CEO and board of directors. We have an outstanding team and regarding the investment, we are in the process of deciding where to invest. But ultimately, I was excited to take the role because our group has a strong DNA on sustainability.'

Having worked at NTT DATA for more than two decades, in various roles and regions, David understood early on that sustainability wasn't simply a promise that appeared in the company's annual report. As he describes, it's been part of the company's DNA since its inception.

'As I said, we have a strong DNA, but we still have a lot of things to improve. What we are now seeing is that there is huge engagement from the top of the company and that's crucial. We always come back to this question, which is, "if you have to choose between growth and operating income or profit – or a bit less growth, operating income and being sustainable – what do you choose?" The reality is that embedding sustainability into processes and decisions is the right thing to do as part of our heritage and DNA. Benefits are countless, but it requires courage and conviction. There are many financial benefits (access to capital, stock performance, cost savings, risk reduction, etc.) and most importantly non-financial benefits (talent attraction, employee satisfaction, positive reputation, innovation required to achieve the goals and of course, the positive impact that can be driven to the planet, the society and the economy). The premium for low carbon intensity varies by sector and is often more reflective of how carbon intensive the leaders in each sector are. If you become genuinely sustainable, you are more attractive to talent, clients and partners, and this trend will accelerate in the years to come. It is a virtuous circle; your company will attract the best talent. The employees will be happier and proud of being part of it. You will make an impact on the clients. And the clients – because sustainability is about the whole value chain – will engage with you. But it has to be in this order. You become genuinely sustainable, and then the rest will come! It's not that you do that because you are seeking the rest. And this is leading to many interesting conversations over the last few months. That's why I like to say I have the best job in the company right now. It's not easy, but it's definitely an exciting one.'

Reflecting on the company's journey, David remarks that NTT DATA's approach to sustainability draws inspiration from the Japanese business philosophy of Sanpo Yoshi, which dates back to the Edo period between the 17th and 19th centuries. Sanpo Yoshi is based on the idea of the three goods – whatever was good for the seller, was good for the buyer, and was good for society (see Figure 3.1). The origins of Sanpo Yoshi can be traced back to the Omi Shonin, a small group of villagers that would travel across the country selling goods from their local Omi region. When returning to their village they would bring back goods from their travels. What separated the Omi Shonin from other merchants of their time was that, because they travelled far distances, they needed to forge long-term trusting relations with the communities they visited, so that they would be welcomed into those communities. They did this by giving back to those communities when they visited, by building bridges and schools, for example.[1]

FIGURE 3.1    Sanpo Yoshi philosophy (adapted from Social Innovation Japan image)[2]

Sanpo Yoshi (三方よし) means 'three-way satisfaction'

Urite Yoshi （売り手よし） – good for the seller

Kaite Yoshi （買い手よし） – good for the buyer

Seken Yoshi（世間よし） – good for society

The Omi Shonin's approach to business made them one of Japan's most successful group of merchants during the Edo period and, put simply, sustainability is at the heart of Sanpo Yoshi. The underlying principle of this philosophy is the idea of shared value creation that benefits all parties. As David describes, this notion of the three goods, which considers the interests of all stakeholders, is central to NTT DATA's modern approach to business. It also serves as the foundation for the circular economy as we know it today, which is another example of a sustainable business model that considers the interests of all stakeholders, including our most precious and valuable stakeholder – the planet.

With its definition rooted in all that is good, Sanpo Yoshi brings to mind another ancient philosophy, eudaimonia, which dates back to the teachings of Aristotle. The word Eudaimonia stems from the Greek words 'eu' which refers to 'being on good terms' and 'daimon' which means your 'highest self'.[3] In the teachings of Aristotle, eudaimonia refers to 'the pursuit of virtue, excellence, and the best within us'.[4] Put simply, Aristotle believed that eudaimonia comes from how we live our lives, or perhaps more specifically – how we choose to live our lives.[5] Aristotle reinforced this belief with the following statement: 'At the intersection where your gifts, talents and abilities meet a human need; therein you will discover your purpose'. When we think about the idea of eudaimonia in the context of our modern world, we can understand how living in accordance with our virtues, or purpose, can lead to living a happier and more fulfilled life.

'At the intersection where your gifts, talents and abilities meet a human need; therein you will discover your purpose.'

**Aristotle**

In his book *The Story of Philosophy*, Will Durant sums up Aristotle's teachings with the following statement: 'We are what we repeatedly do. Excellence, then, is not an act, but a habit'.[6] When we think about how companies approach sustainability, Aristotle's teachings hold – perhaps even more so today than ever before. Sustainable transformation in organizations will not occur through a single action or decision. Rather, it is the culmination of many acts that, when repeated, will lead to continuous improvement and enhanced performance. Leaning on the teachings of Aristotle, in the context of corporate sustainability, companies are not what *they say they will do* – they are what *they repeatedly do*.

## The benefits of defining corporate purpose

As we've gleaned from our discussions with CSOs – and from the wisdom of ancient philosophies – people's motivation to pursue a career in sustainability is often rooted in their personal experiences and beliefs, which shape their values and perspectives of the world. When these values align with professional aspirations, it sets the stage for a purpose-driven career.

As the world continues to grapple with many global challenges affecting people and the environment, pressure is mounting on nations and organizations to do more to reduce their adverse impacts and to drive positive change – for both humanity and the planet. Organizations that are heeding the call and leading with purpose are benefiting from their efforts. Isabelle Grosmaitre, author of the book *Purpose-Led Companies: How the next generation of leaders can really change the world*, underscores the need for businesses to put sustainability, or purpose, at the centre of their business models.[7] In an interview with Forbes, she pointed to companies such as Unilever, Patagonia and Ikea as examples of organizations that have reinvented their approach to business, leading the way forward for their industries.

In terms of how or where to start, Isabelle believes companies need to start with clearly defining, or in some cases redefining their purpose. Looking beyond profits, companies need to ask themselves *why do they exist?* With its clearly defined purpose of 'we are in business to save our home planet', Patagonia is a shining example of a world-leading enterprise whose entire business model revolves around its clearly defined purpose and mission.[8]

Having a clearly defined vision, mission and purpose is vital for organizations to be able to effectively communicate why they are in business. Being able to convey a company's *why* is a powerful way for companies to connect with their stakeholders. In his book *Start with Why: How great leaders inspire everyone to take action*, best-selling author and inspirational speaker Simon Sinek emphasizes how purpose-driven leadership can have a transformative impact on individuals and organizations.

By asking why, what Simon is really asking is '*What is your purpose? What is your cause?*' In the context of business, he emphasizes that people don't buy *what* you do, they buy *why* you do it. In other words, the *why* is what connects companies to people. He also underscores the power of purpose in organizations, stating that purposeful leadership inspires loyalty among employees and customers, as well a culture of trust and collaboration.[9]

While having a clearly defined purpose seems intuitive, many companies fail to clearly define and communicate their purpose to their stakeholders. As Simon points out, for companies that do not have a clearly defined purpose, or are struggling to find their purpose, starting with asking *why* is a good place to start.

## The importance of purposeful leadership in business

Jennifer Dulski is a best-selling author and thought leader on the topic of leading with purpose. In her book *Purposeful: Are you a manager or a movement starter?*, Jennifer provides key insights aimed at helping managers become leaders – and more than that, to help them lead with purpose. In an interview with the NSLS (National Society of Leadership and Success) in 2023, Jennifer explained that she came to understand the power of leading with purpose early in her career, when she was working as a teacher.[10] It was during this time that she saw how meaningful it was to help others unleash their potential. Her passion to elevate others led her to create a not-for-profit focused on helping first-generation students become college graduates. Keen to scale up her efforts, she moved over to the tech sector. Leaning on her education and tech experience, and on her passion to help others realize their potential, Jennifer later went on to be the CEO and Founder of Rising Team, a platform designed to train managers to lead with purpose and empower their teams. Reflecting on the objective of Rising Team, Jennifer explains that it is more than a platform. It is a movement that is driven by passionate leaders. Speaking about the impact of leading with purpose, Jennifer emphasized that strong movements do not rely on a single leader; rather, purposeful leaders focus on building strong communities and networks that can carry the movement forward.

'The best legacy is that the movements we start can live on without us.'

Jennifer Dulski

As an expert leading teams at some of the world's largest tech firms, including Google, Facebook and change.org, Jennifer fully understands the benefits of purpose-driven leadership for businesses and leaders alike, not least of all how rewarding it can be.

It is clear that leading with purpose brings great satisfaction to leaders on a personal level. But why is purposeful leadership important at an organizational level? A 2016 study by EY and Oxford University Saïd Business School set out to answer this question. The study revealed six factors that are driving companies to lead with purpose:[11]

1  Trust deficit in corporations: since the 2008 financial crisis there has been a decline in public trust of organizations, in particular among the younger generations.

2 Sustainability: amid the increase in challenges being brought on by climate change, pressure is mounting on companies to address these issues and to operate more responsibly.

3 Social inequality: inequality across the globe continues to rise, with one per cent of the world's population controlling 50 per cent of the planet's wealth; the pay gap between employees and executives is also increasing, leading to a decrease in morale.

4 Diminishing brand control with rise of social media: public perceptions and discourse around brands, and the reputation of those brands, is influenced exponentially by the increased use of social media. Companies need to be transparent about their actions and engage in the conversation.

5 Demand for longer-term thinking: there is an increase in pressure on organizations to consider their long-term impacts and gains that consider people and the planet, rather than to focus solely on short-term gains, namely profits.

6 Digitization: digital innovations and technologies are emerging at a rapid speed. Companies need to be agile in their abilities to embrace technology and adapt in a digital world.

Altogether these factors are driving organizations to consider the importance of clearly defining and communicating their purpose to their stakeholders. Those that do will stand out from their competitors. Reinforcing the point that leading with purpose provides a competitive advantage, Mark Weinberger, Global Chairman and CEO at EY, stated that businesses that are leading with purpose are seeing the gains in their performance metrics.

'Businesses today are finding that doing good also means doing well. For instance, companies with an established sense of purpose – one that's measured in terms of social impact, such as community growth, and not a certain bottom-line figure – outperformed the S&P 500 by 10 times between 1996 and 2011.'

When it comes to truly leading with purpose, companies need to go beyond simply defining and communicating their purpose. Purpose needs to be embedded into the fabric of the organization. It needs to drive the company's strategy, operations and decision-making processes. A 2021 article by McKinsey reinforces this point, stating that companies should look introspectively and ask very specific questions such as: Does your company meaningfully consider its role in society? And do your executives use the company's purpose as their North Star when making difficult decisions? Companies that are serious about their ambition to lead with purpose will go even further by integrating purpose metrics into executive performance assessments and renumeration.[12]

## Purpose drives employee engagement and attracts talent

Companies that lead with purpose garner a multitude of benefits that enable them to stand out from their competitors. Among the many benefits linked to purposeful leadership is a company's enhanced ability to attract and retain talent, drive innovation, and foster greater employee engagement, morale and productivity. Companies that lead with purpose are also seeing improvements in their financial performance. Research shows that engaged employees lead to more productive and more profitable organizations. Companies who value and prioritize the interests of their employees, and invest in their well-being and professional development, stand to benefit from their efforts. They also stand to gain a competitive advantage by standing out from their competitors. This is even more true during difficult times, when retaining employees is vital for organizations, as was seen during the Great Resignation, a term coined in 2021 during the Covid-19 pandemic by UCL School of Management Professor Anthony Klotz, which described the record number of people quitting their jobs. During the Great Resignation, employees were choosing to leave their jobs in search of opportunities that aligned with their personal goals and preferences.[13] According to a 2021 study by McKinsey, nearly two-thirds of US-based employees surveyed stated the pandemic led them to reflect on their purpose.[14] The study reinforces the point that purpose is key to keeping employees engaged.

Furthermore, according to an article published by the *Harvard Business Review* in 2023, purpose is one of the most powerful magnets for talent. The article points to Patagonia as a primary example of a company whose employees are so engaged and tied to the company's purpose that they couldn't imagine working anywhere else. When asked about the company's talent strategy, Patagonia founder Yvon Chouinard mentioned that he once invited an industrial psychologist to assess his employees. The outcome of the assessment, in short, was 'These people are really unemployable.' Meaning, they were so invested and aligned with the company's purpose that they couldn't imagine working anywhere else.[15] Patagonia's renowned leadership position, driven by purpose, serves as an admirable model for other companies to aspire to.

In addition to attracting and retaining talent, a 2015 study by the *Harvard Business Review* and EY revealed that purpose-driven organizations are more likely to drive innovation and sustainable transformation across their organizations. The study, which surveyed 474 executives, found that 53 per cent of respondents who said their company has a clearly defined purpose said their companies have enhanced their innovation efforts and results, compared to 31 per cent who are struggling to define their purpose. Furthermore, the study shows that purpose-driven companies are seeing greater and consistent revenue growth compared to those who are either trying to define their purpose, or simply do not have a clearly defined purpose. According to the study, 58 per cent of purpose-driven companies say they saw a growth of 10 per cent over three years, compared with 51 per cent of those who are defining their purpose and 42 per cent who have not defined their purpose.[16] This study clearly shows that purposeful leadership impacts not only the people and culture of an organization – but also the bottom line.

---

**KEY TAKEAWAYS**

- **Personal inspiration**: Many Chief Sustainability Officers (CSOs) draw their inspiration from personal experiences and a deep appreciation and connection to nature.

- **Overcoming barriers**: CSOs often face significant challenges and require resilience, courage and stamina to drive long-term sustainability goals within their organizations. They are driven by the belief that positive, impactful change is possible.

- **Purpose-driven leadership**: Leading with purpose is essential for CSOs. Their motivation often stems from a desire to create a better world for future generations.

- **Corporate purpose**: Companies with a clearly defined purpose inspire loyalty and engagement among employees and customers. Purpose-driven organizations benefit from enhanced innovation, sustainable transformation and consistent revenue growth.

- **Purpose drives employee engagement and retention**: Purpose-driven leadership positively impacts employee engagement and talent retention.

Companies that align their purpose with their employees' values and prioritize their employees' well-being gain a competitive advantage and attract top talent.

- **Cultural and strategic integration**: Purpose needs to be embedded into the core strategy, operations and decision-making processes of an organization. Companies that integrate purpose into their business models are more likely to drive long-term success and positive social impact.

## Notes

1   Lewis, R (2018) Sanpo Yoshi: The Japanese business principle of success through responsibility, *Social Innovation Japan*, 28 November, https://medium.com/social-innovation-japan/sanpo-yoshi-japans-responsible-business-philosophy-15db037a840e (archived at https://perma.cc/AH3R-3WDG)

2   Lewis, R (2018) Sanpo Yoshi: The Japanese business principle of success through responsibility, *Social Innovation Japan*, 28 November, https://medium.com/social-innovation-japan/sanpo-yoshi-japans-responsible-business-philosophy-15db037a840e (archived at https://perma.cc/AH3R-3WDG)

3   Chelliah, V (2021) Eudaimonia: The stoic happiness triangle, 17 April, www.youtube.com/watch?v=USvBd6Mxewo (archived at https://perma.cc/UBQ3-E5LN)

4   Debevoise, N D (2024) How purpose-driven leadership is changing the world, Forbes, 13 March, www.forbes.com/sites/nelldebevoise/2024/03/13/how-purpose-driven-leadership-is-changing-the-world/?sh=30343d596942 (archived at https://perma.cc/MZ9A-LNPW)

5   Moore, C (2019) What is Eudaimonia? Aristotle and Eudaimonic wellbeing, PositivePsychology.com, 8 April, https://positivepsychology.com/eudaimonia/ (archived at https://perma.cc/TQ2B-GQ6K)

6   Durant, W (1926) *The Story of Philosophy*, Simon & Schuster, US

7   Michelson J (2023) The new business model for sustainable competitive advantage. A top C-suite adviser speaks, Forbes, 30 October, www.forbes.com/sites/joanmichelson2/2023/10/30/the-new-business-model-for-sustainable-competitive-advantage-a-top-c-suite-adviser-speaks/?sh=13585c912aea (archived at https://perma.cc/XX9A-SBFE)

8   Patagonia (2024) Patagonia's Mission Statement, www.patagonia.com.hk/pages/our-mission (archived at https://perma.cc/GZ8U-ZA8Q)

**9**  Mack, T (2024) Unveiling the power of purpose: Insights from 'Start with why' by Simon Sinek, LinkedIn Pulse, 11 March, www.linkedin.com/pulse/unveiling-power-purpose-insights-from-start-why-simon-travis-t-mack-6habe/ (archived at https://perma.cc/X33Y-XGUD)

**10**  The National Society of Leadership and Success (2023) Leading with passion and purpose: featuring Jennifer Dulski, 13 November, www.nsls.org/blog/leading-with-passion-and-purpose (archived at https://perma.cc/Q6HV-SWH2)

**11**  Ernst & Young, Oxford University Saïd Business School (2016) The state of the debate on purpose in business, EY Beacon Institute, May

**12**  Dhingra, N, Samo, A, Schaninger, B and Schrimper, M (2021) Help your employees find purpose – or watch them leave, McKinsey, 2 April, www.mckinsey.com/capabilities/people-and-organizational-performance/our-insights/help-your-employees-find-purpose-or-watch-them-leave (archived at https://perma.cc/5DFU-QJEL)

**13**  UCL School of Management (2023) Is the 'Great Resignation' a thing of the past?, 9 June, www.mgmt.ucl.ac.uk/news/great-resignation-resigning-itself (archived at https://perma.cc/Q4M8-ME4Q)

**14**  Dhingra, N, Samo, A, Schaninger, B and Schrimper, M (2021) Help your employees find purpose – or watch them leave, McKinsey, 2 April, www.mckinsey.com/capabilities/people-and-organizational-performance/our-insights/help-your-employees-find-purpose-or-watch-them-leave (archived at https://perma.cc/5DFU-QJEL)

**15**  Fernández-Aráoz, C (2023) A strong purpose can make your company a magnet for talent, 9 November, https://hbr.org/2023/11/a-strong-purpose-can-make-your-company-a-magnet-for-talent (archived at https://perma.cc/YPP4-V62C)

**16**  Harvard Business Review Analytic Services Report (2015) The business case for purpose, 2015, https://hbr.org/resources/pdfs/comm/ey/19392HBRReportEY.pdf (archived at https://perma.cc/NLH9-R8DF)

# 4

# There is no single path to becoming a Chief Sustainability Officer

Through our conversations with inspiring Chief Sustainability Officers (CSOs), a clear realization emerged: there is no single path to becoming a CSO. Despite sharing the common title of Chief Sustainability Officer, or a version thereof, the leaders in sustainability we engaged with came from diverse educational and professional backgrounds. Much like the multi-dimensional nature of sustainability itself, the CSOs we interviewed showcased a broad spectrum of knowledge, experience and expertise.

The career origins of these CSOs were varied, spanning fields such as engineering, law and finance, to name a few. For some, pursuing a career in sustainability was clear from the beginning. For others, their path to becoming a CSO was less predictable from the start.

## An unpredictable path to sustainability

When Garrett Quinn stepped into the role of Group Chief Sustainability Officer at Smurfit Kappa in 2021, it was a move that he would not have predicted at the onset of his career. Smurfit Kappa, now known as Smurfit Westrock, after its combination with WestRock in 2024, is a global leader in sustainable paper and corrugated packaging based in Dublin, Ireland and listed on the New York Stock Exchange (NYSE: SW).

Prior to stepping into the role of CSO, Garrett worked in various operational roles within the company for 16 years. Garrett began his career as a graduate trainee working on the operations side of the business at Smurfit Westrock's plants In Ireland and Argentina. From there he moved into plant management roles at the company's plants in Ireland. In 2008, Garrett spent a year in France where he held the role of PA to the Head of the European business. From 2009, he led some of the company's manufacturing plants that produced and distributed boxes across the UK and Ireland. During his time in operations Garrett worked closely with employees on the production and distribution lines. He also worked directly with customers and local businesses. His dealings ranged from building relationships with startups who were seeking small orders, to dealing with large consumer packaged goods (CPG) companies who were bringing forward their comprehensive lists of sustainability certifications and requirements that needed to be adhered to.

Reflecting on his experience, Garrett credits the knowledge and skills he gained from the time he spent working in operations as being pivotal to paving the way to his role of CSO. By interacting with a wide range of stakeholders across all areas of the organization, Garrett learned first hand the ins and outs of the company's operations, the challenges that arose, as well as the different needs of each stakeholder he encountered along the way. It is this level of understanding that positioned Garrett well for his next role as the Head of Investor Relations at Smurfit Kappa, which he stepped into in 2016. As Garrett pointed out during our discussion, typically someone in an investor relations role would have a financial background. In Garrett's case, his leadership team recognized the value of having someone from operations lead the investor relations function. The rationale was simple. Armed with a deep knowledge of how the business works, an operations expert would be well-poised to engage investors on important yet complex issues such as sustainability, as they would have the know-how to engage different areas of the company to find solutions that would meet the interests of investors and the company alike.

The experience and perspectives gained from working in both operations and investor relations functions ultimately enabled Garrett to transition into the role of CSO at Smurfit Kappa, which he stepped into in 2021. He did not have a sustainability, environmental or financial background that one might expect of a CSO. What he did bring, however, was the knowledge and expertise of how the company operated. Having a deep knowledge and understanding of how a business operates is incredibly valuable for CSOs, as it enables them to engage stakeholders by looking at issues not only through a sustainability lens but also through the lens of what it means for a specific business area. Garrett's combined industry experience and sustainability knowledge made him well-positioned to collaborate with all business areas on solutions that kept Smurfit Westrock's business and sustainability goals in mind. Garrett's path to becoming a CSO may not have been clear from the start. What is clear, however, is that the experience he gained over the course of his career proved to be of tremendous value that helped shape and define his role as Smurfit Westrock's CSO.

Jeffrey Whitford is another sustainability leader whose path to becoming a CSO was anything but straightforward from the start. In 2023, Jeffrey Whitford was appointed Vice President of Sustainability and Social Business Innovation for the Life Science business of Merck. Merck Life Science is a leading global life science and biotech company with its headquarters based in Darmstadt, Germany.

When Jeffrey graduated from the University of Missouri in 2004 with a journalism degree, his ambition was to pursue a career in the advertising industry. He never imagined that one day he would go on to lead sustainability at a global science and technology company. Soon after his graduation an opportunity arose for Jeffrey to pursue a postgraduate internship at Sigma-Aldrich, a chemical science company. In 2015, Sigma-Aldrich was acquired by Merck. Although Jeffrey was excited about the prospect of an intern placement, working for a science and technology company was not part of his plan. Reflecting on his decision to take the internship opportunity, Jeffrey recalls the advice he received from his father at the time.

'I had an opportunity that came to me for an internship post-graduation. And my dad said to me, you've got two choices. You can ask people if they'd like fries with that, or you can go take that internship in St Louis. And so, no offence to the golden arches, but I packed myself up and went to this place called Sigma-Aldrich.'

With his newly acquired journalism degree in hand – and with his father's advice in mind – Jeffrey packed up and moved to St Louis where he began his three-month postgraduate internship. It was a significant move that, unbeknownst to Jeffrey at the time, marked the start of a long and rewarding career path that would lead him to become head of sustainability for Merck Life Science some 10 years later.

Upon completion of his internship, Jeffrey was offered a full-time position working on the company's corporate social responsibility community initiatives. The CSR division was initially focused on regional activities in the St Louis region. From there, the scope expanded to be national, and then international. Leaning on his communications and advertising background, Jeffrey was initially charged with covering all things related to advertising, branding and communications. And then the unforeseeable happened. Jeffrey's boss left, opening the door for Jeffrey to be promoted and to lead the company's CSR division. In 2009, the CSR division evolved, and Jeffrey became the Manager of Global Citizenship, which encompassed several areas and topics including carbon emissions, green chemistry, engineering and supply chain.

Although his background in advertising and journalism seemed, at least to Jeffrey, to not be relevant or applicable to his role at Merck Life Science when he first joined the company, Jeffrey quickly came to realize that, to the contrary, his diverse communications and creative-driven background proved to be a tremendous asset. His creative and communication skills enabled Jeffrey to bring a different perspective to the science-driven organization. Furthermore, Jeffrey quickly discovered that a key part of leading sustainability in a large multinational organization is having the ability to take complex topics and communicate them in a way that can be readily understood by different stakeholders across an organization. As such, Jeffrey's journalistic background proved to be a benefit rather than a hinderance to his career.

'I think for me, it's a journey that you wouldn't necessarily have seen. But one of the things that I love about what I get to do is I bring a different perspective to the conversation. And I think we all have different perspectives that we bring, but especially in a science-based company, I am really an outsider. But it also allows me to kind of push boundaries in a different way that maybe others might not have been able to do.'

Like Jeffrey Whitford, Klaus Kunz's journey to sustainability was not exactly planned from the start. Klaus Kunz is the Founder and Managing Director at Ephrin, a sustainability-focused business consulting firm. Previously, Klaus held the role of VP of ESG Strategy at Bayer AG (Bayer). Bayer is a German multinational company that specializes in the life sciences fields of health and agriculture.

Prior to joining Bayer, Klaus studied at the University of Münster where he completed a PhD in Chemistry, as well as at FernUniversität in Hagen, where he completed an MBA at the same time. Soon after graduating, Klaus started working as a researcher at Bayer in 2002. A few years later he moved over to the regulatory division. Klaus recalls that his experience working in the regulatory area of the company was an eye-opening one for him, as it shed light on the importance for organizations to be transparent about their actions and the steps they are taking to reduce their impact. This is especially true for organizations that are perceived to have a negative impact on the environment. For these companies, providing science-based facts and data about their impact, through sustainability reporting and disclosure for instance, does not go far enough. Given that corporate reputation is at risk, these organizations also need to be able to communicate this information more broadly and transparently to various stakeholders through their marketing, PR and communication efforts. As Klaus pointed out, rather than ignoring the public discourse around an important issue, it is best for companies to engage and be part of the conversation.

'As I reflect on my experience working at Bayer, initially in the research and regulatory areas, it is clear that although I only began to formally work on sustainability in 2018, the experience I gained from working in research and regulatory was intrinsically linked to various aspects of sustainability. That experience paved the way towards my career in sustainability.'

## A clear path from the beginning

As we've seen through the experiences shared by Garrett Quinn, Jeffrey Whitford and Klaus Kunz, professionals or graduates seeking a job in sustainability can come from various occupational and educational backgrounds, bringing with them a diverse set of skills, knowledge and perspectives that shape and define their roles as sustainability leaders. For others, however, the path to becoming a CSO was much clearer from the start.

Charlotte Wolff-Bye, for instance, took a much more direct path to her role as CSO at Petronas, which she stepped into in July 2021. For Charlotte, she always knew from the onset of her career that she would be working in a sustainability-focused role that would help businesses to operate more responsibly – keeping people, communities and the planet in mind. Reflecting on her own experiences, Charlotte points to her home country of Finland as being the place where her love and appreciation for nature began.

'I'm one of those few people that can probably say that I didn't just end up in sustainability. This was a clear career path for me from day one. It is something I had my eye on even before the profession existed. And something I've been busy doing for a very long time now.'

It was this focused drive and determination that led Charlotte to start her professional journey in finance. In today's landscape, where sustainability and financial reporting practices are more integrated than ever, Charlotte's financial background has equipped her with the foundational knowledge and tools essential for navigating the complexities of sustainability and performing the role of a Chief Sustainability Officer.

Similar to Charlotte, Elisa Moscolin always knew she would work in sustainability. In 2023, Elisa became the Executive Vice President of Sustainability and Foundation at Sage. Her career as a sustainability professional goes back much further, however. Elisa's decision to pursue a career in sustainability links back to an experience she had when she was a teenager. During her high-school years, she spent one year living and studying in a very small Andean village in South America. During that trip Elisa met a seven-year-old boy who cleaned people's shoes to feed his younger sisters. The boy dreamt of becoming a doctor but was out of education with no means to get out of poverty. Elisa recalls the deep sense of injustice and inequality she felt, which pushed her later in her life to find ways to fix that. That boy, that sense of unfairness and injustice has stayed with her – and it would, in some ways, shape her career path from that point forward.

After graduating from high school Elisa went on to study diplomacy. She was motivated and determined to really try and find a way to change the world for the better. During her studies Elisa stumbled upon a field known as corporate social responsibility (CSR). As Elisa puts it, it was love at first sight. She saw immediately the potential that CSR had to make a meaningful difference in the world. Back then, and perhaps even more so later in her career, Elisa recognized the important role that small and medium-sized enterprises (SMEs) could play to help create a better world for future generations, stating, 'SMEs are the backbone of economies. They have a lot of power.'

Determined to help businesses become better corporate citizens, Elisa has always worked in the field of sustainability. She is probably one of a few people who can say they have spent their whole career working in sustainability. In the beginning Elisa worked in the ITC and financial sectors, specializing in supporting organizations through their sustainable transformation journeys. Her focus was to help companies really integrate sustainability into the core of their business models and operations and move beyond a CSR approach, which often happens on the sidelines of a business or business strategy. Over the course of her career, Elisa worked in local roles, leading a multinational organization's operations in specific regions of Europe and Africa. She also worked in global roles that saw her lead global sustainability agendas. In these roles Elisa had the opportunity to learn how issues and strategies can vary in different industries and geographies, and then finding ways to work through those challenges.

Having worked in the field of sustainability throughout her entire career, Elisa has worked in many roles and her remit kept expanding, from developing sustainability reports in line with the GRI (Global Reporting Initiative) standards, to leading transformation working with the board and executives.

Motivated by the firm belief that if she could help rewire the way companies operate, and get them to be more sustainable while keeping them commercially successful, then she could contribute to rewire markets and the economy towards a model that will benefit the current as well as the next generation. Reflecting on her experience and what motivates her throughout the day-to-day challenges of the CSO role, Elisa says that she hopes to be able to look at that little boy in the middle of the Andes and say, 'I know the world is unfair, but I have done everything I could to make it better.'

## No two paths are the same – but there are some common traits

We can see from the experiences and stories of the sustainability leaders we met with that there isn't a single path to becoming a CSO. And while each story is different, there were some common themes and traits that stood out.

### Hone your area of expertise

Although the educational backgrounds of each CSO differed, each sustainability leader had an area of expertise they honed and leaned on throughout their career.

Having worked on the operations side of the business for many years, Garrett intrinsically knew how the company operated. This area of expertise proved invaluable as it enabled him to bridge the gap between investor expectations and the company's ability to fulfil those objectives. It also allowed him to streamline operations and identify opportunities to effectively grow the business.

Elisa Moscolin emphasizes the importance of companies investing in subject matter expertise, stressing that it is not enough to take a sustainability course to add on to someone's credentials. 'I think that companies need to equip themselves with solid subject matter experts. Long gone are the days where it was okay to just wing this. I am a big believer that companies need to invest in the right sustainability skills and subject matter expertise.

In addition to a strong central team of subject matter experts, I think it is also important to empower employees with the skills they need to make more sustainable decisions. Sustainability cannot be delivered just by a small central team; it needs to be embedded in the fabric of the company. I've seen, throughout my career, companies underestimating the power of that and the importance of investing in this area.'

## The importance of communication

In our discussion with Jeffrey Whitford, we learned about the importance of having strong communication skills for any role in business, but especially for a sustainability leader. The topic of sustainability is complex and immense, covering multiple dimensions of environmental, social and governance issues. Having the ability to take these complex topics and communicate them in a way that can be readily understood and applied by different stakeholders of an organization is an incredibly important and useful skill. Strong communication skills are also vital for gaining much-needed support from various stakeholders to drive sustainability forward in any organization.

Part of what makes a good sustainability communicator is being a good interpreter. The field of sustainability is evolving at a rapid pace, and so too are the regulations that are being defined and redefined and put into legislation. For companies big and small, the risks of not complying are high – and the path forward is clear: companies can do their utmost to transform and get ahead of impending regulations, or they will run the risk of being left behind.

Amid the influx of information, sustainability leaders and their teams need to stay on top of the changes. Moreover, they need to discern from all the different sources what it all means for their company and each of its stakeholders. And then they need to be able to transfer their knowledge by breaking it all down – as clearly and effectively as possible – into bite-size pieces of information for each stakeholder. The challenge is enormous – but it is also crucially important. Equally important is having strong communications skills to meet the challenge.

## Driven by passion

All the sustainability leaders we met with shared a similar trait: they are all passionate about sustainability and about their work in this field. Whatever industry or organization they work for, they are all driven by a common goal of helping businesses to operate more responsibly for people and the planet. This passion is evident not only in their work, but also in how they talk about their work, and how they engage and inspire people along the way. It underpins the point that being a sustainability leader is much more than doing a job or meeting a company's business objectives. It's a way of living and a way being.

## Education and training

As we've learnt through our interviews with sustainability leaders from different industries, the experience gained from working in different professional fields, or in various roles within an organization, is incredibly valuable to the role of a sustainability leader. Having a solid knowledge base in a specific area of sustainability and being able to transfer that knowledge more broadly is a key part of a CSO's role. Equally important to choosing the right career path is choosing the right educational and training opportunities to develop one's skills and knowledge base in the area of sustainability.

As demand for sustainability professionals continues to rise, the number of sustainability courses and training modules on offer by institutions globally has also skyrocketed over the last decade. A quick online search will show a myriad of courses to choose from that cover a wide range of topics including reporting, finance and investing, management and leadership, to name a few. Among the multitude of programmes available, some courses require a significant amount of time and investment, while other shorter courses are designed to be more accessible and are offered for free. The SDG Academy is an example of a free online educational platform developed by the United Nations Sustainable Development Solutions Network (SDSN). The SDG Academy offers free online courses that cover key topics specific to the UN's Sustainable Development Goals.[1]

For undergraduate or graduate students looking to delve deeper into the field of sustainability, there are many post-secondary and postgraduate courses and degrees offered by institutions worldwide. Students have the option to pursue a sustainability degree or select individual courses as part of their curriculum in their chosen field of study. More than ever, beyond sustainability-focused degrees or courses, the topic of sustainability is being woven into the curriculum across all disciplines of study.

For business professionals, there are an equally high number of executive education and training opportunities available for those looking to expand and broaden their sustainability knowledge base and skills. Additionally, sustainability-focused training and professional workshop opportunities are available to companies who are looking to upskill their business leaders and employees in the area of sustainability. Companies can look to bring on consultants or firms that specialize in the field of sustainability to develop training workshops specifically for their organizations, with the aim of elevating an organization's understanding of sustainability and what it means to their business. Deciding which is the best course to pursue depends on the area of sustainability that the company is looking to develop, as well as the level of time and resources that the company is willing to dedicate towards training and educational opportunities.

## Choosing the right path

It may seem somewhat paradoxical, how the field of sustainability itself is embedded in a web of complex global standards, regulations and frameworks, and yet, there is no clear path or set of guidelines for business leaders or graduates on how to become a CSO.

Compared to more traditional career paths that require specific training, degrees and qualifications that are verified by a governing body – as is the case with pursuing a career in law, medicine or accounting, for example – the path to becoming a CSO is less defined and less structured. Whereas lawyers, doctors and accountants must obtain specific degrees and qualifications to practise in their respective fields, CSOs are not yet required to have a specific set of certifications or qualifications. Sustainability remains a relatively new field that does not have a governing body in place to oversee practitioners' credentials. Sustainability is also still in the early stages of adoption on the part of many organizations. Therefore, it is not surprising to see that the profile of CSOs is mixed, with professionals coming to the role with expertise from various educational and professional backgrounds. Looking forward, as sustainability continues to evolve as a discipline – and more specialized certifications become available – the path to becoming a CSO will likely become more structured over the next decade, in line with other more established professions.

And while the path to becoming a CSO is less structured, this isn't a bad thing. To the contrary, this is what makes the field so interesting and appealing to many. The field of sustainability in and of itself is widespread – there is freedom and flexibility to define and shape the role based on one's area of expertise and interests. In many instances, the role is also defined by the nature of the organization or even industry. A CSO working for a large manufacturing company, for example, is more likely to come from the operations, manufacturing and engineering side of an organization. Conversely, a CSO working for a consumer packaged goods company may bring marketing and communications experience, given the importance placed by the company on engaging directly with consumers.

For business leaders looking to pursue a career in sustainability, or to one day become a Chief Sustainability Officer, choosing the right path can seem daunting. For starters, the field of sustainability covers such a vast array of topics across environmental, social and governance domains that it does not seem possible to be an expert in all areas. Added to this the many emerging and changing regulations, as well as the number of sustainability training and courses that have sprung up over the last decade – deciding which is the right path to take can be overwhelming. So, where should one begin?

In our conversation with Michelle Davies, Global Head of Sustainability at EY Law, Michelle emphasized it was really important for anyone at the start of their career, and particularly for anyone interested in pursuing a career in sustainability, to take a moment to really reflect on their strengths and interests, stating, 'I think in sustainability it's really important to take a step back and think about where you can be most impactful and valuable, because that's where you're going to really enjoy your role.' Reflecting on the question of where to begin, Michelle offered some wise advice, stating that the best place to start is by looking introspectively and asking: Where can I be most impactful? Where can I be most valuable? The question compels one to reflect on their strengths and interests. It is sound advice that, in essence, can be applied to any profession or professional.

> 'I think in sustainability it's really important to take a step back and think about where you can be most impactful and valuable, because that's where you're going to really enjoy your role and be more successful.'
>
> **Michelle Davies, Global Head of Sustainability at EY Law**

Given how multidisciplinary the field of sustainability is, reflecting on these questions is an excellent place to start. By pausing to identify a specific area or areas they would like to focus on developing in terms of their skills and knowledge base, aspiring sustainability leaders can begin to map out a clear career path that will move them towards achieving their career goals.

Indeed, the field of sustainability is multidisciplinary by nature, spanning all areas of environmental, social and governance domains. It may come as no surprise, therefore, that the role of CSO is also multidimensional. And while there is no single or clear path to guide business professionals or graduates towards becoming a CSO, what this means is that – on the plus side – there are many different avenues and opportunities that can lead to a career in sustainability. More importantly, as Michelle aptly pointed out, by following a path that stays true to one's interests and strengths, aspiring sustainability professionals will no doubt find enjoyment and satisfaction in whichever path and work they choose.

KEY TAKEAWAYS

- **No single path**: There are multiple paths that can lead to becoming a Chief Sustainability Officer (CSO). Professionals from various backgrounds – including engineering, law, finance, journalism and chemistry – have successfully transitioned into sustainability leadership roles.

- **Understanding of operations**: Experience in operations can be incredibly valuable for CSOs. Understanding the intricacies of a company's operations helps in bridging the gap between sustainability goals and business objectives.

- **The importance of communication skills**: Strong communication skills are crucial for sustainability leaders. They need to translate complex sustainability issues into understandable and actionable insights for diverse stakeholders.

- **Regulatory and public engagement**: Understanding regulatory environments and public perception is vital. Transparent and open communication with the public on important issues is key to driving sustainability initiatives forward.

- **Education and training**: Continuous education and training are essential. Aspiring CSOs should seek relevant courses and certifications to enhance their expertise and stay updated with evolving sustainability standards and practices.

- **Driven by passion**: A common trait among successful CSOs is a deep passion for sustainability. This drive motivates them to lead their organizations towards more responsible and sustainable practices.

## Note

1  United Nations Sustainable Development Solutions Network (2024) SDG Academy, https://sdgacademy.org/ (archived at https://perma.cc/5APM-ZYXN)

# 5

# Essential skills and traits for Chief Sustainability Officers to thrive

As pressure mounts on organizations to elevate their environmental, social and governance performance in line with the global sustainable development agenda, companies need leaders who have the right skills, knowledge and training to navigate the complexity of the multifaceted discipline of sustainability.

According to a study by LinkedIn, which was conducted with its nearly 800 million users, sustainability job postings grew at a rate of 8 per cent per year over the span of a five-year period (between 2016 and 2021). At the same time, the number of profiles that listed green skills grew by only 6 per cent per year over the same period – signalling a skills gap. The study projects that this skills gap will widen over the next five years.[1] As the study highlights, the need for skilled sustainability leaders has never been higher.

## Minding the green skills gap

In this chapter we discuss the key *hard* and *soft* skills CSOs need to excel in their role. Drawing on our discussions with sustainability leaders from different industries, several skills emerged as being *essential* to the role of CSO. Beyond the technical skills, we also explored key traits and characteristics that help CSOs remain motivated and perseverant when faced with challenges on this journey.

## Essential skills

### *Business acumen*

Business acumen encompasses having a comprehensive understanding of how a business operates, how decisions are made, and how it can generate value for stakeholders and drive profits. In the realm of corporate sustainability, the role of the CSO is firmly positioned at the intersection of sustainability and business. To drive a company's sustainability agenda forward, the CSO needs to work closely with the executive team to ensure sustainability is integrated into the core business. Making the business case for sustainability is an integral part of any CSO's role. CSOs who understand the needs of their businesses, and how sustainability can help further an organization's plans for growth and profitability, will have greater success at getting the buy-in they need from an organization's executive team and board.

Getting buy-in for sustainability can be relatively easy when things are going well, from a fiscal perspective. After all, what business does not want to positively impact society and the planet? It is when a business is under financial pressures, due to external factors such as escalating inflation rates and cost of living, for instance, that companies are forced to make some difficult decisions. Maintaining a steadfast commitment to sustainability in the face of such pressures is no easy feat. During these more trying times, having strong business acumen becomes especially important for CSOs to persevere and gain the support they need to see the company's sustainability plans through.

To make the business case for sustainability, CSOs need to adopt a dual mindset that considers sustainability and business objectives simultaneously. Understanding and communicating inherent risks alongside potential growth opportunities becomes paramount. Adopting a dual-minded approach can enable CSOs and companies to effectively identify and navigate both risks and opportunities, ensuring resilience for the future.

Charlotte Wolff-Bye, Chief Sustainability Officer at Petronas, emphasized the importance for CSOs to adopt a business mindset to drive a company's sustainability agenda forward. Prior to starting her career in sustainability, Charlotte studied business and economics in her home country of Finland. She always knew she was going to pursue a career in sustainability, and she knew that having a business background would be an asset on her journey. Having grown up in a Nordic country and being surrounded by nature,

Charlotte was always passionate about the role companies could play to help create a better world for society and the planet.

'When you work in sustainability for a corporation you are at the intersection between business and society. So, one of your tasks is to translate back into business what's going on in society, and in which direction social norms are evolving. You develop insights that answer key questions, such as: How is a societal matter or change relevant to your business? Will it impact you and how should you respond? And then vice versa, you engage on the business response back with society. This is one way of describing it. It's about making sure that while you're creating value, you create value for more stakeholders around you, including the physical environment and those whom you affect that don't have a voice. To sum up, corporate sustainability is to a large extent an exercise about understanding how your business impacts society, how to measure them, and hopefully this leads you, through your work, to leave society in a better place.'

For Charlotte it's clear that for a business to have a positive impact on the planet and society, it needs to be profitable. There is no doubt when leaders approach business with a dual mindset, both the business and the planet will benefit.

## Financial skills

Closely linked to having business acumen is having strong financial skills, or a solid understanding of financial literacy. Central to a CSO's role is being able to translate the impact of sustainability, very clearly, in financial terms. Specifically, being able to communicate the financial risks and growth opportunities to CEOs and CFOs is critical. By looking at sustainability through a business lens, CSOs are well-positioned to discuss important issues, such as cost savings that can be gained in the long term or exploring new market opportunities stemming from new sustainability-focused products and services. Equally important is assessing the cost of not engaging with sustainability, and the associated medium- to long-term risks to the business. Having a strong financial background will help CSOs to build the business case for sustainability investments. Additionally, given the minefield of data that needs to be assessed in the field of sustainability, having strong analytical and critical thinking skills is integral to the role of CSO.

Giulia Genuardi, Managing Director at Enel Foundation and former Head of Sustainability at Enel, credits her economics background for giving her the foundational skills she needs to excel in her role. When Giulia first joined Enel in 2003, she worked in the company's internal audit division, which focused on conducting financial audits and risk management. Fast forward nearly 10 years and the internal audit division decided to create a similar audit for sustainability, applying the same approach, rigour and methodology used for the financial audit. Giulia credits her financial background with preparing her for her role in sustainability. She notes that she was the first person from finance to work in sustainability at Enel, something that wasn't very common at the time.

'I studied economics and I emphasize this because it was an important element when I decided to change my work and go into sustainability. I think this was really useful for my transition to sustainability, especially because I focused on the code of ethics, which was the starting point of our sustainability approach for the company. But what was different was that, around 2010, when I was working in the internal audit division, we decided to create a new initiative that was related to the internal audit of the sustainability report. It was something that didn't exist at the time in the other companies within the Enel Group, or in companies in Italy in general. And so, while I was in the audit division, I was tasked with verifying our sustainability report. For a few years I prepared a long list for the action plan – to cover the gaps identified in the sustainability report. After three years, the Head of External Department, who was in charge of this area, said to me, "Please stop listing the action plan of what we have to do. Please go directly to sustainability and change the processes". So, I decided to transition over to sustainability for this reason – to action the plan we developed.'

Giulia's economics background proved to be incredibly useful in her sustainability role.

As the field of sustainability has evolved, so too has the practice of reporting. More companies are applying the same rigour and level of detail to sustainability reporting and disclosure as they apply with annual financial reports. Companies that are even further along on this journey are developing integrated reports that combine financial and sustainability performance metrics. At present, much of this is being done voluntarily on the part of organizations, but as tighter disclosure and reporting regulations soon come into play, such as the EU's Corporate Sustainability Reporting Disclosure, which comes into effect in 2025, more detailed reporting requirements will soon become mandatory. Companies that are taking steps to improve their reporting practices by applying the same rigour they do with financial reporting will only stand to benefit when the regulations come into play.

## Communication skills

A key part of a CSO's job is their ability to foster relationships, build internal and external networks, and influence key stakeholders on this journey. To achieve these goals, being an effective communicator is paramount. When it comes to sustainability, which can be a complex field to navigate, communication is one of the most valuable skills a CSO can harness.

As Jeffrey Whitford, Vice President of Sustainability and Social Business Innovation at Merck Life Science, emphasized during our discussion – communication skills are a valuable asset for any profession, not least a CSO. As someone who graduated with a journalism degree focused on advertising, Jeffrey appreciates how much his communications background has helped him advance in his career as a sustainability leader. Jeffrey's communication background has enabled him to bring unique and more creative and innovative perspectives to his role, and especially to a science-driven company such as Merck Life Science.

'This is where my background helps me, in terms of that strategic communication, because I'm really thinking about the framing of this myriad of things that we're doing in sustainability. I had a boss who, as we were planning and prepping the next projects that we were working on, asked me, could we just do two or three projects? And my initial thought was "I wish I could just do two to three things; it would be much simpler!" But the communication component here is how do you connect the dots between the reasons why we're doing all of these things? You have to be able to connect things like the data sources to understand where the impact is coming from; but then also explain why the actions you're taking or the strategy you are implementing is going to be effective at changing the course of where your emissions footprint sits, where your water footprint sits, how you are dealing with social sustainability issues, and other topics. All of that factors into being able to tell a compelling, comprehensive and data-rich story that connects with business leaders to say this is a business imperative. There are technical challenges that go with sustainability as well, but I think some of them are easy communications challenges that, if we looked at them differently and put them in the context of business, I think it's such a powerful tool.'

Telling a compelling story that accurately and effectively conveys a company's sustainability efforts is essential for engaging stakeholders and keeping them informed about the company's goals, initiatives and performance. Additionally, when considering the increased scrutiny around sustainability claims and greenwashing, it is imperative that companies get their sustainability terminology and messaging right. Marketing expert Giuseppe Stigliano underscores the power of an effective purpose-driven marketing and communications strategy on a company's sustainability journey.

'Marketing, when done right, is not just about helping companies sell their products and services – it's about creating real value by informing company decisions with insights into customer needs, wants and desires. This alignment potentially reduces waste, minimizes unnecessary production and distribution, and ultimately creates the conditions for a more sustainable world. By understanding and anticipating customer preferences, marketing can become a powerful force for good, driving companies towards more informed, responsible and sustainable decisions.'

When we set out to define the role of CSO in Chapter 1, some of the words used to describe the role were interpreter or translator. Our discussions with sustainability leaders made it clear that a CSO's ability to interpret, translate and effectively communicate complex topics is essential. To fully appreciate the importance of communication skills in business, one needs to look no further than the research and work of Dale Carnegie. In his best-selling book *How to Win Friends and Influence People*, Dale Carnegie draws attention to the importance of communications and building relationships – in business and in life. Since its first publication in 1936, more than 30 million copies of the book have been sold. And although the book has undergone many revisions since the first edition was published, the core principles remain and have stood the test of time. *The New York Times* emphasized this point in an article that marked the book's 75th anniversary, stating 'The book's essential admonitions — be a good listener, admit faults quickly and emphatically, and smile more often, among them — are timeless. They need updating about as much as Hank Williams's songs do.'[2]

The ideas and principles presented in the book stemmed from decades of research and from a course Dale Carnegie established in 1932, which shared the same title.[3] One of the most successful and well-known business-minded people in the world, Warren Buffett, is a proud alumnus of Dale Carnegie's course. In 1952, when Warren Buffett was 20 years old, he decided to invest US$100 to take the course. Looking back on that experience he has remarked it was his 'greatest investment'.[4] Putting the principles he learnt into action, Warren Buffett points to communication as being the single most important skill to use and refine in business – above everything else.

'If you can't communicate and talk to other people and get across your ideas, you're giving up your potential.'

**Warren Buffet**

## Collaboration and networking

As we learnt through our discussions with CSOs, this is not a job that one leader can do alone. To drive a company's sustainability agenda forward, it is important for CSOs to collaborate with colleagues across every area of a business. CSOs who approach their role holistically make a concerted effort to forge relations with key decision-makers in every area of the business – be it finance, HR, operations, IT, marketing, communications and legal, to name a few. Equally important to collaborating internally is building a strong network externally, as sustainability pushes organizations to develop ecosystem strategies for shared-value creation. This becomes especially important when striving to address issues that fall outside of an organization, such as within its value chain. One of the most effective ways to build networks and exchange knowledge is by participating in various industry and cross-industry events. In our conversation with Sean Jones, Chief Sustainability Officer at Microsoft Germany, he highlighted that networking, both internally and externally, is an integral part of a CSO's role.

'I think a CSO needs to be a leader who has networked, both within the company as well as externally. They need to be someone who has a lot of communications capabilities as well – being able to explain the story, but also being able to listen to what the requirements are from the marketplace. And that can be in external communications with investors, or in presentations that they're doing internally. So, I think networking is an important skill for CSOs.'

## Bold and purpose-driven leadership

Bold, purpose-driven, unwavering and steadfast are just a few of the words we heard to describe the type of leader a CSO needs to be to flourish in their role. Drawing on the many inspiring conversations we had with the

CSOs we met with, we would add inspirational and passionate to this list. As Elisa Moscolin stated when asked to define the role of CSO, she described it as being a tough gig. And because it is a tough gig, Elisa emphasized the pressing need for bold leadership in the field of corporate sustainability.

'I believe this agenda needs bold and purpose-driven leaders. I don't think it is an overstatement to say that this is a defining moment of human history. The decisions that leaders make today will define the future of the next generation and probably of humanity. This is because if we don't reverse things now, they probably won't be reversible later, and science is quite clear about this, particularly around climate change. I think sustainability professionals, CSOs, have an incredibly important role to play to guide leadership teams to take the right decisions but let me be clear, these are not easy decisions, and I think CSOs must recognize the conundrum many executives and boards find themselves in. The decisions leaders take today may determine the next famine, drought, death toll and even war, but the markets today do not incentivize them to do the right thing. Doing the right thing may come at a high personal cost.'

Given the many obstacles that sustainability teams encounter in their roles, an unwavering leader who can navigate challenges, garner support and mobilize employees across an organization will be well-poised to advance an organization's sustainability efforts.

'I think the decisions that leaders make today will define the future of the next generation and probably of humanity. I know this may sound like an overstatement, but if we don't reverse things now, they probably won't be reversible later. The leaders of today have a great responsibility and are faced with very difficult decisions where they will have to balance short- vs long-term gains.'

Elisa Moscolin,
**Executive Vice President of Sustainability and Foundation at Sage**

## Key traits and characteristics

### Resilience

In the field of positive psychology, resilience is defined as the ability to cope with whatever life throws at you. People who are knocked down by challenges but return stronger than before are resilient.[5] When it comes to sustainability, having the ability to persevere and carry on in the face of adversity is essential. Montse Montaner, former Chief Sustainability Officer at Novartis, underscored the importance of resilience on this journey.

'You need to have a lot of resilience. I need to tell you resilience is super important. The motivation comes when I go back home and I see my children and I say to myself, what is the legacy that you are leaving with them? So that, of course, pushes you – pushes you to do more, and to do things differently. You need to be able to provide a better planet for them, or to avoid these injustices that there are across the globe, which are really unfortunate. So, these external factors from outside the company are the ones that are really keeping me motivated and inspired. Unfortunately, there are also many negative external factors that you need to be always looking at, which are also really pushing you to do the things differently, right? Now on this journey there are ups and downs – but you need to keep being consistent. Consistent on changing the world, on fighting against injustices, on fighting against lack of diversity and inequality. So, keep doing that despite all of the challenges. And I think the overall balance is still much more positive when you keep doing that, and when you keep trying to do things in a proper way.'

Considering the many challenges that CSOs encounter in their role, it is clear that having resilience is an important trait. One question that came to mind following our discussions with CSOs was whether resilience could be taught and learnt. To seek the answer to this question, we turned to the work of the father of positive psychology, Martin E P Seligman, who is a Professor of Positive Psychology at the University of Pennsylvania and renowned for this work and research on the topic of resilience. Specifically, his research focused on assessing how to distinguish those who grow after failure from those who collapse. Following decades of research, Seligman and his colleagues discovered that the answer to this query was optimism.[6] Those who persevered when faced with adversity were more likely to interpret the setback as temporary, and as something that was changeable. In other words, they could learn from the situation and do something to change course. The research showed that by simply thinking more optimistically, one can feel less helpless when faced with adversity. What Seligman's work also revealed was that, fortunately, resilience is a characteristic that can be learnt and developed. This is especially important to note for leaders who are building and leading sustainability teams, who can feel, at times, that they are rowing against the current.

## Grit

Closely related to resilience is grit. In her best-selling book *Grit: The power of passion and perseverance*, Angela Duckworth, psychologist and Professor of Psychology at the University of Pennsylvania, defines grit as 'passion and perseverance for very long-term goals'.[7] Prior to becoming a psychologist, Angela worked as a management consultant and then as a seventh-grade maths teacher in public schools in New York and San Francisco. It was during her job as a teacher that Angela realized that IQ wasn't the only predictor of success. This led Angela to leave her job as a teacher to go on and study and work in the field of psychology. Together with her research team, she set out to study different groups of people in very different environments with the aim of predicting who was going to be successful. She surveyed cadets at a military academy, children participating in spelling-bee competitions, rookie teachers working in tough neighbourhoods, and salespeople working in private companies. In each setting, Angela's research centred around one key question: Who is successful here and why? Following years of research, grit emerged as being the single most important predictor of success above all other indicators, including IQ. In an interview about her work, Angela offered an important distinction between resilience and grit, stating that 'resilience is a response to adversity that is at least as positive as if the adversity didn't happen'. She highlighted that some people can even grow from adversity and become net positive. Angela explained that where resilience overlaps with grit is that if someone is working towards a long-term goal, they will inevitably experience adversity along the way. How they respond to that adversity is a test of their resiliency. In turn, resilience is an element of grit. Where resiliency differs from grit is that someone can be resilient, but they may lack a sense of purpose or drive towards a long-term goal.[8]

Based on this definition, which combines passion and perseverance towards long-term goals, grit inherently captures the essence of what it means to be sustainable. In the context of sustainability, being purpose-driven and focused on achieving long-term goals is at the heart of a CSO's role. CSOs who embody this essential trait will not only be well-positioned to lead their teams through adversity – but they will also foster their growth and resilience along the way.

## Humility and curiosity

Leading with humility and being curious were characteristics that also arose as being essential to the role of CSO. We have intentionally paired these two traits together because – in our view – being humble and being curious are valuable traits that, when put together, can foster a culture that is open to new ideas and innovation. A common misconception in business is that leaders need to have all the answers. In reality, having the humility to be transparent about what one does not know is a strength – it also helps build trust with colleagues and teams. In an interview with consulting firm McKinsey & Company, Adam Grant, organizational psychologist and Wharton Professor, underscored the importance of leading with humility.

'It sounds like low self-esteem or having a low opinion of yourself or being meek. That's not actually what humility is. If you go back to the Latin roots, one of them means "from the earth". Being humble is about being grounded, recognizing that you're only human, that you're fallible. And I think it takes real confidence to say, "You know what? Here are the things I'm not good at. Here are the questions that I don't have answers to. Here's what I don't know. Here's where I was wrong." What the research shows consistently is that leaders who are secure enough in their strengths to admit their weaknesses and vulnerabilities actually get better ideas from the people around them, they learn more, and that ultimately enables them to lead more effectively.'[9]

Equally important to leading with humility is being curious enough to continuously seek answers. It is this combination of humility and curiosity that lays the foundation for leaders to foster a culture that embraces a growth mindset. First introduced by Stanford psychologist Carol Dweck and her colleagues, a growth mindset is the belief that a person's capacities and talents can be improved over time. The opposite of a growth mindset is a fixed mindset, which is the limiting belief that the capacity to learn and improve cannot be meaningfully developed.[10] In sustainability, adopting a growth mindset is vital. Part of a CSO's role is to seek new and innovative solutions to address grand challenges facing organizations.

## Kindness

As we've learnt through our discussions with sustainability leaders, sustainability can take on many different meanings. In the context of sustainable development, in 1987 the United Nations Brundtland Commission defined sustainability as 'meeting the needs of the present without compromising the ability of future generations to meet their own needs.'[11] Earlier in this book we shared our modern definition of sustainability, in the context of corporate sustainability. If we had to define sustainability in a word, however, that word would be kindness. Being kind to people and the planet is at the heart of what it means to be sustainable. It is also a trait that is often undervalued, or even perceived as a weakness in the context of business. But what if this wasn't the case? What if more companies included viewing kindness as being an essential trait for employees, and listed it as a key qualification on job postings, for instance? Could hiring kinder and more compassionate managers have a positive impact on a company's culture and overall performance?

Dr Bonnie Hayden Cheng, author of *The Return on Kindness*, believes the answer to this question is an overwhelming yes. Based on her years of researching this topic, Dr Cheng's research shows that kind leadership leads to the creation of high-trust companies whose workers are *more engaged* and *more productive* than companies that scored lower on the kindness barometer.[12] Rather than being considered a weakness, Dr Cheng believes kindness is a powerful tool that can help leaders foster strong organizational cultures where both people and companies can thrive. Looking at kindness through a sustainability lens – if we all approach business in a way that considers the well-being of both people and our natural world, surely the world will be in a better place.

## Optimistic

Despite the many global challenges facing the world and businesses today, the CSOs we met with were all optimistic about the future, albeit cautiously so. The overall sentiment was that the CSOs we met with were encouraged by how much sustainability has evolved over the past decade – shifting from a PR focus to one that sees sustainability being integrated into the core of a business. This, combined with the progress made by various sectors over the last decade, such as in the field of renewable energy, which has seen tremendous growth, suggests there is reason to be optimistic. Sean Jones, Chief Sustainability Officer at Microsoft Germany, pointed to COP 28 (the 28th United Nations Climate Change Conference) which took place in Dubai in late 2023, as an example of this progress. Traditionally, COP events are largely attended by government representatives and policy makers. What made COP 28 notably different was the increased presence of businesses – as well as the amount of business activities that were happening at the event. With more businesses pushing for change, and more fossil-fuel companies joining the conversation, indeed there is reason to be optimistic. Perhaps we should remain only cautiously so, however, because as Sean aptly pointed out, despite the progress being made – we are still not going fast enough.

## Sustainability expertise

In addition to all of the essential skills and traits listed above, there are some technical skills or subject areas that CSOs need to have a solid understanding of to perform their jobs well, and to lead in these areas. Having awareness of compliance, legislation and regulations, especially as it relates to their specific organizations and industries, is key. Understanding the impact of a company's value chain, and the resources that are needed to support their value-chain partners on this journey, is also critical. CSOs also need to have a solid understanding of the various frameworks that can help companies with their disclosure and reporting efforts. Finally, having a good understanding of the tools, technology and resources that are available to help companies navigate and collect data, as well as measure and track their performance, is crucial. As we've gleaned from our discussions with CSOs, we recognize that being an expert in all areas of sustainability isn't realistic. But having a solid foundation of each of these technical areas, combined with a strong network and team of experts to lean on, is imperative.

## Sustainability knowledge is transferable

Another notable trend identified in our discussions with CSOs is the widespread transferability of knowledge and skills across sectors. This transfer of knowledge is pivotal for companies looking to elevate their understanding of sustainability. Given that sustainability is still a relatively new and emerging field – encompassing environmental, social and governance aspects – identifying a sustainability expert with extensive sector experience may be challenging. Organizations looking to bolster their teams with sustainability expertise should prioritize the valuable contributions a sustainability expert can make, rather than give emphasis to the sector-specific experience they may or may not bring. In an interview with *Sustainability Magazine*, conducted in August 2023, Sarah Gould, Principal Sustainability and ESG Consultant at Shirley Parsons, underscores this point.

'You are hiring the Head of Sustainability for their expertise in sustainability, leadership, commercial awareness and personality skills,' Sarah explains, 'and not for their 10 years of working in the sector.'[13]

Additionally, Sarah emphasizes that industry-specific experience can be learned and gained over time. Elisa Moscolin shares Sarah Gould's view that companies need to invest in the technical expertise of sustainability experts, and not see sustainability simply as a label that can be added to an existing function or role.

'Companies are struggling with a war for talent in the area of sustainability. There is very high demand and not enough supply. We haven't created the pipeline of talent yet. So, what happens more often than not is that companies get someone who is a brilliant leader and then add the label of sustainability to their job title. That has been one of the root causes of greenwashing and has weakened the credibility of the sustainability practice. The same way you wouldn't give the Chief Technology Officer title to your Chief People Officer or vice versa, companies should avoid giving the CSO title to people that do not have the right level of expertise and experience in the field. If you really want to drive progress, you do need to have the right technical skills in addition to the leadership. The challenges that the sustainability agenda poses are complex. Although it is true that there are not too many people who have done this for a long time and who have that deep subject-matter expertise, companies should invest in the right talent if they want to have a solid and credible sustainability strategy.'

As we've learnt through our conversations with sustainability leaders, being a subject matter expert in all areas of sustainability is not realistic. But, as Elisa stresses, being a subject matter expert in a specific area, combined with having a strong foundational knowledge of corporate sustainability and a strong team of experts to lean on, is vital to succeed in this demanding role.

## The importance of sustainability training and upskilling

Sustainability is not an all-encompassing skill set that can simply be added to one's list of credentials following a single course or training session. It is an area of expertise and a career path that is developed through a journey of continuous learning and growing. And just as there are various avenues students and professionals can take to become a CSO, there are also several options for training and upskilling across all facets of sustainability, such as sustainability strategy, regulation, auditing and reporting, to name a few. Going back to the advice offered in Chapter 1 by Michelle Davies, Head of Global Sustainability at EY Law, knowing which path to choose starts with knowing one's area of interest, and where one can have the greatest impact.

A study by Microsoft and Boston Consulting Group (BCG) asserted that formal training and credentials of sustainability leaders varies. The study looked at the training and credentials of sustainability professionals at major global companies and found that the majority of those surveyed did not have formal training in sustainability. Of the nearly 250 sustainability professionals surveyed across 15 organizations, the study found that only 43 per cent had sustainability-related degrees and 68 per cent were hired internally.[14] The study also revealed that 60 per cent of those hired on sustainability teams did not have any expertise in the field. To fill this skills gap, more companies are starting to invest in training and upskilling their employees on the topic of sustainability. By investing in their people, they are investing in future-proofing their business.

Whether through formal education or on-the-job training and experience, there are many different opportunities to develop one's knowledge, skills and expertise in this still nascent and evolving field. What matters more than which route one takes is one's steadfast commitment to continuous learning and growing on this journey. Those who choose to develop the essential skills outlined in this chapter – and embrace a growth mindset – are undoubtedly paving their way towards a rewarding and bright future.

---

KEY TAKEAWAYS

- **Business acumen**: CSOs need a comprehensive understanding of business operations and decision-making processes. This skill helps in making a strong business case for sustainability and ensuring that sustainability initiatives align with a company's growth and profitability goals.

- **Financial skills**: A solid understanding of financial literacy is crucial for CSOs. This includes the ability to translate sustainability impacts into financial terms, communicate risks and opportunities, and support sustainability investments with strong financial reasoning.

- **Communication skills**: Effective communication is vital for fostering relationships, building networks, and influencing key stakeholders. CSOs must be able to convey complex sustainability topics clearly and effectively to ensure buy-in from both internal and external stakeholders.

- **Collaboration and networking**: CSOs must collaborate with various business functions and build strong external networks. This holistic approach helps in addressing sustainability issues across the value chain and facilitates knowledge exchange through industry events and cross-industry collaborations.

- **Bold and purpose-driven leadership**: Successful CSOs are bold, purpose-driven leaders who inspire and mobilize their teams, navigate challenges and make impactful decisions with future generations in mind.

- **Resilience and grit**: CSOs need resilience to persevere in the face of adversity and grit to stay committed to long-term sustainability goals despite obstacles.

# Notes

1  LinkedIn Economic Graph (2022) Global Green Skills Report 2022, https://economicgraph.linkedin.com/content/dam/me/economicgraph/en-us/global-green-skills-report/global-green-skills-report-pdf/li-green-economy-report-2022.pdf (archived at https://perma.cc/L4XT-A3ZV)

2  Garner, D (2011) Classic advice: Please leave well enough alone, *The New York Times*, 5 October, www.nytimes.com/2011/10/05/books/books-of-the-times-classic-advice-please-leave-well-enough-alone.html (archived at https://perma.cc/6MD6-PWTF)

3  Dale Carnegie website, www.dalecarnegie.com/en-gb/approach/heritage (archived at https://perma.cc/E7KJ-E96K)

4  Krausz, J (2021) Speak like a billionaire: Warren Buffett's simple approach to Communication, Media Shower, 28 October, https://mediashower.com/blog/speak-like-a-billionaire-warren-buffetts-simple-approach-to-communication/ (archived at https://perma.cc/RT72-C8FC)

5  Fontane Pennock, S (2017) Resilience in positive psychology: How to bounce back, 3 March, https://positivepsychology.com/resilience-in-positive-psychology/ (archived at https://perma.cc/LQZ9-AEE6)

6  Seligman, M E P (2011) Building resilience, *Harvard Business Review*, April, https://hbr.org/2011/04/building-resilience (archived at https://perma.cc/N7K8-U22Z)

7  Ted Talks Education (2013) Grit: The power of passion and perseverance with Angela Lee Duckworth, www.ted.com/talks/angela_lee_duckworth_grit_the_power_of_passion_and_perseverance (archived at https://perma.cc/GPP2-MYFY)

8  The Kenan Institute for Ethics (2021) Angela Duckworth: What is the difference between resilience and grit?, www.youtube.com/watch?v=05XmoKKrj4M (archived at https://perma.cc/JYE3-67BZ)

9  McKinsey & Company (2021) Adam Grant on leadership, emotional intelligence and the value of thinking like a scientist, 24 May 24, www.mckinsey.com/about-us/new-at-mckinsey-blog/adam-grant-on-modern-leadership (archived at https://perma.cc/2E6H-95RU)

10 Psychology Today, Growth mindset, www.psychologytoday.com/us/basics/growth-mindset (archived at https://perma.cc/82EP-RLW5)

11 United Nations Academic Impact, Sustainability, www.un.org/en/academic-impact/sustainability (archived at https://perma.cc/5MZ9-LPNV)

12 Peesker, S (2024) Kindness isn't weakness in leadership, *The Globe and Mail*, 19 March, www.theglobeandmail.com/business/article-kindness-isnt-weakness-in-leadership/ (archived at https://perma.cc/FE9M-3WHW)

13 Buchholz, L (2023) What does it take to be a Chief Sustainability Officer?, *Sustainability Magazine*, 20 August, https://sustainabilitymag.com/articles/what-does-it-take-to-be-a-chief-sustainability-officer (archived at https://perma.cc/N7LA-G2CL)

14 Microsoft (2022) Closing the sustainability skills gap: Helping businesses move from pledges to progress, 2 November, https://blogs.microsoft.com/on-the-issues/2022/11/02/closing-sustainability-skills-gap/ (archived at https://perma.cc/D79U-ZWDY)

# 6

# Structuring sustainability for long-term success

Despite the level of maturity of an organization, when it comes to sustainability, one thing is clear – to improve a company's ESG positioning, sustainability needs to be systematically embedded across the organization. Given sustainability is still a relatively new and growing function in business, the way it is structured and integrated across organizations varies. Through our discussions with CSOs we have seen how sustainability has become a growing priority for many business leaders – rising from the bottom of the corporate agenda to the top. In this chapter, we delve into how sustainability is organized across organizations big and small. Additionally, given the many business areas that intersect with sustainability – such as strategy, compliance, reporting and stakeholder relations – we also explore whether there is an ideal reporting structure for sustainability, particularly for the CSO.

## Sustainability leadership

In recent years we have seen an increase in the number of corporations coming forward with their bold commitments and ambitious targets. As we have gleaned from our discussions with CSOs, bold commitments require bold leadership. And by this we mean leadership from the top. As any CSO will attest, navigating the complexities of sustainability can be challenging. Without the unwavering support of the executive team and board of directors, these challenges are even greater. Given the complexities of sustainability issues, it is equally important for executive teams to be able to lean on the expertise of a sustainability expert to guide the company's sustainability strategy and goals. For organizations that may just be starting their journey of sustainable transformation, recruiting and hiring an experienced CSO is a good place to start. Appointing a dedicated CSO who is knowledgeable and experienced underscores the importance of sustainability within an organization. Leaning on their years of experience working in the field, CSOs can develop and steward a company's sustainability strategy, set realistic and measurable goals, and ensure sustainability is integrated into the company's core business and operations – and perhaps most importantly, its culture.

In Chapter 5 of this book, we discussed the essential skills CSOs need to succeed in their role. What we also discussed, and think is worth restating, is that when it comes to sustainability leadership specifically – sustainability expertise trumps industry expertise. What we mean by this is that sustainability expertise, by and large, is transferable from one industry to another. The knowledge, skills and experience that CSOs bring to the table can be applied to any organization and industry. Of course, having industry knowledge and experience is incredibly valuable. For industry experience, however, the CSO can draw on the expertise of others in the organization who can bring that knowledge. For this reason, it is also crucial that CSOs are working in lockstep with other areas of the business – so that knowledge can be transferred in both directions. Through this collaborative approach, CSOs will gain a better understanding of the tangible business and operational challenges that companies are facing when striving to decarbonize their business, for instance.

## Reporting lines

Placing the CSO in a position that allows direct access to the executive team is imperative for ensuring that sustainability initiatives receive top-level support. In recent years, we have seen more CSOs establish direct reporting lines to the CEO or CFO. This shift in reporting lines is demonstrative of how much the field has evolved over the last decade. When sustainability first emerged as a key issue for companies to focus on, it was often approached as a CSR initiative that was part of the company's PR or marketing function. Having a seat at the executive table ensures that sustainability is no longer approached peripherally as a CSR initiative, rather it is integrated into the core decision-making processes of the organization. An article published by *Harvard Business Review* highlights this shift. In the article, the authors argue that given the need for CSOs to adhere to more rigorous sustainability reporting standards, similar to financial reporting, establishing a direct reporting line to the CFO is ideal. To further support this viewpoint, the authors also point to the fact that sustainability is increasingly becoming an important topic for investors, and as such CSOs are being asked to join meetings and discussions with investors.[1] More and more investors are keen to dive deeper into a company's ESG activities and performance. This rising interest from investors is yet another reason for the CSO to be closely positioned to the executive team.

Garrett Quinn, Group Chief Sustainability Officer at Smurfit Westrock (formerly Smurfit Kappa), supports the idea that given the increased scrutiny that is coming to sustainability reporting, as is the case with the CSRD in Europe, having the CSO report to the CFO makes a lot of sense. At the same time, he argues that where sustainability is positioned in the organization, whether it is under the CEO or CFO, depends largely on where a company is positioned more broadly on sustainability.

'I think it really depends on the company. I don't think there's a right or wrong answer. For instance, if you work for a company where sustainability is approached more as PR and opportunistic, and it's not really integral to the business, then there's a good argument to say the CSO should report to the CEO – because you need to drive that culture change. And you need the leader of the company to drive that culture change. So that's where I would see that structure might be a bit more obvious, where you need to drive the change. In a company like Smurfit Westrock where in our business – and I know there's an element of bias here – recycling is core to our business. We need old boxes to make new boxes. And we've been doing it since the 1930s.

'So, the idea of sustainability, both operationally and commercially, is ingrained in the company and it always has been. And so, the decision was made actually to move the reporting structure. Previously, the person who was in charge of sustainability reported to the CEO. And later, due to the reporting that was coming, the intention was to move it to the CFO. The thinking was, let's not lose the good things that we're doing, let's continue to develop where the opportunity is. But, equally, given where the regulations are going and where the reporting is going, we need to capitalize on the good reporting practices that exist within the finance department to support that.'

Offering a slightly different perspective on the optimal positioning of the CSO in an organization, Sean Jones, Chief Sustainability Officer at Microsoft Germany, believes positioning sustainability squarely under finance could, in some ways, be limiting. While he appreciates the many benefits of having sustainability under the finance function, reporting efficiencies being a clear one, Sean argues that positioning the CSO under the CFO may limit their focus to compliance and reporting, rather than on establishing long-term strategies. For this reason, Sean believes the CSO would be better positioned to report directly to the CEO.

'Simplistically speaking, if you're going to position the CSO somewhere, it should be under either the CEO or the CFO – and that's okay. The issue, however, with placing the CSO under the CFO is that they will focus primarily on reporting and controlling requirements, which are very important, of course. Companies under CSRD (Corporate Sustainability Reporting Directive) will need to follow the requirements in their reporting – and that will be a big effort. Then of course there are the controlling requirements, which are delegated functions from the CFO into each of the business units to figure out how they are performing from a finance perspective. And then you also need to consider transformation of people, processes and technology. CSOs still need to make sure that everybody in the different business units and the different functions understands what sustainability means. And there's a huge lack of understanding – no doubt it's complicated too.

'So, taking complex topics and making sure that everybody in the organization understands those topics, just like profit and loss, is key. Everybody understands revenue and margins and profits and working capital in business now – but nobody understands carbon, water and waste, let alone social aspects. So that all needs to be part of it. And that has to be part of the CSO's role. In my view, this will not be the role of the CFO. It has to be part of the CSO's role to really enable and empower and educate the organization on sustainability.'

Sharing the view that, in an ideal structure, the CSO should report to the CEO, we find David Costa, Chief Sustainability Business Officer at NTT DATA. As we discussed in Chapter 3, prior to stepping into the role of CSO, David outlined three key conditions he felt were essential for newly appointed CSOs to thrive in their role. The first was the need for the CSO to report to the CEO. As David puts it, to really shift the culture and mindset of a company, this requires bold leadership that comes from the top. The second was a commitment to build a strong team with the best talent. And the third condition was a promise for empowerment and investment capacity. Combined, these three conditions would provide the foundation for a CSO to build a sustainability-driven culture and strategy to deliver on the company's medium- to long-term goals.

'What I like to say is that this is not just the sustainability area mission – it's the corporate mission. And most of the conversations I've had with executives over the past year revolve around where their responsibilities are. And it's interesting, because if you look at the details of what the Chief Financial Officer, Chief HR Officer, Chief Marketing Officer, and what the CEO should do; at the end, if they take their responsibility in regard to sustainability and work by it, there is nothing left for me to do. So, if we, as a team, do a good job – in the future the company should be sustainable by itself. This is why we are ready for the challenge – and we like to say that we have the best job in the company.'

**David Costa, Chief Sustainability Business Officer at NTT DATA**

Based on our research and discussions about optimal reporting structures, whether the CSO reports to the CFO or CEO is less critical than ensuring the CSO holds a prominent position at the executive table. Even more important is ensuring they have unwavering support from the entire leadership team across the organization. Placing the CSO in a position that allows direct access to the executive team is crucial for ensuring that sustainability initiatives receive top-level support and are aligned with the company's business objectives. Furthermore, this executive-level reporting structure and approach ensures that sustainability is not operating as a silo, rather it is integrated across different functions of the business and into core decision-making processes.

## Organizing sustainability in the boardroom

Sustainability is not a function that belongs solely on the desk of the CSO. Executive teams and boards of directors must also ensure they are engaged and knowledgeable on sustainability matters, especially given the rising interest from stakeholders, including investors. According to PwC's Global Investors Survey 2023, 75 per cent of respondents consider how companies manage sustainability-related risks and opportunities in their investment decision-making.[2] If pressure from stakeholders is not reason enough, the increase in regulations developed to hold companies accountable for their environmental and social impact will undoubtedly spur organizations to elevate their efforts. Being accountable is precisely the reason boards need to take sustainability seriously. The pressure mounting from stakeholders and more stringent regulations underscores the need for boards to establish robust governance policies and procedures that ensure effective oversight and transparency on sustainability matters.

Research conducted by Andreas Rasche, a Professor at Copenhagen Business School, focused on assessing the different ways boards can effectively engage with sustainability. Andreas's research explores whether boards should adopt a fully integrated approach to sustainability, where they can discuss sustainability topics during regular board meetings, or if it would be more effective to form a separate subcommittee, where board members can explore sustainability topics more deeply. Indeed, within a committee setting, board members can dedicate more time to gain a deeper understanding of the issues and risks and identify potential business opportunities.

Andreas acknowledges that, theoretically, adopting an integrated approach that considers sustainability issues alongside business objectives is a good approach. In practice, however, Andreas's research has shown it can be challenging for boards to effectively incorporate sustainability into their broader discussions, particularly if the board is still in the early stages of knowledge and understanding of sustainability. Andreas cautions that if boards are still in the early stages of learning and understanding, a fully integrated approach may not be the best option.[3]

'Forming a sustainability committee, or extending an existing committee, are viable alternatives, especially for boards that are still building up capacity and that are in the process of finding their way on sustainability. Committees also have downsides, but they allow for more granular discussions of how material ESG topics and corporate value drivers interact.'

As part of his research, Andreas offers four possible structures for boards to effectively integrate sustainability into the boardroom: 1) Full integration into the board, 2) Sustainability committee, 3) Individual board champion, 4) Extension of existing committee.[4] In our view, the ideal structure depends on two key factors: the size of the organization, and its level of sustainability maturity. For example, the optimal structure for a large organization that is at a nascent stage of sustainable transformation may be to lean on the expertise of a 'sustainability champion' or 'sustainability committee' to help educate and steer the board's focus towards matters that have the greatest impact on the business. For smaller organizations, where sustainability is already embedded into the culture, a fully integrated approach may be the best option. In this scenario, board meetings can serve as a forum for more in-depth training to elevate knowledge of specific topics impacting the business. Through this approach, sustainability knowledge can cascade into all areas of the business. Additionally, in a smaller boardroom setting, where board members can build a solid understanding of sustainability issues – associated risks and opportunities can be deliberated more effectively as part of strategic decisions and long-term planning discussions.

As we can glean from Andreas's research, there are several approaches boards can take depending on where they are positioned on their journey of sustainable transformation. While there are indeed optimal structures suitable to different scenarios, in our view, so long as sustainability has a seat at the boardroom table – be it in the form of an individual champion or a committee – the most important thing is that organizations are making strides to ensure sustainability is on the corporate agenda.

In addition to strengthening a board's governance and proficiency around sustainability, to really drive meaningful results in line with a company's sustainability goals, boards can also look to introduce executive remuneration policies. According to an article published by EY in 2023, companies are more likely to achieve their sustainability targets if the remuneration of their executives is tied to those objectives.[5]

## Building a sustainability team

In addition to having solid leadership at the top of the organization, in the form of a supportive executive team and unwavering CSO, in an ideal setting the CSO is supported by a strong sustainability team. Even with strong sustainability leadership in place, no CSO or executive team can do this work alone. A central part of a CSO's role is to build a team that can help steward the company's sustainability agenda across the organization. Investing in building and developing a team of subject matter experts and providing them with the resources they need to excel in their roles is key.

Given the many dimensions of sustainability, in an ideal structure a sustainability team would be comprised of diverse subject matter experts, each specializing in different areas of sustainability. For example, one member of the team would specialize in sustainability reporting, diligently staying abreast of the latest disclosure regulations pertinent to their company and industry, regionally and globally. Another team member might focus on environmental initiatives, with a particular focus on strategies to mitigate a company's carbon footprint through targeted measures and processes.

Another member could specialize in social matters. As part of their role, they would be focused on implementing policies that aim to ensure the well-being of employees, suppliers and partners. Central to this team and how it functions is the transfer of knowledge. By sharing their expertise and knowledge within the team, but also more broadly through internal training and upskilling initiatives across the organization, the sustainability team plays a pivotal role in ensuring sustainability is embedded across different functions of the business. Additionally, this focus on training and upskilling also contributes to fostering a sustainability-focused culture.

Given the many dimensions and complexity of sustainability, combined with the magnitude of new or impending regulations that CSOs need to be versed on, being an expert in every subject area is simply not realistic. When we asked CSOs how they manage to navigate the tsunami of information that flows towards them weekly or even daily – many pointed to key pillars that they lean on to help them grow, and to help them stay abreast of trends and new information. The first was the pillar of being surrounded by a *strong team of experts* – and the importance of building and supporting that team. The second was about the importance of *building a network* of like-minded leaders. Attending industry events and exchanging knowledge with leaders from other organizations and industries is imperative for CSOs to excel in their role.

## Sustainability steering committees

To ensure sustainability is ingrained into the fabric of a business, it cannot be driven solely by a centralized sustainability team. It needs to be embedded across every function of a business.

Establishing a cross-functional steering committee is one approach companies are taking to steward sustainability across their organizations. As part of Canon's approach to sustainable transformation, Peter Bragg, Sustainability and Government Affairs Director EMEA at Canon, set up a steering committee in collaboration with other departments. Peter explained that by including key decision-makers from different business areas on a steering committee, the company can ensure sustainability issues are being considered as part of decision-making processes company-wide. Furthermore, by engaging representatives from other business areas, accountability for sustainability performance and goals extends beyond the sustainability team – something that Peter believes is incredibly important on this journey.

'To engage other business areas on sustainability, you have to engage the right level of decision-making and influences within those key business units and functions as well. At Canon, what we have is our sustainability steering committee, which we set up in 2022. And we made sure that we had representatives from the different functions who had an influencing role within their own area of the business. And we use this as a forum to drive progress. To support our agenda, we have status reports and dashboards that we're now producing so that we can monitor all of the different activity. We have a lot of functions that operate quite differently and actually the way our business units are split between consumer and business means that we have very different activities depending on where you are in the business.

'As such, trying to monitor progress across all those different areas can be challenging, and this is where this committee has proven effective. We also use it as a chance to give them updates and information, and then cascade that information. Whether that's coming down from our parent organization in Japan, or conversely if there is something we want to share with them about new policy and strategy as well. So that works very well in terms of dealing with that sharing of information across business units, and also at a more senior level.'

As Peter points out, the decision to form a sustainability steering committee has proven effective and valuable for the multinational organization. As we've seen in the example at Canon, having a dedicated cross-functional steering committee enables a company to not only embed sustainability across different areas of the business, but it also allows for improved communication and transfer of information between business areas, as well as with the executive team. Ensuring key decision-makers are engaged as part of this cross-functional committee also allows organizations to be agile in making informed decisions quickly and effectively.

## Structuring sustainability across a multinational organization

One of the biggest challenges facing multinational organizations is determining how to navigate the avalanche of sustainability regulations that are emerging globally. For example, companies that operate in Europe need to adhere to the latest disclosures put forward by the CSRD (Corporate Sustainability Reporting Directive), which call for more robust data in their reporting, as well assurances of the information they report on. For companies that are also operating in other regions of the world, they will need to ensure they are following the different sets of requirements specific to those regions. Where this becomes more complex is when regional requirements overlap and conflict, as is the case when considering a company's value chain. Klaus Kunz, Founder and Managing Director at Ephrin, points to the vast differences in reporting requirements between the EU and the US as just one example of this complexity.

'I'll just give you one example of the many challenges global businesses face. We are just learning about the new CSRD in Europe, and what the new regulation to disclose non-financial data is going to look like. When you look at the topic-related requirements, they are very bold. For example, they require companies to report specific data like biodiversity – whereas, of today, we don't even know what to report. And also, when looking along the value chain, we often don't know what to report. And regarding the value chain, it means we will need to ask customers to provide data to us, which we have to include in our annual reports. But there may be geographies, take the US for example, where it might be even legally forbidden to collect this data. And I want just to point out that in Europe, of course, this agenda is very progressive, forward-looking and energetic – but if you don't get the other regions, the other leading countries, behind this, you basically lead the entire industry into a trap where in the end we have to choose the court where we are not compliant, because the legal situation becomes very complicated.

'On the political levels, I'm really an advocate for discussing these issues – we need to sit and talk and agree on the way forward. We need to come to internationally recognized standards, and not only regionally recognized standards. And we need to understand the maturity of each of these areas, and how far can we go.'

Reflecting on the different perspectives and underlying regulatory concerns that arise across different regions, Klaus believes it is important that companies actively listen and make a concerted effort to understand the concerns in order to address them regionally and globally while they can also help to build bridges, like in the international standard-setting discussion.

Given the multitude of regulations that are emerging around the globe, it is not surprising to see that many companies are struggling to understand and navigate many different requirements. To help companies address these challenges globally, establishing a global steering committee with a dedicated CSO appointed to each region the business operates in, is a good place to start. Depending on the size of the organization, in an ideal scenario each regional CSO is supported by a team that is focused on sustainability matters specific to their region. Sean Jones, Chief Sustainability Officer at Microsoft Germany, sits on Microsoft's global sustainability team. Being part of a global team allows Sean to transfer knowledge about the issues that are pertinent to Germany, and more broadly Europe, while also staying well-informed on issues that are impacting the business globally.

'At Microsoft today, we have a highly mature organization developed around environmental sustainability. It is led out of a group under the leadership of Brad Smith, who is our Vice Chairman and Head of CELA, which is our compliance and legal division. And under Brad Smith is Melanie Nakagawa, who is our Global Chief Sustainability Officer at Microsoft. Under Melanie, we have a whole global team that defines a strategy and develops our sustainability reports on an annual basis. We started that process in 2020, and we have produced three reports so far. We'll do our next one in 2024. And then within Melanie Nakagawa's group, she has several programme managers that are identifying and working with other functions within the organization to drive our measures. If you take a look at carbon as an example, our biggest carbon impacts are in Scope 3, so our supply chain.

'So there's a whole supplier category management group that looks at how we source materials for our Xboxes and our surface laptops, for instance. And then there's a whole group that focuses on how we build our data centres. Those three areas combined account for about 80 per cent of our total carbon emissions. And we have expanded that now from carbon, to also look at water and waste. And for an American company that's not really impacted yet by European regulations, I think we're one of the leaders.'

Although some large corporations are not yet impacted by European regulations, Sean aptly points out that soon they will be. As a multinational organization operating in the European Union, Microsoft will indeed be impacted by CSRD's regulations that require large corporations to disclose a comprehensive list of data in their reporting practices. To prepare for this directive that is coming from the EU, Microsoft is already thinking about how to gather and bring together all of the different data that is required across environmental, social and governance spheres. Under the new directive, companies also need their sustainability disclosures to be audited. Given this impending requirement, companies that are further along on their sustainability journey are beginning to merge their sustainability reports with their annual reports, thereby creating integrated reports.

## *Investing in sustainability-focused resources and solutions*

For sustainability to be effectively structured and embedded into processes and operations across an organization, companies need to invest in training and resources to support their teams. If a company hires a sustainability expert specialized in decarbonizing operations, but then fails to invest in technology or R&D projects aimed at reducing its carbon footprint, then it isn't being serious about reducing its impact. Commitments alone will not propel companies towards achieving the goals they have set out. Commitments need to be backed by meaningful actions, achievable only through investments in resources dedicated to sustainability.

On the topic of investing in sustainability, Klaus Kunz points to the need for governments and investors to mobilize capital towards the green economy. Pointing to initiatives such as the EU's Green Deal, which aims to mobilize a green economy by investing in green companies and technological solutions only, Klaus believes this approach is fundamentally flawed as it fails to stimulate transition and mobilization of new capital towards sustainability.

'The whole idea of the Green Deal is to enable investors to make better-informed green decisions to mobilize capital. We need to mobilize capital to do the right thing. The way taxonomy is constructed as of today, the money only goes to the already very green companies. That's a big concern for me because the impact lies in the transformation and transition. And this deal does not stimulate the transition. It stimulates those who are already there. Take a look at what the UK is doing. The Financial Conduct Authority in the UK introduced a label called Sustainable Impact which directs investments into companies in transition. I believe this is where the impact lies.

'So, I am a little concerned here on the EU side that the frame they are setting is not necessarily helping investors to stimulate impact. Additionally, the data requirements the EU has put up will create an avalanche or Mount Everest of data that companies will need to report. And how do you make decisions based on a Mount Everest of data? Assessing the correct aggregation of data into something meaningful is another challenge. And finally there's the different maturity level of the different topics. Carbon versus biodiversity, for instance – we are not talking about the same maturity in measuring these things. These are not at the same level. Don't get me wrong, I'm fully behind integrating non-financial reporting into the annual report. I think this says sustainability is part of the business. But as you can see, it's difficult when you see already that carbon offsets are part of the greenwashing discussion, and with carbon you have an agreed framework on how to measure. So, it is very foreseeable that the same will happen to biodiversity if we do not ensure that it's done properly.'

As we've discussed throughout this chapter, there are multiple approaches and structures companies can adopt to ensure sustainability is firmly embedded within the business and culture of an organization. Adopting a holistic approach where sustainability is systematically structured across an organization is key – and this begins at the leadership level. Having in place a strong governance structure and leadership team that is committed to ensuring sustainability is incorporated into the company's core strategy and decision-making is vital. Equally important is ensuring sustainability is integrated into different areas of the business and, perhaps even more importantly, into the culture. This can be facilitated by establishing sustainability teams and steering committees that are focused on driving the company's strategy forward. Finally, investing in sustainability-focused training initiatives and technology that supports employees, suppliers and partners on this journey is imperative.

As we noted at the beginning of this chapter, how sustainability is structured varies depending on the size of an organization, as well as its level of sustainability maturity. What is also worth noting, however, is that as a business inevitably evolves – so, too, will its structure. As such, it is important for leadership teams to continually re-evaluate and adjust the structure to ensure that sustainability remains a priority for the business – not least of all in the boardroom.

---

KEY TAKEAWAYS

- **Systematic embedding of sustainability**: To improve ESG positioning, sustainability needs to be systematically embedded across the organization. This includes integrating sustainability into the core business operations and company culture.

- **Leadership commitment**: Bold commitments require bold leadership. The support of the executive team and board of directors is crucial for the successful navigation of sustainability complexities. Recruiting experienced CSOs who can guide the sustainability strategy and goals is a good starting point for organizations.

- **Optimal reporting lines**: The CSO should have direct access to the executive team. Reporting directly to the CEO or CFO ensures that sustainability is integrated into core decision-making processes. This positioning also facilitates engagement with investors who are increasingly interested in a company's ESG performance.

- **Board engagement**: Boards need to be knowledgeable and engaged in sustainability matters, especially with rising stakeholder interest and tightening regulations. Establishing robust governance policies and possibly forming sustainability committees can ensure effective oversight and integration of sustainability into strategic decisions.

- **Building a strong sustainability team**: A CSO needs support from a diverse team of subject matter experts. This team should include specialists in areas like sustainability reporting, environmental initiatives and social matters. Knowledge transfer within the team and across the organization is vital for embedding sustainability.

- **Sustainability steering committees**: Forming cross-functional steering committees helps embed sustainability across all business functions. These committees ensure that sustainability issues are considered in decision-making processes and improve communication and accountability. Establishing a global steering committee with regional CSOs can also help multinational companies to navigate the complexities of local legislations better.

- **Continuous evolution of structure**: As businesses evolve, so should their sustainability structures. Leadership teams must continuously re-evaluate and adjust their sustainability strategies and structures to ensure they remain aligned with the company's goals and transformation initiatives.

## Notes

1  Eccles, R G and Taylor, A (2023) The evolving role of Chief Sustainability Officers, *Harvard Business Review*, July to August, https://hbr.org/2023/07/the-evolving-role-of-chief-sustainability-officers (archived at https://perma.cc/Q56N-Z45T)

2  PwC (2023) PWCs Global Investor Survey 2023, www.pwc.com/gx/en/issues/c-suite-insights/global-investor-survey.html (archived at https://perma.cc/U7D6-PHUG)

3  Rasche, A (2025) *Sustainability in the Boardroom*. Cambridge University Press, Cambridge, New York

**4** Rasche, A (2025) *Sustainability in the Boardroom.* Cambridge University Press, Cambridge, New York

**5** Hobbs, A (2023) How corporate governance can help build a more sustainable world, EY, 21 February, www.ey.com/en_uk/public-policy/how-corporate-governance-can-help-build-a-more-sustainable-world (archived at https://perma.cc/3M3B-Z3QD)

# 7

# Engaging employees on a company's sustainability journey

## The importance of employee engagement in organizations

At the heart of any company's sustainability strategy or bold commitments is their most valuable resource – their people. Having an engaged workforce that is aligned with a company's purpose and values is vital for an organization to fulfil its ambitious sustainability targets and long-term business objectives. While the focus of this book is about how to be more sustainable – as a company, a leader and an individual – from a corporate sustainability perspective, it is important to recognize that before companies can engage their employees on sustainability, they first need to ensure they are fostering an organizational culture where employees are valued, respected and heard. In other words – a culture where employees are, first and foremost, engaged in their work. Employee engagement refers to an employee's psychological commitment to their work, their team and their organization.[1] And while ensuring employees are engaged in their work is fundamental and essential for an organization to thrive, in practice, too many organizations are failing to genuinely and successfully engage their employees. According to Gallup's 2023 State of the Global Workplace Report, 59 per cent of employees surveyed stated they were 'quiet quitting' or 'not engaged' in their roles. Gallup describes highly engaged employees as employees who find their work meaningful and feel connected to their team and organization. As the research shows, unengaged employees – or quiet quitters – are costing companies, and more broadly the global economy, immensely. Gallup estimates the global cost of unengaged employees to be US$8.8 trillion or 9 per cent of global GDP.[2] On the flip side of this equation is the opportunity for growth. Companies that prioritize employee engagement as a core part of their business strategy gain a competitive advantage. They cultivate a culture with more motivated employees, higher retention rates, and improved performance – resulting in increased productivity and profitability.[3]

Given the high level of unengaged employees globally, it is important to ask, why are so many employees feeling disengaged from their work? According to another study conducted by Gallup in 2023, which looked at employee engagement trends in the US, one of the largest factors driving disengagement among employees was a lack of role clarity.[4] The findings underline that having a clear understanding of one's role, responsibilities and expectations can lead to improved productivity and employee satisfaction. When we consider these findings through a sustainability lens, the same can be said. Unless employees understand how sustainability topics and issues relate to their particular function or role, it is unlikely they will be engaged or feel they can contribute to the company's goals. This underscores the need for companies to educate employees on sustainability to help them understand what it means to the business and to their specific function, and more specifically, to help them understand the important role they play to support the company's strategy – individually and collectively.

## Examples of how CSOs are engaging employees on sustainability

During our discussions with CSOs we asked how they set out to engage employees on sustainability, and in particular employees who may not have sustainability within their titles or job functions.

To effectively engage employees on the topic of sustainability, Peter Bragg, Sustainability and Government Affairs Director EMEA at Canon, believes sustainability needs to be embedded into every area of the business, and this starts with ensuring the leaders and decision-makers of each business unit are engaged and on board with the company's sustainability agenda. In Chapter 6, where we discussed the various ways sustainability can be structured within an organization, Peter shared with us Canon's approach of creating a sustainability steering committee whose focus is to ensure sustainability is embedded into each business unit across the organization. In addition to forming a steering committee of representatives from each business area, employees have access to dashboards where the progress of specific initiatives can be readily tracked and monitored. These sustainability-focused processes ensure that sustainability is not only embedded into the day-to-day activities of the organization but also, as Peter points out, enables information to be transferred and communicated efficiently across all levels of the business.

'Our steering committee serves as a forum to drive progress, but it also gives us insight into the various business areas. In a large organization such as ours, the various business functions operate quite differently, and the way our business units are divided – between consumer and business – means we have very different activities depending on where you are in the organization. So, our processes aim to monitor progress across all those different areas. At the same time, we also use this forum to provide updates so that information can cascade, be it information coming from our parent organization in Japan, or information my team wants to share about a new policy or strategy. It is an effective way of engaging and communicating, at least with the more senior level of each business unit. And to engage the rest of the employees more broadly, we also do an annual engagement survey to gain a better of understanding of how well sustainability is understood and integrated across the organization.'

As Peter explains, conducting an employee engagement survey allows him and his team to better understand employees' understanding of sustainability. More importantly, the survey gives insight into how employees feel about their own ability to contribute to the company's sustainability strategy. By simply asking employees about sustainability and how they feel about their role, the company can gain valuable insights that can inform decisions about the resources needed to support and empower employees on this journey.

'With our annual engagement survey, we set out to measure how sustainability is understood across our business. But also, we ask what I think is a fundamental question, and that is, we ask people to reflect and share how they feel about their ability to support Canon on its journey towards becoming more sustainable. We ask that because we want people to understand that every role, no matter how small it is, plays a key part in supporting the work we are doing on sustainability. And this all comes back to our corporate philosophy of kyosei, which refers to our dedication to seeing all people – regardless of culture, customs, language or race – harmoniously living and working together in happiness into the future. And when we think about the work we are doing on sustainability, it is rooted in this philosophy. It is all about everyone pulling together towards a more sustainable future.'

As Canon describes on its corporate website, kyosei is the combination of the two Japanese words of kyo (共) and sei (生), which literally mean 'co-living'.[5] Put together, kyosei forms Canon's corporate philosophy of living and working together for the common good. Sustainability is at the core of this philosophy, which underscores the company's vision and mission to be a responsible corporate citizen. Going beyond words, Canon's kyosei philosophy aims to encourage employees to be mindful of the world, and the impact of their individual decisions and actions, stating that if each person takes responsibility for the impact their actions have on the environment – and makes a concerted effort to adopt a more sustainable way of living – each person can make a positive difference.[6] With the phrase kyosei written on the walls around the company, it serves as a subtle yet powerful daily reminder of the company's philosophy and vision for a better future.

Peter emphasizes that the functions of corporate communications and marketing are central to pulling everyone together towards a common goal, both internally and externally. Ensuring the company's stakeholders have a clear understanding of the company's strategy and goals, as well as its progress, is incredibly important on this journey of sustainable transformation. It is also essential from a regulatory perspective, given regulations about ESG claims are tightening. Despite best intentions, far too many companies make claims about net zero or carbon neutrality when they may not know what these terms actually mean, from a science-based target perspective. In turn, these companies find themselves facing backlash for greenwashing. In addition to the reputational risks that come with greenwashing, companies can also face significant regulatory fines. In Europe, for example, as of January 2024, the EU Parliament introduced its Greenwashing Directive. The new Directive is designed to ban unsubstantiated green and social impact claims on the part of organizations.[7] To hold organizations to account, the Directive requires that companies provide more specific details and information to justify their claims. Companies who fail to comply with the new regulations face being excluded from procurements and face a minimum fine of 4 per cent of their annual turnover. Given the heightened level of scrutiny that organizations face when it comes to their sustainability claims and commitments, as Peter underlined, it is more important than ever for companies to communicate their efforts and progress clearly and transparently for their stakeholders – not least of all for their employees.

Part of engaging employees on this journey involves providing the resources, tools and training that can help them to elevate their knowledge of sustainability topics, as well as their skills. In the example of Canon, Peter Bragg explained sustainability-focused training sessions were conducted to help employees understand how sustainability impacts their function and roles and, equally important, how their roles can contribute to the company's strategy. Peter emphasizes that one of the aims of the training session was to create a cultural or mindset shift that encouraged employees to think about sustainability as something that can be part of their job, and not an additional activity. Peter points to the example of recycling and placing items in the right bins, every day, as a small act that helps and adds up – contributing to the company's overall sustainability efforts.

Charlotte Wolff-Bye, Chief Sustainability Officer at Petronas, shares Peter's viewpoint that employees can engage with sustainability and have a positive impact regardless of where they are positioned within an organization. When we asked Charlotte how she sets out to engage employees on sustainability, she emphasized that sustainability is not a topic that resides solely within the function of the sustainability team, and engaging employees is an essential part of a company's journey. Done well, it should permeate into all the different business areas and roles across an organization. To engage employees across an organization as large as Petronas, which has approximately 50,000 employees globally, Charlotte points to an initiative that Petronas has created which has fostered a culture that harnesses employees' enthusiasm for sustainability, supporting their efforts to make a positive impact in surrounding communities.

'One of the ways we are engaging employees here at Petronas is through our Petronas Young Professionals Club. It's an initiative designed to engage our vibrant and passionate group of young professionals to get involved in various projects, and through this programme they are supported through budgetary means. The programme provides a platform for the younger voices within our organization to be heard. And they are doing really interesting and impactful work, which is impressive to me. Another thing that always impresses me is how much Petronas values education. Petronas has supported around 38,000 people through university, at some of the best universities in the world; a true investment into the future generation – not just for Petronas, but for the country of Malaysia. I've been here as CSO for three years, and I think we've achieved a lot. But actually, we've been able to achieve a lot because the ground has been fertile and fertilized for a long time.'

Petronas' approach to actively listening and supporting younger professionals is a shining example of how organizations can harness the enthusiasm employees have and channel that energy towards making a positive difference. Not only does Petronas' Young Professionals Club programme benefit local communities and projects, but it also serves to develop and empower the next generation of leaders and corporate citizens. Furthermore, by investing in the projects and initiatives that employees care about, Petronas is also investing in building a more engaged and productive workforce, which, as the Gallup study showed, also benefits the business.

To effectively engage employees on sustainability, Michelle Davies, Global Head of Sustainability at EY Law, believes sustainability needs to be engrained into the company's DNA. This requires ensuring sustainability is embedded into decision-making processes and actions across all levels of the organization. Michelle concedes that sustainability is a journey, and while organizations are not always going to get it right, the important thing is that they strive to improve and move towards becoming more sustainable.

'To engage employees, you have to make sustainability part of your DNA, which is what we're doing at EY. And it is still a journey for us. So, I'm responsible for global sustainability at EY Law, and I have a team that is very committed and very driven. They are keeping up to date with sustainability, and they are thinking about sustainability in everything they do. Part of my role is to also ensure that all the lawyers across our legal firm, and we are one of the largest legal teams in the world, are also building sustainability into everything they do. In terms of us being sustainable and behaving sustainably within the workplace, I rely on the wider EY machine to deliver that. But what we do is we have constant communication and updates. You can't really go anywhere in the office without seeing stuff about sustainability. It's all over our messaging, in our reception. It is throughout the organization. And that's what we're trying to do – just build it into our DNA. We get things wrong. I came into the office one day, and I had a wet umbrella, and the guy in reception immediately took me to this machine to put it into a plastic bag. And every organization will get things wrong, but the point is that there will be people coming through this reception and they'll be very aware of that, and they will also pick up on it. So, I would say out of any organization I've worked in, this one really is building sustainability within its DNA.'

As Michelle points out, for organizations to become more sustainable, fostering a sustainability-focused culture is key. By building sustainability into every decision and action at the boardroom level, companies can ensure that a sustainability-driven culture and mindset cascades throughout the organization.

As we've gleaned from our discussions with CSOs, engaging employees is integral to a company's sustainable transformation journey. If organizations are serious about fulfilling their sustainability commitments, they need to make a concerted effort to engage and support their employees. As research has shown, an engaged workforce is a company's greatest competitive advantage. An engaged workforce can drive innovation and profitability – positioning their companies for long-term success.

As we saw in the examples of Canon, Petronas and EY Law, central to each company's approach to engaging employees on sustainability is ensuring that first and foremost, sustainability is embedded into the DNA of the organization. It needs to be part of the company's everyday decision-making processes, behaviours and actions. Sustainability also needs to be part of the company's common language that is communicated at every touch point – from the boardroom agenda to the writing on the walls.

## The power of education to drive employee engagement, creativity and innovation

While there are many different initiatives and steps organizations can take to engage their employees, one recurring theme that emerged from our discussions with CSOs was the important role of education in driving awareness and engaging employees. Training employees across all levels of the business about sustainability, and how it impacts the business, is key to ensuring everyone has a clear understanding of the company's sustainability strategy and long-term business objectives.

In the context of corporate sustainability, where more companies are committing to contributing to the sustainable development goals (SDGs) set by the UN, the power of education cannot be overstated. This is especially true in this era of digital transformation, where emerging technologies such as AI require companies, and employees, to commit to a path of continuous learning and growth. With the right support, training and resources, employees can be empowered to experiment and develop innovative solutions that advance an organization's business and sustainability-focused efforts. Companies that prioritize educating and training their employees across all levels about sustainability, and its relevance to the business and its purpose, are on the right path towards building more sustainable businesses with the future in mind. Harnessing the power of education to cultivate awareness about sustainability and engage employees is key. Equally important is for companies to leverage education to spark creativity, drive innovation and unleash the potential of their employees.

During his 2006 Ted Talk, British author, speaker and global adviser on education Sir Ken Robinson, illuminated the vital role education and creativity play in unleashing human potential. During his talk, which was titled *Do schools kill creativity?* Sir Ken Robinson argued that our traditional approach to education is not preparing our children to meet the needs of the future. He points to the fact that educational systems around the world place greater value on subjects such as maths, languages and literacy than they do on the arts and creativity. As a result, Sir Ken Robinson argues that children are growing out of creativity, rather than into it. He makes the point that while this trend begins within our school systems, it is one that persists and is mirrored in the way we run our companies. His contention is that all kids have creative talent, and current educational systems are designed to squander that talent. During his talk he tells the story of a little girl who didn't always pay attention in class, and during one particular art lesson her teacher noticed she was very focused on her drawing. When her teacher asked what she was drawing, the girl stated she was drawing a picture of God. Surprised by the girl's response, the teacher said, 'But nobody knows what God looks like', to which the girl replied, 'they will in a minute.'[8] Sir Ken Robinson used this story to illustrate that when children don't know the answer, they are not afraid to be wrong, and they will still give it a go. And as he astutely points out, being prepared to be wrong is exactly what is needed to be creative and innovative.

'If you're not prepared to be wrong you will never come up with anything original. By the time they get to be adults most kids lose that capacity; they have become frightened of being wrong. And we run our companies like this by the way, we stigmatize mistakes. Picasso once said, "All children are born artists. The problem is to remain an artist as we grow up." I believe this passionately, that we don't grow into creativity, we grow out of it – or rather we get educated out of it.'

Sir Ken Robinson's Ted Talk went on to become the most watched Ted Talk of all time, garnering more than 77 million views to date. His ideas resonated with audiences when he first shared them back in 2006 – and his message continues to resonate today at a time when the world is in dire need of creative and innovative solutions to address some of the greatest challenges facing humanity. At the heart of Sir Ken Robinson's message is the belief that if we want to address grand global challenges, we need to harness creativity in our children, and in turn in our employees, rather than stifle it. In the business and organizational context, companies that foster a culture where employees are encouraged to try new things, get things wrong, and try again are well-positioned to drive innovation and propel their organizations forward.

Establishing a culture where employees feel psychologically safe to share their ideas and opinions is perhaps the single most important step leaders can take to engage their teams. The tech industry is a good example of an industry that cultivates a culture of innovation, where employees are encouraged to try, fail, learn and repeat.

Investing in innovation and R&D efforts aimed at developing new solutions to address the world's greatest challenges is key for organizations to prepare their businesses for the future. As is the case with any new and innovative business venture, there is a certain level of risk that companies need to be prepared to take if they want to drive their organizations forward. Taking calculated risks and giving employees freedom to experiment and get things wrong needs to be factored into the cost of doing business.

With its renowned 80/20 policy, Google encourages employees to dedicate 20 per cent of their time to work on work-related projects of their choice. Many of the company's most successful and innovative products were born from the 20 per cent share of employees' efforts, including Gmail and Google News.[9] The company's policy proved so successful in empowering employees and driving innovation that the 80/20 rule was adopted by many other companies across various sectors. As Google's example shows, providing a safe culture that encourages employees to experiment, and make mistakes, creates an environment where creativity and innovation can thrive.

Adam Kingl, educator and author of *Sparking Success: Why every leader needs to develop a creative mindset*, shares the viewpoint that companies need to cultivate an environment that sparks creativity and innovation if they want to position themselves for sustainable success. He pointed to Gallup's study, which showed that the vast majority of the global workforce feel emotionally detached from their work, as being a telling sign for a much-needed revolution in the way we run our organizations. To build our companies with the future in mind – and set them up for long-term success – Adam Kingl argues the world needs to rediscover the art of creativity and play.

'In rediscovering art and play, two virtuous habits that spark and nurture those characteristics of innovation including divergent thinking, collaboration, mindfulness, inspiration, exploring untraditional ideas and picturing the future, we uncover anew the state of mind and spirit that we have always naturally possessed. We begin to encourage an environment that allows our companies collectively to discover what we know individually that we have always craved.'

**Adam Kingl, educator and author**

Adam Kingl advocates that creativity is needed to drive innovation in any industry. He cites Steve Jobs as an example of a leader who valued creativity, art and design as much as technology and science in the tech sector, attributing it as being a key to Apple's success to Jobs' own creative background, including a calligraphy course he took back when he was a student in university.[10]

In his 2005 commencement speech at Stanford, Steve Jobs talked about the valuable learnings he gained from that calligraphy class, stating, 'I learnt about serif and sans serif typefaces, about varying the amount of space between different letter combinations, about what makes great typography great. It was beautiful, historical, artistically subtle in a way that science can't capture, and I found it fascinating.'[11] He didn't know it at the time, but years later he would lean on the experience he gained from that course to design fonts for the first Macintosh computer, which was, as Steve Jobs described, 'the first computer with beautiful typography.'[12] Driven by his creativity and attention to detail, simplicity and design, Steve Jobs revolutionized the home computer sector.

As demonstrated by Steve Jobs' example, creativity is essential to drive innovation, not only for a company but also for an entire sector. Apple's creative and revolutionary spirit was captured in its iconic 1984 'Think Different' advertising campaign. The campaign, which is considered by many to be one of the greatest ads of all time, boldly positioned Apple as a tech company that, above all else, valued individuality and creativity.[13] What separated Apple from its competition was not its superiority in technology, rather it was its superiority in design and simplicity that gave its products a competitive edge. It is a sentiment that Adam Kingl shared and underscored in his book with the following statement: 'A creative, humanistic mindset isn't a luxury, it is your competitive advantage'.

While fostering a creative mindset and culture is essential to drive innovation, there is only so much that companies can do to inspire and engage employees in their work. Leaders can inspire people – but ultimately motivation comes from within. Steve Jobs stated that the secret to success is to have passion in what you do. He emphasized this is especially true when the work is hard.[14] Going back to his famous commencement speech, Steve Jobs emphasized the importance of passion in work.

'I'm convinced that the only thing that kept me going was that I loved what I did. You've got to find what you love. And that is as true for your work as it is for your lovers. Your work is going to fill a large part of your life, and the only way to be truly satisfied is to do what you believe is great work. And the only way to do great work is to love what you do.'[15]

According to Steve Jobs, passion is what will motivate people to persevere and stay engaged. It is why, as we discussed in Chapter 3, companies that clearly define and communicate their purpose are better positioned to create a meaningful connection with their employees.

## Unleashing employees' greatest potential

Helping people unlock their potential is the focus of best-selling author and behavioural psychologist Adam Grant's area of research and expertise. In his book *Hidden Potential: The science of achieving greater things*, Adam Grant talks about how many of us are unaware of our strengths, leading us to think we lack potential. In an interview with the *Talks at Google* podcast series, he explains that potential is not determined by how good someone is at something when they start, rather the ultimate question of potential is: how far can you travel? He believes that we are our own worst judges, so to really identify and unleash our potential, we need to find knowledgeable people who can hold a mirror up and show us what we are capable of achieving.

On the topic of engaging employees and unleashing their potential, during the interview Adam Grant discusses how Google's playful spirit and culture is designed to make hard work motivating and fun. He argues that individuals and companies should take a similar approach to work, stating the key is to not make work or practice feel like a grind. While he recognizes that hard work and repetition is indeed needed to work towards expertise or honing a skill, if companies or individuals only focus on the task at hand – and not approach it in a deliberately playful way – they run the risk of burning out in the long run.[16] Before they get to this point, however, Adam Grant stresses employees could hit another point that psychologists call *boreout*.[17] It is at this point that employees start to disengage. To curb these trends, Adam Grant suggests that companies need to adopt a deliberate play approach that turns the daily grind into a source of daily joy. In other words, fostering a culture that promotes play and creativity will lead to a more motivated and engaged workplace.

## Steps leaders can take to drive employee engagement in their work and on sustainability

While the high level of disengaged employees globally is certainly cause for concern, fortunately for organizations, steps can be taken to reconnect and re-engage employees in their work. This starts with having engaged and purpose-driven leadership that puts the interest of employees at the top of the organization's agenda. In light of its dim 'State of the Global Workplace' study findings, with its '2024 Employee Engagement Strategy' report Gallup set out to offer employers a list of practical steps they can take to improve employee engagement within their organizations. Gallup's recommendations include: checking in on the well-being of managers; preparing managers to have meaningful conversations with their employees; clearly promoting the company's mission and purpose with employees; measuring engagement; and lastly, taking action and following through on the employee engagement survey results.[18]

In addition to the recommendations put forward by Gallup, an article published by *Forbes* in 2023 listed three ways organizations can improve engagement.[19] The first way is to make employees feel like individuals. To do this, leaders need to recognize an employee's individual contributions and efforts. Secondly, companies to need to foster a culture that values employee health and well-being. And thirdly, leaders need to prioritize value-driven work across all levels of the organization. Employees need to know *why* their work matters and how it aligns with the company's overall *purpose*.

Relatedly, fostering a purpose- and value-driven organization requires leaders to proactively and broadly consider and develop a human-centric organization. In essence, as highlighted by various practitioners and summarized well by Phanish Puranam, an expert on the future of work, when leaders place human fundamental needs and values at the core of management and leadership, it creates a culture where employees are valued as humans and the work environment is genuinely motivating and engaging.[20]

Dr Sunny Lee, director of MSC People Analytics and Human-Centred Management at University College London, details the values and needs particularly relevant to an organization's endeavour to develop a human-centric and purpose-driven organization which genuinely cares about and motivates employees.[21]

'As top management scholars, such as Douglas McGregor and Phanish Puranam, have argued, organizations can achieve sustainable success and growth when they pursue business efficiency and organizational mission in consideration of employees' fundamental values and needs. The scope of such values can differ by specific organizational context, but research highlights the importance of addressing employees' needs on autonomy, fairness, curiosity, self-mastery and belongingness. Securing these values, for example, by giving employees ownership of certain tasks, maintaining fair HR practices, and exposing them to new opportunities, helps leaders fundamentally address employee engagement, well-being and values.'

When it comes to engaging employees on sustainability specifically, we would be remiss not to refer to the example of Unilever under the leadership of Paul Polman, who served as the company's CEO from 2009 to 2018. In an article Paul Polman co-authored with CB Bhattacharya for Stanford in 2016, the authors offered a list of eight practical steps companies can take to engage employees on their sustainability journey. The eight steps included: define the company's long-term purpose; spell out the economic case for sustainability; create sustainability knowledge and competence; make every employee a sustainability champion; co-create sustainable practices with employees; encourage healthy competition among employees; make sustainability visible inside and outside the company; and showcase higher purpose by creating transformational change.[22]

These recommendations serve as a roadmap, bridging an employee's personal values with the company's purpose. As research shows, aligning with a company's overall purpose is what ultimately connects employees to their organizations and their work. We think it is worth restating here that Gallup describes highly engaged employees as employees who find their work meaningful and feel connected to their team and organization. Put simply, if companies want to engage their employees – having a clearly defined purpose that they communicate at every touchpoint is the best place to start. Furthermore, it is clear from our conversations with CSOs that no leader can do this job alone. It is only with the support, dedication and enthusiasm of engaged employees that a company can realize its sustainability goals and commitments.

---

KEY TAKEAWAYS

- **Importance of employee engagement**: Engaging employees is crucial for achieving a company's sustainability targets and long-term business objectives. An engaged workforce leads to higher productivity, retention and overall performance.

- **Understanding role clarity**: Clear understanding of roles and responsibilities is essential for employee engagement. Educating employees on how sustainability relates to their specific functions helps them understand their contributions to the company's goals.

- **Embedding sustainability into business units**: Sustainability needs to be integrated into every area of the business. Creating steering committees and using dashboards to track progress can help embed sustainability into daily operations.

- **Annual engagement surveys**: Conducting annual engagement surveys provides valuable insights into employees' understanding of sustainability and their perceived ability to contribute to the company's sustainability strategy.

- **Empowering employees across functions**: Employees passionate about sustainability can often have a greater impact within their current roles rather than being part of the sustainability team. Encouraging employees to embed sustainability into their day-to-day work is essential.

- **Education and training**: Providing sustainability-focused training sessions helps employees understand the impact of sustainability on their roles and how they can contribute. Education drives awareness and engages employees at all levels.

- **Cultivating creativity and innovation**: Fostering a culture of creativity and innovation is vital for engaging employees and driving sustainable transformation. Encouraging employees to experiment and embrace mistakes can lead to significant innovations.

- **Leadership and purpose**: Purpose-driven leadership is essential for employee engagement. Leaders need to clearly communicate the company's mission and purpose, making employees feel valued and connected to their work.

## Notes

1  Pendell, R (2022) Employee engagement strategies: Fixing the world's $8.8 trillion problem, Gallup, 14 June (updated 11 September 2023), www.gallup.com/workplace/393497/world-trillion-workplace-problem.aspx (archived at https://perma.cc/MK8C-2TJE)

2  Gallup (2023) State of the Global Workplace 2023 Report, Gallup, www.gallup.com/workplace/349484/state-of-the-global-workplace.aspx?thank-you-report-form=1 (archived at https://perma.cc/L2W3-D5KL)

3  Beheshti, N (2019) 10 timely statistics about the connection between employee engagement and wellness, *Forbes*, 27 September www.forbes.com/sites/nazbeheshti/2019/01/16/10-timely-statistics-about-the-connection-between-employee-engagement-and-wellness/?sh=28976a4e22a0 (archived at https://perma.cc/DX5V-32VV)

4  Gallup (2024) 2024 Employee engagement strategies checklist, Gallup, www.gallup.com/workplace/388685/2024-guide-employee-engagement.aspx (archived at https://perma.cc/RWR8-ZWVD)

5   Canon (nd) Together is more than just a word, www.canon.co.uk/view/
    kyoseiforliving/ (archived at https://perma.cc/KYR9-U7LM)

6   Canon (nd) Together is more than just a word, www.canon.co.uk/view/
    kyoseiforliving/ (archived at https://perma.cc/KYR9-U7LM)

7   European Parliament (2024) Greenwashing: How EU firms can validate their
    green claims, European Parliament News, 14 February, www.europarl.europa.eu/
    news/en/press-room/20240212IPR17624/greenwashing-how-eu-firms-can-
    validate-their-green-claims (archived at https://perma.cc/T5YY-CNMK)

8   Ted (2006) Do Schools Kills Creativity? February, www.ted.com/talks/
    sir_ken_robinson_do_schools_kill_creativity?language=en (archived at
    https://perma.cc/YVW4-GCC6)

9   Krastevam S, Sharma, P and Wagman, L (2015) The 80/20 rule: Corporate
    support for innovation by employees, Research Gate, November,
    www.researchgate.net/publication/273710559_The_8020_Rule_Corporate_
    Support_for_Innovation_by_Employees (archived at https://perma.cc/
    Z4BZ-G6CV)

10  Kingl, A (2023) *Sparking Success: Why every leader needs to develop a creative
    mindset*, Kogan Page, 2023

11  Stanford Report (2005) Steve Jobs to 2005 graduates: Stay hungry, stay foolish,
    12 June, https://news.stanford.edu/stories/2005/06/steve-jobs-2005-graduates-
    stay-hungry-stay-foolish (archived at https://perma.cc/T979-RPF8)

12  Meta, R (2016) Steve Jobs Speech, Research Gate, May, www.researchgate.net/
    publication/301899412_Steve_Jobs_Speech (archived at https://perma.cc/
    Z4BZ-G6CV)

13  Himanshu (2023) Case Study: What makes Apple's design and creative strategy
    unique and ensures no other brand comes even remotely close to it in creativity
    and innovation, Medium, 14 May, https://medium.com/@himanshusocial/
    case-study-what-makes-apples-design-and-creative-strategy-unique-and-
    ensures-no-other-brand-comes-fc7f40b4ff83 (archived at https://perma.cc/
    JY56-8ASN)

14  The Coach (2007) Steve Jobs passion in work, YouTube, May 30, 2007,
    www.youtube.com/watch?v=PznJqxon4zE&t=90s (archived at https://perma.cc/
    FM8N-DGAK)

15  Stanford Report (2005) You've got to find what you love, Jobs says, 12 June,
    https://news.stanford.edu/stories/2005/06/youve-got-find-love-jobs-says
    (archived at https://perma.cc/R7CH-448U)

16  Talks at Google (2023) Adam Grant – Hidden potential: The Science of
    Achieving Greater Things, 24 October, www.youtube.com/
    watch?v=EZBz5c5IWTU (archived at https://perma.cc/QN7Q-JPBQ)

17  Talks at Google (2023) Adam Grant – Hidden potential: The science of
    achieving greater things, 24 October, www.youtube.com/
    watch?v=EZBz5c5IWTU (archived at https://perma.cc/QN7Q-JPBQ)

**18**  Gallup (2024) 2024 Employee Engagement Strategies Checklist, Gallup, 2024, https://www.gallup.com/workplace/608675/new-workplace-employee-engagement-stagnates.aspx (archived at https://perma.cc/BX3F-LMZQ)

**19**  Sonnenberg, S (2023) How leaders impact employee engagement, *Forbes*, 24 July, www.forbes.com/sites/forbesbusinesscouncil/2023/07/24/how-leaders-impact-employee-engagement/?sh=19c454191354 (archived at https://perma.cc/NT96-SZH4)

**20**  Taylor, D (2023) Creating a human-centric business approach, *Forbes*, 20 September, www.forbes.com/sites/forbesbusinesscouncil/2023/09/20/creating-a-human-centric-business-approach/ (archived at https://perma.cc/SDA7-ECVU)

**21**  Lee, S (2024) *RE-HUMaNiZE: How to build human-centric organizations in the age of algorithms*, December, Penguin Random House

**22**  Polman P and Bhattacharya C B (2016) Engaging employees to create sustainable business, Stanford Social Innovation Review, Fall, https://ssir.org/articles/entry/engaging_employees_to_create_a_sustainable_business# (archived at https://perma.cc/PL26-XRSF)

# 8

# Industry-leading practices of sustainability-oriented innovation

Despite the many challenges CSOs face in their roles, every CSO we met with felt optimistic about the role companies can play to drive positive changes for society and the planet. They also shared a common belief that human creativity and ingenuity – channelled towards a common goal – can lead us towards creating a better world for future generations.

It is this combination of human ingenuity and a drive to create a better world that has led to some of the most extraordinary advancements in sustainable and technological solutions aimed at addressing the world's greatest challenges. In our conversations with CSOs from different industries, we learnt about initiatives that are at the forefront of R&D and managerial efforts focused on resolving various global issues – be it climate change, social inequalities or poverty, to name a few. Central to all of these initiatives is sustainability-oriented innovation (SOI).

The importance of SOI was remarked by Thijs H J Geradts and Nancy M P Bocken in an influential article published in the *Sloan Management Review* in 2018. Large multinational corporations are increasingly focused on sustainability-oriented innovation, which encompasses improvements for social good, not just 'green' initiatives.[1] This shift is driven by pressures from governments, NGOs, investors and employees to address the environmental and social impacts of business activities. Companies are seeking new growth opportunities by leveraging the creativity and entrepreneurial potential of their employees to develop products, services and business models that create value for both the company and society.

This chapter will explore various industry-leading practices and innovations that embody this approach, showcasing how organizations are leveraging sustainability to drive technological advancements and create a positive impact on society and the environment. The examples presented will illustrate how collaboration with stakeholders, top management commitment and strategic business model adjustments are essential components of sustainability-oriented innovation, paving the way for a more sustainable and profitable future.

Before we delve into some of these forward-thinking initiatives, it is worth noting that we are being intentional with our choice of words, stating *industry-leading practices* rather than *best practice*s. On the topic of best practices, Adam Grant, organizational psychologist and professor at Wharton University, offers his perspective on why best practice is not the best phrase for organizations to use – advocating instead for companies to strive for *better practices*. In a conversation with McKinsey & Company, Adam provided the following rationale on why the term better practice is, simply put, *better* than best.

'I think the language of best practices creates this illusion that there's an end point, that we've already reached perfection. And so, we don't need to change anything. What I would love to see more organizations do instead is to strive for better practices, right? To say, "Okay, you know what? No matter how good a practice becomes it can always be improved. And we're open to trying whatever ideas you have for trying to evolve the way that we do things around here."'[2]

We concur with Adam's viewpoint. Sustainable transformation is a journey – and on this journey we believe, more than ever, that words matter. For this reason, we opted to use *industry-leading* in the title of this chapter, as it offers a more fitting description of the current innovative developments we have come across through our discussions with CSOs. Similar to better, leading does not imply an end point. Rather, it leaves room for improvement. Furthermore, we recognize that the practices that are leading today will not be the ones that will lead in the future. They do, however, provide important stepping stones that will no doubt lead to better innovations of tomorrow and will help to define new standards in industry.

## Decarbonizing a business rooted in agriculture

In our conversation with Klaus Kunz, Founder and Managing Director at Ephrin and former VP of ESG Strategy at Bayer, we learnt about the industry-leading actions Bayer has been taking on its path to net zero. Klaus explained that the life science and pharmaceutical sector is closely linked to agriculture. Given that agriculture is directly impacted by climate change, Klaus underscored that as an industry leader Bayer has been committed to reducing greenhouse gas emissions (GHGs) by developing a carbon-reduction initiative rooted in agriculture.

Reflecting on his experience at Bayer, where he worked for over two decades, Klaus understood that due to the company's involvement in pesticides, there was a public perception that Bayer was contributing to the decline of biodiversity through its use of pesticides. Klaus emphasized, however, that what some people refer to as pesticides, others refer to as crop protection. In other words, there are two different labels for the same product, which sheds light on the fact that there are two very different perspectives as well. Klaus emphasized this was an issue that affected not only Bayer but the entire life-sciences sector. Addressing these complex issues can be challenging, especially for large multinational organizations. As Klaus points out, changing an organization's culture and perspective on these matters can be equally difficult.

'To reduce our impact we basically stimulated the introduction of a carbon business in agriculture, coming from the idea that we need to reduce GHG because climate change is real – and agriculture is linked. This conversation was not always easy – changing the cultural perspective was equally tough. We needed to acknowledge – and be absolutely clear – that also, biodiversity loss and agriculture are linked. It required a real mindset shift in the organization to make a commitment to reduce the environmental impact of our own products, of our pesticides. Insecticides are designed to fight pests – and of course we cannot claim that we can do medicine without any side effects. So, we need to be very open. And again, coming back to bridging conversations, I think it's important that if we talk about medicine, we talk about effects and side effects. That's why, in my former role as VP of ESG Strategy at Bayer, we set the target to reduce environmental impacts of all our crop protection by 30 per cent by 2030.

'When it comes to setting the ambition level, we faced very different geographical frameworks. If you go to France, people say "that's not enough". If you go to the Americas, they may say "wow, that's astonishing that you are really going in this direction". And that is fine. That is all great feedback for organizations, because we always need to calibrate our targets against this external feedback. And as an industry we have come a long way because it's difficult to measure environmental impacts of crop protection. When I was at Bayer we worked with the University of Denmark and Copenhagen and many other universities to define the methodology for measuring. It is extremely important, for credibility reasons, that somebody else defines the methodology and the way to measure and that companies don't do this themselves. What is also important to note is that Bayer did all of this because the company wanted to do this and not because others wanted them to do this. I think that is a very important point.'

The example of Bayer highlights that certain sustainability problems cannot be solved by business alone. Collaboration with other stakeholders, at times with competitors too, is key for success. In this context, collaboration with premium research institutions is a common trend we have observed through our interviews, as top universities can share the latest science on complex topics such as climate science or crop science that can help businesses to innovate and strategize for sustainable transformation.

At University College London for example (academic home of the authors of this book), the UCL Centre for Sustainable Business carries out groundbreaking research focused on AI applied to ESG problems, human-centric organizations and innovative models to integrate sustainability into core business – in collaboration with tens of leading organizations that use, test and implement this science.

However, addressing complex issues, internally and externally across an organization, can be challenging, as Klaus has highlighted. Shifting a company's perspective on complex matters, while maintaining an open and honest conversation with the public, is no small task. Being clear and transparent about the trade-offs, side effects and impacts linked to a company's products, services and activities is key to building trust with customers on this journey. If CSOs are able to lead the organizations to find this balance, while reducing the environmental impact of their organizations at the same time, they can rest assured that the steps they are taking are leading their organizations in the right direction.

## Carbon budgeting

It is clear from our discussions with CSOs that the field of sustainability has evolved significantly over the last decade. Sustainability as a function has moved closer to the C-suite, with more CSOs reporting directly into the CEO or CFO. Additionally, sustainability reporting has also been more closely intertwined with financial reporting. This shift is demonstrative of how much companies are taking sustainability more seriously compared to just a few years ago.

Bain & Company has made great strides in integrating sustainability into the company's core business in recent years. In 2023, the consultancy firm introduced a new carbon budget initiative that aims to systematically reduce the organization's global carbon footprint. Sam Israelit is a Partner and Chief Sustainability Officer at Bain & Company. Sam shared with us that while the primary objective of this initiative was to reduce the organization's carbon emissions, it has also led to a cultural shift where sustainability has become embedded into day-to-day operations and conversations.

'One initiative that we are particularly proud of and that we completed within the last year was our carbon budgeting process. We implemented carbon budgets in the firm for all internal functions and practice areas. This is something that took us roughly nine months to complete. It was a very involved process. We interacted with 60 or 70 leaders across the firm to engage them in the process. What we did was we designed a process where, in July, when everyone gets their financial budget package and they have to start putting together a financial plan, there's also a template in there for them to develop their carbon plan. And the idea is that the two have to synchronize, so that if you say you're going to travel this much from a financial perspective, you also have to have the appropriate carbon allocation there.'

The company's innovative carbon budget process was introduced and implemented across all internal functions and process areas. Sam recognized that for the initiative to work and be adopted company-wide, it was important to engage key stakeholders early in the process. As part of the process, he and his team interacted with the leaders of all internal functions and practice areas from across the firm to work with them to educate them on the potential ways they could reduce their emissions and build the budgets for their area.

Sam and his team engaged individual function leaders from across the organization. Together with each leader, they walked through the 2019 baseline carbon footprint of each business area, and then discussed all the different levers they could pull to actually reduce their emissions. Sam explained they looked at everything from, '*do you actually need to have a global meeting, or could you do it as a local meeting, or could you do it virtually?*', all the way through to, '*can you change the meeting cadence so that maybe you don't meet as frequently in person or can you schedule meetings to happen in the same window as other meetings?*'

One example of how the company strived to reduce their emissions was by scheduling meetings more efficiently so that less travel would be required.

For example, the firm's worldwide partner meeting is one of its highest carbon emissions events of the year. Rather than booking additional trips for separate partner meetings to discuss a specific practice area, such as consumer products or performance improvement, extra time was added during and around the global partner meeting to allow for the separate meetings, and so that extra travel could be avoided. This approach not only reduces the company's carbon emissions, but it also saves on costs.

A similar approach was taken with every area of the business, including within its recruiting and training processes. The outcome of the discussions with each business area was the development and design of a carbon budget process that essentially mirrored the organization's financial process, which was well-established and embedded in the organization's systems and vernacular.

The initiative has been rolled out across all areas of the organization. Just as every function area is responsible for a financial budget, each area is now also responsible for a carbon budget. To support each division with this process, a dashboard has been developed that displays how much carbon each division has emitted over the course of the year, eventually moving to monthly updates. The carbon budget is updated as new emissions data is received from the business's travel partners – allowing for regular discourse about how the company is progressing. As Sam pointed out, not only is the initiative helping the company monitor and reduce its emissions on an ongoing basis, but it is also creating more awareness about sustainability from a cultural perspective – with more leaders thinking and talking about sustainability as part of their day-to-day operations.

'I think the reason this is really good is that just going through the process got people talking about carbon emissions and how their decisions actually impact emissions. And that really elevated the conversation. And it ties in with the finance function as well, because now when you get a financial update, you get a carbon update. But I think the biggest impact has been getting people to talk about it. While it might not be daily, it's at least monthly that they're getting a reminder that they need to be thinking about carbon. And the impact was significant. I mean, just those discussions led to a roughly 35 per cent reduction in our internal travel. And without a significant impact on the culture of the firm or what we were trying to accomplish, and we expect to continue to use these to manage our footprint going forward. We did put in place the process for a carbon tax as well. We haven't had to face this situation yet, but it is possible that if someone were to exceed their carbon budget, then they would be assessed with a carbon tax based on the overage. And we can use the price of sustainable aviation fuel as the carbon fee for that incentive. And so, they'd effectively have to offset that cost as part of their operations.'

Bain & Company's carbon budget initiative is a powerful example of how companies can seamlessly integrate sustainability into existing processes. By developing a carbon budget that follows a financial template that is familiar to department leaders, reducing emissions becomes as topical as hitting quarterly profits. It is also an example of how sustainability becomes ingrained in a company's culture, as it becomes a part of regular discourse, and what better measurement of a company's culture is there than what is being discussed at the water cooler?

'I think the biggest impact has been getting people to talk about it. While it might not be daily, it's at least monthly that they're getting a reminder that they need to be thinking about carbon. And the impact was significant.'

Sam Israelit, Partner and
Chief Sustainability Officer at Bain & Company

## Bringing rigour to the carbon market

As Global Head of Sustainability at EY Law, Michelle Davies's attention in 2024 has been directed at improving practices and standards related to the carbon market. Unlike the financial market, which operates within well-oiled infrastructure, auditing and regulatory procedures; at present, the carbon market is operating a little bit like the Wild West, with very little structure and oversight. As interest and investments in the carbon market continue to grow, so too will the need for greater governance and assurances, especially for buyers with big net-zero pledges. In an effort to bring some clarity and rigour to this emerging space, EY has been involved with supporting the Global Carbon Market Utility (GCMU) with the development of accounting and auditing processes designed specifically for carbon market activities.

'One initiative that I am proud of recently at EY is the work we're doing on carbon markets. In particular, EY is involved with this Global Carbon Market Utility, which is looking at how to make carbon credits easier to trade. And the easier they are to trade, the more effective they and the gener-ating market will be. Solutions around standardizing and securitizing credits are going to become increasingly important. But we just think clients need to be aware of this opportunity now. Even though it's going to take time, they need to start building into the design of their sustainability strategies the potential to access the carbon markets in a very different way to how we have done previously. That's probably what I'm most proud of because I think we probably were one of the first organizations to really focus on how you can not only operationalize sustainability but also how you can mone-tize it in the context of transition planning. Monetizing sustainability is a critical component of our ability to deliver net zero.'

In a press release issued in December 2023, the GCMU stated that carbon markets enable the financing of avoidance and removal activities by organ-izations and nations that have committed to net-zero targets. With its new initiative, the GCMU is committed to ensuring climate integrity. Leaning on EY's expertise in the area of financial market infrastructure, climate data and accounting policy, the GCMU is committed to bringing rigour and over-sight to the carbon market by designing ledgers for carbon offset purchases that can withstand the financial and regulatory audit requirements. As the GCMU states in its press release, with this initiative corporate buyers, civil societies (and the climate) can be assured of the integrity and impact of their carbon transactions – in line with their net-zero targets and commitments.[3]

## Transforming a carbon-intense cement industry

Another example of how organizations are leading sustainable transforma-tion can be seen in the work that is being done in the cement industry. The cement industry is responsible for more than 7 per cent of global GHG emis-sions.[4] Given the cement industry is a carbon-intensive sector, it is generally not viewed as being sustainable. Magali Anderson, a sustainability expert and engineer by training, is focusing on steering the industry towards more sustainable practices. There is one initiative that Magali helped drive and that she points to as being truly transformative for the cement industry in particular.

In 2019, Magali was appointed Chief Sustainability Officer at Holcim, a Switzerland-based building materials company. In September 2020, under Magali's stewardship, Holcim became the first cement company to pledge its commitment to net zero by 2050, with its pathway validated by Science

Based Targets initiative (SBTi), making it one of the first companies in the world to pledge to net zero *and* have SBTi validation. Most companies at the time had committed to one or the other, but not both. Magali explained that the company's net-zero plans and commitments were a year in the making, as it took that long to engage leaders from across the organization in the process. Magali explained that it was important to have an action plan in place that would ensure the company could deliver on its pledge – and getting company-wide support was integral to that process.

'I am really proud of this work. And the reason it took one year to get to that point is because we engaged the entire organization to do it, to make sure that we had an action plan associated to it, and we knew we could deliver it. But the result that came out of that – outside the fact that we engaged an entire company, and we got an entire company moving together, which was absolutely incredible – was the positive feedback we got from more or less every employee. But also, it was the first in the industry. And being the first mover opened the track for everyone else to get on it. Because once someone has made a move, everyone else wants to make that move. And after that, together with the Global Cement and Concrete Association (GCCA), we launched a programme to get all of the GCCA members to commit to net zero by 2050. That represents 80 per cent of the cement made outside China. And that was an initiative that I co-chaired. Therefore, not only did our work move the company forward, but we moved the entire industry, and I'm extremely proud of that.'

As Magali has highlighted, sometimes it takes just one organization to boldly lead the way forward for others to follow. With its ambitious commitments and action plans, Holcim helped mobilize the cement industry towards better practices. What she also emphasizes, however, is the importance for companies to have action plans in place to meet the ambitious goals and targets they set and communicate to their stakeholders. As the saying goes, hope is not a plan. CSOs need to ensure they have the support and buy-in they need to achieve a company's medium- to long-term sustainability objectives.

## Artificial photosynthesis

Another industry-leading sustainability initiative is one that was developed by NTT Data, a Japanese multinational IT and consulting firm with head-quarters based in Tokyo. Beyond helping companies navigate data, NTT

Data is leveraging its technological expertise to tackle some of the biggest environmental challenges the world is facing, including reducing GHG emissions. David Costa is the Chief Sustainability Business Officer at NTT Data. As part of his role, David is focused on helping clients improve their data management processes related to their sustainability initiatives and performance. In an effort to help organizations reduce their carbon footprint, David shared an example of how the company is using technology to directly remove $CO_2$ from the atmosphere. Inspired by the process of photosynthesis in nature, NTT Data recreated the process of photosynthesis using technology. Photosynthesis involves plants taking $CO_2$ and water from the air and soil. At the plants' cellular level, the water is transformed into oxygen and released into the air, while the carbon dioxide is transformed into glucose and stored within the plant.[5]

Given NTT Data works with businesses from various industries, including carbon-intensive industries such as the airline industry, a key focus for NTT Data is to provide services and solutions that help companies reduce their impact.

'Let me share two examples of our sustainability-focused technologies with you. The first is artificial photosynthesis. An artificial photosynthesis simulates what a tree does. And a square metre of these materials generates the same impact as a tree of 20 metres tall. We are also working now on algae that capture $CO_2$. They grow faster and they help to feed fish. So, it helps also with the human value chain. These investments that we are doing will have a positive impact in the future. For me, incremental change is not going to make a big change. We need to transform. And to transform, we need to find this type of solution. One of the questions I was asking our engineers was, "okay, how many algae should I plant or grow to compensate the whole emissions that we generate every year?" And we need to calculate that. The same applies to buildings; imagine that by using those materials in buildings you could again compensate the impact. These are the complexity levels and the types of technological solutions we are working on.'

The examples David shares showcase how sustainability-focused solutions can be leveraged to address multiple issues at the same time. Take the algae example, for instance. The process of photosynthesis in algae contributes to reducing $CO_2$ emissions while, at the same time, provides a sustainable source of food to fuel our food chain. With one innovative solution, NTT Data is helping its clients contribute to multiple sustainable development goals at the same time. It is these kinds of forward-thinking solutions, accelerated by technology, that will propel us forward on this path towards a more sustainable future.

## Making science more accessible and inclusive

On the social front of sustainability, Jeffrey Whitford, Vice President of Sustainability and Social Business Innovation at Merck Life Science, shared with us an example of how the science-based organization is striving to make science more accessible to groups that have been, and continue to be, under-represented in the field.

'We have a programme here in the US and in Europe called the Curiosity Cube Mobile Science Lab. It's a shipping container that we've transformed into a mobile science lab that moves across the European continent and in the UK and in Ireland. And the main idea of the programme is to really reach underprivileged students who have typically been excluded in the sciences. In the US specifically, that primarily means children of colour and girls. Those are the audiences that have not been included. When you move into other places those topics still exist, but they may exist in a different form or fashion. And sometimes those topics are much more culturally sensitive to talk about. And we're having to figure out how we navigate those conversations, and to really raise it without pointing fingers because that's not what it's about – but it's to remind ourselves that we need to be inclusive. At the end of the day, what is that kind of centralizing message? It's about inclusivity, right? How do we make sure everyone is welcome at the table so that they can participate?'

Since its launch in 2017, Merck Life Science's programme has expanded to include four mobile labs that travel across North America and Europe and will continue expansion into new geographies in 2025. In addition to engaging and sparking curiosity in almost 200,000 primary school children, the programme also engages Merck Life Science's employees who run the labs in each community it visits. The company's staff volunteer their time to impart their skills, enthusiasm and passion with students. In addition to engaging students on the topics of STEM (science, technology, engineering and mathematics), by inspiring the next generation of scientists from diverse places and socio-economic backgrounds, the programme aims to fill the skills, gender and diversity gaps that exist in the field. Merck Life Science's programme is an inspiring example of how organizations can play a pivotal role to address important societal issues. It is also a powerful example of the role that education plays to spark interest and inspire future generations to consider a future career in STEM.

## Adopting a circular business model

As one of the world's largest manufacturers of imaging products, Canon is looking at ways to reduce the company's environmental impact, especially when it comes to waste. To minimize its impact, the company has developed a business model that centres around the circular economy. To reduce waste at the end of the life of its products, Canon has introduced refurbishment and remanufacturing services for popular office printing devices and some camera lines. The company has a long-established facility in Germany that is fully dedicated to refurbishment, remanufacturing and repairing its products; this also includes harvesting older machines for parts to reuse as much as possible and responsibly recycle the rest.

'The refurbishment process involves taking a used device and putting it through a full remanufacturing process. At the end of that process the device looks and operates as good as new. And it's fantastic, as it's taking our used products and giving them a second life. Although it represents a relatively small proportion of our business, compared to all new products, it's growing, with increased demands from our customers wanting this second-life option. We see this area as being very important as it is changing the thinking around product design, how you use products, and how you extend the lifetime of products as well, which is obviously what sustainability is all about.'

Since introducing this circular model, the company has seen demand for refurbished products grow in the marketplace. In addition to reducing waste, the company's remanufacturing operation also supports Canon's circular economy business model, with it also extending to refurbished consumer products selling through its own e-commerce store. By giving products a second life, Canon is meeting its objective to reduce waste while at the same time growing the business.

## Sustainability is a lever for competitive advantage

In this chapter we have shared some industry-leading examples of innovative initiatives that companies are spearheading to address global challenges threatening the environment and society.

The examples provided in this chapter align with the framework proposed by Ram Nidumolu, C K Prahalad and M R Rangaswami in a notable article published in the *Harvard Business Review*, which outlines five stages of sustainability-driven innovation.

These stages include viewing compliance as an opportunity, making value chains sustainable, designing sustainable products and services, developing new business models, and creating next-practice platforms.[6] Each of the initiatives discussed demonstrates how companies are not only addressing environmental and social challenges but also innovating their business models to create value for both the company and society. By progressing through these stages, organizations are positioning themselves to lead in sustainability and reap both economic and social benefits.

In addition to having a positive impact on society and the planet, companies that are adopting a holistic approach to sustainability are also gaining a competitive advantage in their industries.

An article published by *Forbes* highlights that companies that are committed to raising awareness for important global issues, while also taking responsibility for their own impact, are standing out. Younger millennial and Gen Z consumers in particular are taking notice.[7] Underscoring this point, a study by Alfac states that 77 per cent of consumers and 73 per cent of investors are more willing to purchase from a company that has made a CSR/sustainability pledge.[8]

In his executive education course titled 'Building competitive advantage through sustainability', Paolo Taticchi, Professor of Strategy and Sustainability at UCL School of Management and co-author of this book, makes the business case for how companies can build a competitive advantage by adopting a holistic approach that integrates sustainability into every area of the business. He also underscores the point that companies that are approaching sustainability as a CSR initiative are not taking the topic seriously.

'We are moving away from approaches based on traditional CSR, where sustainability is based on a 'give back'/'philanthropic' logic, to embrace business models where sustainability creates real economic value and helps companies to be more competitive in the market. To truly leverage sustainability as a lever for competitive advantage, organizations must embed sustainability into the company's core business strategy, operations and decision-making processes. Furthermore, to really transform an organization towards more responsible business practices, sustainability needs to be at the top of the executive agenda and embedded into the company's values and culture.'

Paolo's modern definition for corporate sustainability, which we discussed in Chapter 1 of this book, underlines the importance for organizations to consider the needs of all their stakeholders, not only shareholders. It also highlights the importance for companies to collaborate and create value for and with their stakeholders. This modern definition of sustainability builds on the idea of 'creating shared value', which was pioneered by Michel Porter and Mark Kramer. Porter and Kramer argue that business can generate economic value by identifying and addressing social problems that intersect with their business.[9] When looking at a business through this shared value lens, companies that consider the interests of all stakeholders – as well as the interests of the planet – can benefit economically while positively impacting society and the natural world. Furthermore, companies that view sustainability as a business opportunity – rather than a risk – are leading the way in their industries. An article by *Harvard Business Review* underscores this point, stating that an investment in sustainability is more than a risk management tool, it is also a driver for innovation.[10]

The benefits companies can gain from a sustainability-focused strategy stretch beyond profits. Research shows that sustainability-driven organizations report higher levels of employee engagement and satisfaction, better recruitment and retention of talent, and higher morale and productivity across their organizations.[11] All of these factors contribute to elevating a company's sustainability and financial performance. In addition to gaining a competitive advantage built on sustainability, sustainability-focused companies are also poised to future-proof their businesses, ensuring long-term success.

As we can see from the industry-leading examples discussed in this chapter, many organizations are dedicated to elevating sustainability practices across their organizations and industries. Moreover, we are seeing how solutions that emerge from one sector can cross over and be adopted by other sectors or be leveraged to address multiple issues, as we saw in the example from NTT Data, which reduced carbon emissions while also supplying the food chain. This serves as a valuable reminder of how even the smallest ideas can lead to big waves of change.

The examples of sustainability-driven solutions shared in this chapter are demonstrative of the positive impact businesses can have in society and on the planet. We can see from these initiatives why the CSOs we met with are optimistic about the role businesses can play to create a more sustainable world. While there is reason to be optimistic, as every CSO we met with also pointed out, much more needs to be done to meet the targets that have been set for this decade and for future generations.

KEY TAKEAWAYS

- **Sustainability-oriented innovation (SOI)**: Leading companies are increasingly focusing on SOI, which involves focusing on business innovation to achieve environmental initiatives and social improvements. This approach aims to create value for both the company and society.

- **Incremental vs. transformational change**: Transformational changes are needed to address global challenges effectively. Incremental improvements may not be sufficient to achieve significant impact; instead, companies must aim for groundbreaking innovations that can accelerate change.

- **Collaboration for success**: Tackling complex sustainability issues often requires collaboration with other stakeholders, including competitors and academic institutions. This collaborative approach is essential for developing credible methodologies and achieving long-term goals.

- **Integration of sustainability into business operations**: To truly leverage sustainability as a competitive advantage, organizations must integrate it into their core strategy, operations and culture. Leading companies are also exploring circular business models, not only to minimize environmental impact but also to create new business opportunities.

- **Long-term benefits of sustainability**: Companies that adopt a sustainability-focused strategy report higher employee engagement, better talent retention, and improved morale and productivity. These factors contribute to both sustainability and financial performance, positioning companies for future success.

# Notes

1   Geradts, T H J and Bocken, N M P (2018) Driving sustainability-oriented innovation, *MIT Sloan Management Review*, 18 November

2   McKinsey & Company (2021) Adam Grant on leadership, emotional intelligence, and the value of thinking like a scientist, McKinsey Leadership blog, 24 May, www.mckinsey.com/about-us/new-at-mckinsey-blog/adam-grant-on-modern-leadership (archived at https://perma.cc/2E6H-95RU)

3   Global Carbon Market Utility (2023) The Global Carbon Market Utility engages EY to build infrastructure to scale voluntary carbon market, PR Newswire, 4 December, www.prnewswire.com/news-releases/the-global-carbon-market-utility-engages-ey-to-build-infrastructure-to-scale-voluntary-carbon-market-302004651.html (archived at https://perma.cc/YQ87-JNQE)

4  Miller, S, Habert, G, Myers, R and Harvey, T (2021) Achieving net zero greenhouse gas emissions in the cement industry via value chain mitigation strategies, *One Earth*, 4 (10), 22 October, www.sciencedirect.com/science/article/pii/S2590332221005339 (archived at https://perma.cc/4DL2-MQCM)

5  National Geographic Education, Photosynthesis, https://education.nationalgeographic.org/resource/photosynthesis/ (archived at https://perma.cc/UQV2-27CN)

6  Nidumolu, R, Prahalad, C K and Rangaswami, M R (2009) Why sustainability is now the key driver of innovation, *Harvard Business Review*, 87, 9 (September), 56–64

7  Newman, D (2020) How leading global companies are using sustainability as a market differentiator, *Forbes*, 24 July, www.forbes.com/sites/danielnewman/2020/07/24/how-leading-global-companies-are-using-sustainability-as-a-market-differentiator/?sh=644c88681ff3 (archived at https://perma.cc/6L6Q-YVSD)

8  Newman, D (2020) How leading global companies are using sustainability as a market differentiator, 24 July, *Forbes*, www.forbes.com/sites/danielnewman/2020/07/24/how-leading-global-companies-are-using-sustainability-as-a-market-differentiator/?sh=644c88681ff3 (archived at https://perma.cc/6L6Q-YVSD)

9  Whelan, T and Fink, C (2016) The Comprehensive Business Case for Sustainability, *Harvard Business Review*, 21 October, https://hbr.org/2016/10/the-comprehensive-business-case-for-sustainability (archived at https://perma.cc/73RT-33FH)

10  Whelan, T and Fink, C (2016) The Comprehensive Business Case for Sustainability, *Harvard Business Review*, 21 October, https://hbr.org/2016/10/the-comprehensive-business-case-for-sustainability (archived at https://perma.cc/73RT-33FH)

11  Whelan, T and Fink, C (2016) The Comprehensive Business Case for Sustainability, *Harvard Business Review*, 21 October, https://hbr.org/2016/10/the-comprehensive-business-case-for-sustainability (archived at https://perma.cc/73RT-33FH)

# 9

# Navigating the biggest challenges facing business

As companies strive to reduce their impact on the planet and contribute to the sustainable development goals (SDGs) outlined by the UN, they are encountering a myriad of challenges on this journey. In this chapter we delve into three big challenges facing businesses, and the approaches CSOs are taking to navigate those obstacles.

Before we delve into the various sustainability issues companies and CSOs are grappling with, it is worth noting that the challenges businesses face are country- and industry-specific and depend on their level of ESG maturity. In addition to discussing some of the most prevalent challenges businesses encounter, based on the expertise of the CSOs we met, we suggest strategies to address and rise above them.

## Challenge #1: Collecting and disclosing ESG data and performance

For organizations big and small, one of the greatest challenges is gathering and assessing data to inform their sustainability strategy and decision-making processes. During our conversations with CSOs, this repeatedly came up. Knowing which data to gather, where and how to collect it, and how to analyse it can be overwhelming for an organization of any size. Add to this the task of gathering data from a company's value chain – as is the case when assessing Scope 3 carbon emissions – the challenge is even greater.

Navigating the complexity of data gathering and data management is a central focus for David Costa, Chief Sustainability Business Officer at

NTT Data, a leading global IT infrastructures and services company. As a sustainability-driven IT company, NTT Data is committed to lead the way by alleviating the complexity that comes with data management and calculations, while also supporting their clients on this journey.

'Data is a big challenge for companies. To begin with, all companies need to make sure they have accurate data about their emissions. And it's not easy. We are in the process of measuring that, and depending on how you do the calculations, this process will vary. So, it is not a shortage of data; it's about how all the calculations are done.

'At NTT Data we have developed a solution that is called C-Turtle, which helps to calculate our emissions. Another challenge is geography. We are now operating in 50 countries and the way you calculate emissions within each country and region differs. Our calculations in India differ from those in Spain, Brazil or the US, for example. Because of these variances, we need to do some hypotheses. And fortunately, we have amazing people in the team. Our leader, Vicky, who is in charge of the transformation and strategy, has a lot of industry experience and understands this field very well. But when we sit down to do those calculations, even we have conversations about what is the best approach to take to calculate this metric or the other one.

'We also have external conversations with Apple and other stakeholders, and realize that we all need one another. We have amazing people who have been doing this for years – so we have a good basis and general overview to start with and we have a good hypothesis to improve as we move forward.'

Determining how to effectively operationalize the process of data collection is central to this challenge. In addition to ensuring that teams have the right skills and training when it comes to data collection and assessment, companies need to also invest in resources and technology to support employees and make the process as efficient and frictionless as possible.

Although gathering data can be a seemingly daunting task, the fact that companies need to adhere to several frameworks and regulations – each with a different set of criteria to check off – makes it even more difficult. While some of the regulations are voluntary, some are legally binding, meaning companies must report specific details related to their sustainability impact. The EU's Corporate Sustainability Reporting Directive (CSRD) is one example of a legally binding regulation that requires companies to report on their sustainability impact.[1] Under the CSRD's most recent requirements, which came into effect in January 2023, all large and listed SMEs are mandated to disclose information related to their social and environmental impact. Estimates suggest that more than 50,000 SMEs in the European Union will engage with sustainability disclosure for the first time in 2024 to 2025.

Another framework that is considered an industry standard, albeit a voluntary one, is the Global Reporting Initiative (GRI). GRI is an independent, international organization that helps companies be accountable for their impacts with a comprehensive guide on how to communicate those impacts. According to consulting firm KPMG, the GRI is the most widely used standard for sustainability reporting globally.[2] In addition to offering a comprehensive list of metrics, the GRI also provides standards that are specific to certain industries and material topics.

Despite the many challenges that come with data collection, reporting and disclosure practices, more than ever, companies are making strides towards improving their sustainability practices and transparently communicating their progress and efforts. For sustainability experts, advocates and enthusiasts around the world, this is encouraging. And while credit should be given to companies that are taking steps to reduce their impact and report on their progress, to a certain extent these companies also face greater scrutiny. The reality is that once a company discloses their activities and impacts, they open themselves to criticism and become subject to the judgement of rating agencies that analyse ESG performance using different criteria and often non-transparent methodologies. However, companies that value the viewpoints of all their stakeholders will view the criticism as valuable feedback.

## Challenge #2: Sustainable supply chain management

Any CSO focused on steering their organization towards achieving its sustainability goals will tell you that for companies to meet their goals, engaging stakeholders along the way is key. When we think about measuring and assessing a company's carbon footprint, for example, we know that the majority of a company's carbon emissions typically comes from its Scope 3 emissions, therefore, its supply chain. Key to a CSO's role, therefore, is ensuring the company is effectively engaging and supporting its suppliers on their own journey of sustainable transformation.

Sam Israelit, Partner and Chief Sustainability Officer at Bain & Company, underscored the importance of engaging supply chains in order to meet a company's own sustainability targets.

'Engaging our supply chain is a key challenge for us. As a professional services firm, we don't manufacture anything, so our direct emissions are very low. Therefore, our supply chain is a really important part of our overall impact. What that means is we have to engage the people who make decisions around what we purchase to affect those emissions, and to do this our approach is simple – we follow the carbon. We look at where we generate the biggest buckets of emissions, and then we look at what we can do to reduce those emissions. And a lot of the time that entails working with people on the front lines in those functions and giving them the data they need to make informed decisions.

'People will naturally want to do the right thing, but they don't always know what that is, and they don't always have the data to actually make those decisions in the right way. So, you have to give them the information and tools to do that. And that's why you would engage people in the procurement function, to educate them on the importance of decarbonization and help them understand what they can do and how their decisions affect our footprint. And then you have to work with the leadership team in that function to really realign the decision criteria they use around supplier decisions. It is only by working together that we will achieve our common goals and objectives.'

It is important to highlight that reducing carbon emissions along the supply chain is just one aspect of this journey. Other aspects to consider when engaging suppliers include a wide range of sustainability topics that cover environmental, social and economic dimensions.

One company that is making strides to engage their supply chain and position themselves as industry leaders on the road to net zero is the LEGO Group. In 2014, the global toy manufacturer launched its Engage to Reduce programme, an initiative designed to help suppliers minimize their GHG emissions.[3] By engaging and supporting suppliers, the programme aims to reduce emissions along the LEGO Group's supply chain in line with the company's 2050 net-zero pledge. Given over 99 per cent of the company's carbon emissions come from its supply chain, the LEGO Group recognizes the pivotal role its suppliers play to help it achieve its target. Building on this initiative, in 2024 the company launched its Supplier Sustainability Programme, which outlines key procurement requirements and actions suppliers need to take to reduce their environmental impact.[4] In addition to providing specific carbon-related data linked to a supplier's products and services, suppliers will also need to provide annual reports about their impact to the LEGO Group going forward. With its ambitious plans and targets in place, the LEGO Group recognizes the challenges suppliers face as they strive to measure, track and reduce their impact in line with the LEGO Group's programme.

To support their suppliers on this journey, the LEGO Group has committed to sharing knowledge, learnings and resources that can help suppliers on this journey. The LEGO Group's team of sustainability experts are also available to provide support and guidance along the way. Annette Stube, Chief Sustainability Officer at the LEGO Group, emphasized the importance of engaging suppliers on the road to net zero, stating, 'To put it simply, a net-zero world is simply not possible unless we find solutions that are greater than our own operations. We will not be able to meet our sustainability targets alone – we have to work in partnership with our suppliers. We want children to inherit a healthy planet and there's no time to waste.' All in all, the LEGO Group's Supplier Sustainability Programme is an industry-leading example of how companies can engage and support their supply chains towards creating a better world for future generations.

In addition to taking steps to address the environmental impacts stemming from a company's supply chain, it is equally important for SMEs and large multinational organizations especially, to put processes in place that ensure fair labour and fair working conditions are being practised across their supply chains. Gone are the days where companies can claim ignorance of the activities that are happening out of sight, or far away from their own operations and sites.

With the increase in global challenges, there has been a rise in the level of awareness on the part of consumers that their purchase behaviours can influence positive change. Due in part to the exposure of various corporate scandals over the years, such as the well-known Nike sweatshop case that came to light in the 1990s, our collective social consciousness has gradually awakened to the many human injustices that persist along global supply chains. In the 1990s, Nike faced intense scrutiny amid widespread media reports alleging violations of human rights in its global supply chain, including instances of child labour.[5] Photos of children stitching footballs in places like Cambodia and Pakistan appeared on the covers of newspapers around the world. Among the many damning activities being reported was the claim that Nike workers in Indonesia were earning as little as 14 cents an hour.[6] The damage to the company's reputation and the consumer backlash that ensued was significant. In 1998, the sportswear giant was forced to lay off employees due to a decline in sales. Additionally, the company paid US$1.5 million to settle allegations about how it treated workers.[7]

Although the scandal could very well have marked the beginning of the end for the sportswear giant, instead it became a significant turning point that put the company on a path towards long-term sustainable growth. To borrow a phrase from the sports world, the scandal propelled one of the biggest comebacks in the history of sports retail. It also became a catalyst for change. In the years that followed, Nike's CEO Phil Knight made it his mission to turn the company around by following a simple and clear strategy – going forward Nike was going to be honest and transparent about its labour issues and activities.[8] What separates great companies from good companies is how they respond in the face of adversity. Nike's response to the scandal led it to become an industry leader for its transparency around labour practices. Following the scandal, Nike committed to improving labour practices and conditions across its supply chain by raising the minimum wage of paid workers and improving its oversight of labour practices and working conditions in its factories. Additionally, in 1999, Nike joined the Fair Labour Association, a non-profit organization that promotes human rights for workers around the world.[9] Reinforcing its commitment to do better and lead the way for the industry, in 2005 the company published a 108-page report that detailed the labour and working conditions in all 700 factories across its supply chain. Michael Posner, Executive Director of the Human Rights First organization, commended Nike for its transparency, describing the company's report as 'an important step forward' for the company and the sector. Underscoring the importance for industries to work together to address labour issues across global supply chains, the company made the following statement in its report: 'We do not believe Nike has the power to single-handedly solve the issues at stake.'[10] Nike's 1990s case is just one example of the many human rights and labour violations that persist within global supply chains.

And while it is imperative that companies are transparent about their activities from a consumer-demand perspective, in many jurisdictions today it is also required by law. For example, the Modern Slavery Act in the UK, introduced in 2015, requires companies with a turnover above US$43.5 million to publicly disclose an annual slavery and trafficking statement detailing how the company is addressing human rights violations across its supply chain.[11] Despite significant improvements in corporate policies and human rights laws since the 1990s, issues remain prevalent across many industries today, including within the fast-fashion, electronics and consumer packaged goods sectors.

A more recent example of human rights violations involved one of the world's most beloved beverages: tea. In February 2023, a BBC news report shed light on human rights violations within global supply chains, revealing instances of sexual abuse occurring on Kenyan tea plantations, many of which are owned by major international companies. Given the seriousness of the allegations reported, the companies involved took immediate action and launched independent investigations.[12] The case highlights the importance of companies taking accountability for actions along their supply chains and implementing measures to safeguard workers at every step. To protect workers within organizations and across their supply chains, companies need to ensure they have formal human rights policies and governance practices in place. For example, having policies that ensure zero tolerance for modern slavery, human trafficking or sexual harassment, to name just a few issues, is imperative.

Today, sustainable supply chain management is key for success. If companies want to be sustainable, they need to be able to extend their corporate sustainability strategies to their supply chains. Research from Formentini and Taticchi in 2016 has analysed how to achieve this, finding that companies need to activate a mix of collaborative and non-collaborative governance mechanisms, both formal and informal, to influence suppliers.[13]

Amid the increasing demands and expectations for corporations to be more environmentally and socially responsible, as well as the rise of social media where news travels faster than ever before, it is no surprise that more companies are striving to not only improve their sustainability practices but also to ensure their efforts are recognized. Recognizing that sustainability is a competitive advantage, many companies are looking to elevate their sustainability performance, branding and positioning by applying for sustainability certifications with organizations such as B Corporation, for example. B Corporation offers a certified designation that a business meets a high set of sustainability performance, accountability and transparency standards.[14] Evidence of sustainable supply chain management is part of B Corp's certification requirements. As of 2024, more than 8,900 companies have earned a B Corp certification.[15] Given the many benefits companies and brands gain from being sustainability-focused, we anticipate this trend will grow in the coming years.

## Challenge #3: Greenwashing and greenhushing

One of the potential risks that companies face when it comes to transparent communication and reporting is being exposed to criticism, or worse, being accused of greenwashing. Greenwashing refers to when a company misleads people by making them believe it is more environmentally responsible than it really is. A classic story of greenwashing is the Dieselgate case. In 2015, German car giant Volkswagen (VW) admitted to fitting their diesel-powered cars with devices that enabled them to cheat on emissions tests. Commenting on the scandal at the time was Frank O'Donnell from Washington-based Clean Air Watch, who aptly stated, 'Volkswagen made a point in selling these cars that they're clean. It's too bad that their technology wasn't as good as their ads.'[16] The scandal ended up costing the company over US$30 billion in fines and damages, making it the most expensive in the history of the automotive sector. And this doesn't take into account the reputational damage caused to the VW brand. According to an article published by *Forbes*, marketing and communications efforts aside, Dieselgate was the product of a corporate culture that was driven by financial targets. In an attempt to learn from its mistakes, in the years that followed the company underwent a significant cultural shift towards becoming a more ethical and responsible organization.[17]

While many organizations are indeed guilty of deceptive greenwashing, in many instances this is happening unintentionally. We see this occur when organizations approach sustainability as a marketing or PR initiative, rather than as an approach that integrates sustainability into the core business strategy. Without the right expertise and processes in place, companies risk making claims that not only are they unable to deliver on – but also that they do not fully understand. One example of unintentional greenwashing was seen in the UK when banking giant HSBC was called out by the Advertising Standards Authority (ASA) for what it claimed were misleading advertisements about the bank's efforts to address climate change. The UK's advertising regulator banned two HSBC campaigns that appeared at bus stops in London and Bristol in the lead up to the UN COP26 climate change summit, which took place in Glasgow, Scotland in early November 2021. According to the ASA, the campaigns 'omitted significant information' about the bank's contribution to $CO_2$ and GHG emissions.[18] One of the posters that appeared during the campaign showed an image of tree growth rings alongside copy that read, 'Climate change doesn't do borders. So in the UK, we're helping to plant 2 million trees which will lock in 1.25 million tonnes of carbon over their lifetime.' While this initiative was well-intended, the ASA argued the bank's claims about addressing climate change were unqualified, given that it was simultaneously financing businesses and projects that were contributing to climate change, namely in the carbon-intensive oil and gas sector.

Another of the bank's advertisements showed an image of waves crashing next to text that read, 'Climate change doesn't do borders. Neither do rising sea levels. That's why HSBC is aiming to provide up to $1 trillion in financing and investment globally to help our clients transition to net zero'.[19] We can see how the use of the term net zero by a bank that counts businesses involved with fossil fuels on its list of clients is problematic.

The HSBC example stands out as a cautionary tale for companies to be transparent about their activities, both the positive and the negative. It is important to point out, however, that HSBC is not the only bank involved with financing fossil fuel projects. A 2024 report developed by the Sierra Club, the Rainforest Action Network and others, showed that, in 2023, a total of $700 billion dollars flowed from 60 of the world's largest private banks to companies working in fossil fuels; HSBC was ranked 12th on the list.[20] On a slightly more positive note, the report also showed there was a slight decline in the financing of oil, gas and coal by banks since 2021. Unfortunately, as researchers of the report have stressed, this decline is not happening fast enough.[21]

On the flip side of greenwashing is another concerning trend that is growing, and that is *greenhushing*. Opposite to greenwashing, whereby companies are effectively shouting their baseless sustainability claims from rooftops, greenhushing refers to when a company is too quiet about their impacts.[22] Rather than exposing themselves to being publicly criticized and scrutinized on sustainability matters, companies are instead choosing not to disclose their goals, commitments and progress.

A 2022 report published by South Pole, a Swiss-based carbon finance firm, revealed that of 1,200 large companies surveyed, 25 per cent are keeping quiet about their sustainability targets and progress.[23] What is surprising is that many of the companies surveyed have net-zero strategies and science-based targets in place, which begs the question, why not talk about it? According to the report, scrutiny from media and NGOs, as well as the threat of being sued are all possible deterrents – even for companies that are making an honest effort to elevate their sustainability performance. A key risk associated to greenhushing is that without transparent reporting and disclosure practices, companies cannot be held to account for their commitments. Worse, companies could be quietly slowing down their efforts altogether.

Klaus Kunz, Founder and Managing Director at Ephrin, believes this trend of greenhushing is cause for great concern. Reflecting on organizational behavioural shifts he has seen around sustainability over the years, Klaus noted that in and around 2018 the world saw a higher level of convergence on the part of corporations, compared to previous years, towards sustainability reporting and practice, and credits activists like Greta Thunberg and others for creating a movement that mobilized large corporations and politicians to all move forward together. Reflecting on the situation in 2024, however, Klaus feels that due to changing political landscapes and a rise in trends such as greenhushing, many organizations and nations are starting to pull back on their commitments and targets.

'I look at the situation now, the political regulatory landscape, and we are moving into divergence. We see that the Europeans are running faster while the Americans are slowing down. I think this is very dangerous for corporations in between. We see with corporations that there are those who are walking the talk and talking the walk. And then there are others who are greenhushing – they are silently escaping from the conversation. They just exit and hope nobody realizes, and I find this very concerning.'

As Klaus points out, the trend of companies choosing to opt out of communicating their impacts is concerning. What is equally worrisome is the fact that some companies are choosing not to engage in certain sustainability practices altogether for fear of being criticized. Klaus points to carbon offsetting as one such example. Carbon offsetting refers to a way to compensate for $CO_2$ emissions by funding solutions that will remove the equivalent $CO_2$ emissions elsewhere.[24] Tree planting is one example of a carbon offset solution. It is true that not all carbon offsets are trustworthy investments, and companies have reason to be concerned and cautious. Conversely, there are many carbon offsets that are indeed credible and do in fact remove $CO_2$ from the earth's atmosphere as they promise to do.

'We see with corporations that there are those who are walking the talk and talking the walk. And then there are others who are greenhushing – they are silently escaping from the conversation. They just exit and hope nobody realizes, and I find this very concerning.'

**Klaus Kunz, Founder and Managing Director at Ephrin**

## Steps companies can take to address sustainability challenges

While the challenges companies face are indeed monumental, they are not insurmountable. There are specific steps organizations can take to mitigate risks and threats to their business. In this section we offer four steps that can help companies navigate and address the challenges they encounter.

### Step 1: Leverage sustainability expertise

As we discussed in the chapter about essential skills, harnessing the right skills and subject matter expertise is key. In this vein, one of the first steps companies can take when starting to engage with sustainability is leaning on the knowledge of sustainability experts.

Having a dedicated team member, or team, that specializes in sustainability reporting and is trained on the regulations and reporting requirements for a particular company will prove incredibly helpful. Having subject matter experts spearhead a company's strategy will also help it avoid missteps that can lead to greenwashing. For companies who are just beginning their journeys and may not have this expertise in-house, leaning on the support of a third-party consultancy is a wise option to consider. In addition to supporting a company though the process of data collection and reporting, consultants can also provide training in this area so that companies can gradually build this expertise internally. With the right expertise in place, companies can be better positioned to identify both risks and opportunities related to sustainability.

Beyond having a strong team of subject matter experts, companies also need to invest in training and upskilling employees across the organization. Elisa Moscolin, EVP of Sustainability and Foundation at Sage, firmly believes that having a strong team of subject matter experts and skills training is crucial for companies to address any sustainability challenges they face. She also emphasizes the multitude of challenges leaders are faced with on this journey.

'Sustainability teams are faced with many dilemmas. How do you deliver on net zero and reconcile your commercial imperatives? How do you use AI and data ethically to elevate the work of humans? You cannot, as a tech company, not experiment with AI and data. You will cease to exist. But at the same time, when you do that, how do you do it ethically? And for many of these dilemmas, not only is there no template but also, many times there isn't an obvious answer that beautifully meets both short- and long-term goals. There is a tension between what markets expect in the short term vs. the long-term implications of business decisions. I therefore believe it is important to work together with boards and CEOs that need to square things up and also accept that sometimes, it simply won't be possible.'

As a sustainability leader who has helped many organizations on their sustainability journeys over the course of her career, Elisa appreciates the complexities and difficulties that executive teams face as they strive to advance their organization's sustainability and commercial agendas and goals. Furthermore, during our discussion Elisa emphasized that sustainability cannot be delivered by a small team of experts alone, stating that for organizations to fulfil their commitments, sustainability needs to be embedded into the fabric of the organization.

### Step 2: Invest in sustainability technology

In addition to investing in sustainability expertise, skills and training, it is imperative that organizations also invest in resources and technology designed to support their data collection, assessment and reporting efforts. Investing, in particular, in data management systems and technology that are designed to gather environmental, social and governance metrics is key. This investment is crucial for streamlining the process and making it as efficient as possible. As the CSO of Microsoft Germany, Sean Jones appreciates the challenge that data gathering presents for businesses big and small. A key part of his role at Microsoft Germany is to support businesses as they strive to navigate the complex web of data they are expected to gather and mind.

'The challenges companies face are multifaceted. From a Microsoft perspective, a key challenge we support businesses with is around gathering data. A lot of the work in sustainability right now is in defining what baselines are, for instance, how much carbon equivalent do you actually emit? What is your water position? What is your waste position? How are you impacting biodiversity? Companies also need to look beyond environment and consider social topics as well, such as, how are you treating your own employees? How are you treating your suppliers? In Germany – there is this good German law and term, it's Lieferkettensorgfaltspflichtengesetz (The Supply Chain Act), it must be one of the longest words in the world, and what it means is that a company is responsible for its suppliers. And it is a regulation that has come into frame in Germany and Europe as well. And it's extremely important for everybody to understand how that all works.'

As Sean points out, a key area for organizations to focus on when it comes to data collection is establishing their baselines across a wide spectrum of sustainability issues. Given the extent of data that needs to be gathered across the wide spectrum of sustainability – covering environmental, social and governance factors – investing in technology or software designed to streamline this process is key. Companies need to consider a multitude of factors that look at their environmental and social impacts. Furthermore, organizations need to hold up a mirror and genuinely assess how well they are governing their overall sustainability strategy and initiatives. Combined, the amount of data and inputs that companies need to gather, assess and make sense of is comprehensive and daunting. It is not surprising, therefore, that data is deemed one of the biggest challenges facing companies big and small.

Investing in sustainability technology is essential for organizations to effectively measure, track and report on their progress. This becomes especially important over the long run when companies need to make year-over-year comparisons as part of their assessments and progress reports.

As a sustainability expert, Allegra Fortunato shares the belief that companies need to invest in sustainability-focused technology that is designed to support and simplify their decarbonization measuring, tracking and implementation efforts. Allegra is the Head of Strategy at Tecno International Ltd, a sustain-tech consulting firm that specializes in offering a comprehensive range of services designed to help companies create value by developing and implementing their digital and sustainable transformation strategies. Drawing on her own experience with supporting companies and SMEs (small and medium-sized enterprises) in particular, on their sustainable transformation journeys, Allegra emphasized the importance for business leaders to elevate their knowledge and understanding of the growing market pressures companies are facing due to heightened sustainability reporting regulations, as well as gain an understanding of the associated risks of not engaging with sustainability. What is equally important, especially for companies beginning to engage with sustainability, is the need for executive teams and boards to lean on the expertise of sustainability experts who can help guide organizations towards making more informed decisions about their medium- to long-term business strategy and approach. Additionally, Allegra underscored the need for companies to invest in resources and technology designed to support employees tasked with gathering and assessing what can appear to be a never-ending stream of data.

'Setting ambitious decarbonization targets is only the beginning of a company's journey towards becoming net zero. To achieve those targets, companies need to invest in resources that can support their teams' efforts to efficiently and effectively measure and track their impact. Doing so will not only enable the company to advance their efforts, but it will also make the business more competitive in the process. In our view, doing the right thing is not only good for the environment – it is also good for business.'

Indeed, investing in the right technology that can support sustainable transformation efforts makes good business sense. At the same time, some technology, while immensely useful, can also present some challenges. AI is one example of a technological advancement that can help companies advance their sustainability performance. As Elisa Moscolin pointed out during our discussion, knowing how to use AI ethically is something that businesses, regulators and standards setters are still figuring out. One way for organizations to navigate this challenge is by investing in training and upskilling. With the right training and skills development initiatives, businesses can elevate their understanding of how to leverage emerging technologies such as AI responsibly and ethically. As technology continues to evolve at the rapid pace that we are already seeing, investing in training and development processes aimed at experimenting with new technologies and solutions, in a responsible way, will prove essential for organizations in the future. The sooner organizations move towards putting the right systems, training and processes in place, the sooner they will be able to leverage technology to advance their sustainability agenda and efforts.

### Step 3: Adopt a change management approach

Charlotte Wolff-Bye, Chief Sustainability Officer at Petronas, describes the everyday challenge that companies face on this journey as 'constant change'. To address these challenges, Charlotte believes the CSO's role is effectively a change management role.

'When you work in sustainability, you're only successful if you can embed those practices into the organization. So, every day the sustainability professional will do something new that the organization has never done before. Therefore, the everyday challenge is that constant change. As a CSO you need to believe in what you do, undertake the necessary groundwork and understand the facts behind what you're trying to achieve. At the same time, you must be able to energize yourself, because change will be resisted. It is about resiliency, the ability to dig deep and bounce back every day. It is something I am used to, no day is a struggle; rather, instead I see every day as a small achievement.'

As Charlotte puts it, central to the role of CSO is change management. CSOs need to focus on building an environment, ecosystem and culture that is open to change and that embraces a growth mindset. They also need to be able to demonstrate that with every challenge there is a business opportunity to identify, explore and seize.

## Step 4: Shift the culture of an organization

For an organization to meet the bold and ambitious targets it sets out in support of the Paris Agreement, or the UN SDGs, sustainability needs to be embedded into the company's values, mission and culture. Organizations that are leading on sustainability understand this better than most. Research shows that sustainability-driven companies that have integrated sustainability into the business gain a competitive advantage. Sustainability-driven organizations benefit by attracting and retaining employees, reducing operational costs, increasing innovation and gaining a competitive advantage. We saw this during the Great Resignation. The Great Resignation refers to a period that arose during and following the Covid-19 pandemic era, when historic numbers of employees left their jobs in a search for something better.[25] According to one study by Deloitte, among the many reasons given by employees for leaving their jobs, especially by Gen Z and millennial employees, companies not having a CSR (corporate social responsibility) agenda was one of them.[26] In response to the Great Resignation, some companies decided to make the well-being of their employees a priority. In an effort to attract employees, and more importantly retain them, in 2021 Walmart announced a $1 billion Live Better U programme which promised to cover the full cost of college tuition and books for their employees.[27]

Montse Montaner is a sustainability and innovation leader with extensive experience working in and advising the pharmaceutical sector. In her view, establishing a culture shift and mindset shift that centre around sustainability is one of the biggest challenges companies and CSOs face.

'For me, the biggest challenge companies face is creating that culture. Today, companies are still not able to translate the sustainability mindset, and they are not really understanding that this could bring very positive impacts to the company – in terms of revenue, for example, or hiring people. We know there is a 40 per cent increase in hiring and retention of people in a company that is sustainable. You can also reduce your cost of goods because if you are reducing carbon, you are saving cash. Therefore, there is still a lot of change that is needed across organizations in terms of creating a culture around sustainability.'

As Montse points out, building a culture and mindset that embraces sustainability is vital for an organization to achieve its medium- to long-term goals. Doing so will also give companies a competitive advantage that will ready their organizations for future challenges and set them up for sustainable success.

---

**KEY TAKEAWAYS**

- **Data collection and ESG reporting**: One of the biggest challenges for businesses is gathering and assessing data for sustainability reporting. Investing in technology, skills and resources is crucial for streamlining data collection and meeting regulatory requirements.

- **Supply chain management**: Engaging and supporting the supply chain is essential for achieving sustainability goals. Companies must collaborate with suppliers to reduce environmental impacts and improve sustainability practices across the value chain.

- **Greenwashing and greenhushing**: Companies face risks related to greenwashing and greenhushing. Transparent communication and credible sustainability practices are necessary to avoid these drawbacks and damage to a company's reputation.

- **Leveraging sustainability expertise**: Having a dedicated team of sustainability experts and investing in training and upskilling employees are key to navigating sustainability challenges and avoiding greenwashing.

- **Investing in sustainability technology**: Technology plays a vital role in measuring, tracking and reporting sustainability performance. Companies must invest in technology that is designed to support their sustainability initiatives effectively.

- **Adopting a change management approach**: CSOs must focus on building an environment and culture that is open to change and that embraces a growth mindset. Furthermore, CSOs need to demonstrate that challenges can be turned into business opportunities.

- **Shifting organizational culture**: Embedding sustainability into a company's values, mission and culture is essential for long-term success. Sustainability-focused companies gain a competitive advantage by attracting talent, reducing costs and driving innovation.

# Notes

1   European Commission, Corporate Sustainability Reporting, https://finance.
    ec.europa.eu/capital-markets-union-and-financial-markets/company-reporting-
    and-auditing/company-reporting/corporate-sustainability-reporting_en
    (archived at https://perma.cc/L88F-EP9N)

2   GRI, About GRI, www.globalreporting.org/about-gri/ (archived at
    https://perma.cc/E7A6-AVW8)

3   The LEGO Group, Reducing our emissions, www.lego.com/en-gb/
    sustainability/environment/reducing-our-emissions?locale=en-gb (archived at
    https://perma.cc/R3RQ-F8ND)

4   The LEGO Group (2024) The LEGO Group calls on suppliers to drive
    towards net-zero target, 3 July, www.lego.com/en-dk/aboutus/news/2024/july/
    net-zero-suppliers (archived at https://perma.cc/2SKN-LBJS)

5   Conway, N (2019) Sweatshops almost killed Nike in the 1990s: Now there
    are modern slavery laws, The Fashion Law (TFL), 27 September,
    www.thefashionlaw.com/visibility-is-central-to-a-successful-supply-chain-
    heres-what-brands-need-to-know/ (archived at https://perma.cc/6C4T-J2JS)

6   Lutz, A (2015) How Nike shed its sweatshop image to dominate the shoe
    industry, Business Insider, 6 June, www.businessinsider.com/how-nike-fixed-its-
    sweatshop-image-2015-6 (archived at https://perma.cc/E8CR-DNV7)

7   Teather, D (2005) Nike lists abuses at Asian factories, *The Guardian*,
    14 April, www.theguardian.com/business/2005/apr/14/ethicalbusiness.money
    (archived at https://perma.cc/N879-XVG5)

8   Lutz, A (2015) How Nike shed its sweatshop image to dominate the shoe
    industry, Business Insider, 6 June, www.businessinsider.com/how-nike-fixed-its-
    sweatshop-image-2015-6 (archived at https://perma.cc/E8CR-DNV7)

9   Lutz, A (2015) How Nike shed its sweatshop image to dominate the shoe
    industry, Business Insider, 6 June, www.businessinsider.com/how-nike-fixed-its-
    sweatshop-image-2015-6 (archived at https://perma.cc/E8CR-DNV7)

10  Teather, D (2005) Nike lists abuses at Asian factories, *The Guardian*,
    April 14, 2005, www.theguardian.com/business/2005/apr/14/ethicalbusiness.
    money (archived at https://perma.cc/N879-XVG5)

11  Conway, N (2019) Sweatshops almost killed Nike in the 1990s:
    Now there are modern slavery laws, The Fashion Law (TFL), 27 September,
    www.thefashionlaw.com/visibility-is-central-to-a-successful-supply-chain-
    heres-what-brands-need-to-know/ (archived at https://perma.cc/6C4T-J2JS)

12  BBC News (2023) True cost of our tea: Sexual abuse on Kenyan tea farms
    revealed, BBC News, 20 February, www.bbc.co.uk/news/uk-64662056
    (archived at https://perma.cc/RX2U-UKZZ)

13  Formentini, M and Taticchi, P (2016) Corporate sustainability approaches and
    governance mechanisms in sustainable supply chain management, *Journal of
    Cleaner Production*, 112, 1920–33.

**14** B Corporation, About B Corp certification, www.bcorporation.net/en-us/
certification/ (archived at https://perma.cc/4DDT-C59M)

**15** B Corporation, Make business a force for good, www.bcorporation.net/en-us/
(archived at https://perma.cc/JR7A-7J7W)

**16** Plungis, J (2015) Volkswagen Emissions Scandal: Forty years of greenwashing:
The well-travelled road taken by VW, *Independent*, 25 September,
independent.co.uk/news/business/analysis-and-features/volkswagen-emissions-
scandal-forty-years-of-greenwashing-the-welltravelled-road-taken-
by-vw-10516209.html (archived at https://perma.cc/Q2S6-LJM2)

**17** Kell, G (2022) From emissions cheater to climate leader: VW's Journey from
Dieselgate to embracing e-mobility, *Forbes*, 5 December, forbes.com/sites/
georgkell/2022/12/05/from-emissions-cheater-to-climate-leader-vws-journey-
from-dieselgate-to-embracing-e-mobility/ (archived at https://perma.cc/
UQ8F-NDNE)

**18** BBC News (2022) HSBC climate change adverts banned by UK watchdog,
BBC News, 19 October, www.bbc.co.uk/news/business-63309878 (archived at
https://perma.cc/7MSK-PSQ3)

**19** BBC News (2022) HSBC climate change adverts banned by UK watchdog,
BBC News, 19 October, www.bbc.co.uk/news/business-63309878 (archived at
https://perma.cc/7MSK-PSQ3)

**20** Bankingonclimatechaos.org, Banking on climate chaos: Fossil Fuel Finance
Report 2024, www.bankingonclimatechaos.org/?bank=JPMorgan%20
Chase#fulldata-panel (archived at https://perma.cc/7TG8-W9CU)

**21** Sharma, N (2024) Big banks still funnel hundreds of billions into the fossil fuel
industry, report shows, NBC News, 13 May, www.nbcnews.com/science/
environment/banks-finance-fossil-fuel-industry-report-rcna151977 (archived at
https://perma.cc/7LCU-XP64)

**22** Visram, T (2023) What is 'greenhushing'? The new negative sustainability
trend, explained, Fast Company, 3 October, fastcompany.com/90858144/
what-is-green-hushing-the-new-negative-sustainability-trend-explained
(archived at https://perma.cc/LD8A-WRBM)

**23** South Pole Team (2022) Going green, then going dark: One in four companies
are keeping quiet on science-based targets, South Pole, 18 October, southpole.
com/news/going-green-then-going-dark (archived at https://perma.cc/X9F3-
JK5A)

**24** Carbon footprint (nd) Carbon offsetting, www.carbonfootprint.com/
carbonoffset.html (archived at https://perma.cc/3D2C-TLNA)

**25** Paysse, M (2022) 5 reasons sustainability is beneficial for business – not just
the environment, *Forbes*, 1 September, forbes.com/sites/
forbesbusinessdevelopmentcouncil/2022/09/01/5-reasons-sustainability-is-
beneficial-for-business-not-just-the-environment/?sh=5ea9d9e3439c (archived
at https://perma.cc/8HAP-L2TD)

**26** The Deloitte Global 2021 Millennial and Gen Z Survey (2021) A call for accountability and action, www.deloitte.com/content/dam/assets-shared/legacy/docs/insights/2022/2021-deloitte-global-millennial-survey-report.pdf (archived at https://perma.cc/25L9-GUTK)

**27** Fuller, J and Kerr, W (2022) The Great Resignation didn't start with the pandemic, *Harvard Business Review*, 23 March, hbr.org/2022/03/the-great-resignation-didnt-start-with-the-pandemic (archived at https://perma.cc/2VJK-SPFX)

# 10

# Decarbonizing business and paths to net zero

The science is precise: as the earth's temperature continues to rise, the world will become a more and more dangerous place to live. The latest IPCC Report states very clearly that with every increment of global warming the world faces greater threats related to rising sea levels, biodiversity loss, water scarcity and food scarcity.[1] Underscoring the critical need for the world to act to mitigate the risks associated with a warmer planet, Secretary-General of the United Nations António Guterres made a poignant speech in a special address to world leaders in New York in June 2024:

> We do have a choice: creating tipping points for climate progress – or careening to tipping points for climate disaster. This is an all-in moment. The United Nations is all-in – working to build trust, find solutions, and inspire the cooperation our world so desperately needs. It's We the Peoples versus the polluters and the profiteers. Together, we can win. But it's time for leaders to decide whose side they're on. Tomorrow is too late. Now is the time to mobilize, now is the time to act, now is the time to deliver. This is our moment of truth.[2]

During his speech, the Secretary-General identified specific actions the world needs to take to change the trajectory of the earth's rising temperature and mitigate the associated threats. Top of the list is the urgent need for nations to cut emissions by setting absolute emissions reduction targets for 2030 and 2035, in line with the 1.5 degrees Celsius limit target set for 2030 as part of the Paris Agreement. This means cutting emissions across all sectors, all greenhouse gases (GHGs), and the whole economy.

When we consider that 78 companies are responsible for more than 70 per cent of historical global GHG emissions, according to a 2024 study published by Carbon Majors Database, it is hard to imagine achieving a net-zero world without large corporations being part of that transition.[3] What is even harder to fathom is that during the same period, 50 per cent of the global industrial emissions can be linked to only 25 corporations and state-owned organizations.[4] Not surprisingly, perhaps, most of these companies operate in the carbon-intensive coal- , oil- and gas-producing sectors. For their part, supported by their supply chains, corporations – and large multinational corporations especially – have a significant impact and influence on creating a more sustainable future.

In this chapter, we look at the various tools available for CSOs and executive teams to adopt as they work towards decarbonizing their operations and achieving their medium- to long-term decarbonization targets. But first, we will take a moment to reflect and discuss why, from a business perspective, addressing the climate crisis matters. Leaning on our research and discussions with CSOs, we explore the impact that threats such as climate change are having on businesses – and the importance for business leaders to take steps to mitigate the risks, identify opportunities and set their organizations up for long-term success.

## The impacts of climate change on business and industries

Arguably one of the biggest issues facing businesses, and more broadly humanity and the planet, is the climate crisis. Many industries and businesses are struggling to deal with the impacts of climate change. Of all the industries affected, agriculture is likely the hardest hit by the extreme weather conditions brought on by climate change. Farmers around the world are directly experiencing the detrimental effects of severe weather conditions that are damaging their crops, harvests and yields.

According to the European Commission's Joint Research Centre, 2022 saw Europe's worst drought in 500 years.[5] 1540 was reportedly the last year on record that saw temperatures in Europe rise to above 40 degrees Celsius. The megadrought, as it became known, brought great devastation to the region. Across the continent, forests and villages burned, rivers ran dry, and a countless number of cattle perished.[6] Nearly 500 years later and Europe is enduring droughts of a similar scale, damaging harvests across the region, including cereals, vegetables, wine and dairy.[7] In 2022, Northern Italy went

100 days without a drop of rain. Parmesan makers in the region struggled to meet production standards due to intense drought of the River Po. The river serves as the primary water source for one-third of Italy's agricultural production. Due to severe drought of the river, cows across the region produced less milk, which impacted production of the region's beloved cheese. Cheesemakers in France's Savoie region experienced similar struggles. The Savoie region is known for producing cheeses like Emmental and raclette. Intense drought scorched Savoie's grassy prairies, central to the local cows' diet, impacting cheese production across the region.[8]

Europe isn't the only region being hit by extreme weather conditions brought on by climate change. Sam Israelit, Partner and CSO at Bain & Company, knows all too well the impact that climate change is having on farmers and farmland located along the coast of California. When he isn't focused on stewarding Bain & Company's sustainability strategy, he spends time growing and harvesting his olive orchard located in the Central Coast region of California. Since becoming olive growers, Sam and his family have harvested and produced three award-winning extra virgin olive oils. Passionate about the process of producing premium olive oil and working together with the local community of growers, Sam became involved with Central Coast Extra Virgin, a group dedicated to producing high-quality olive oil in the region and supporting local growers. Reflecting on his experience working in agriculture, and the lessons he has learnt, Sam appreciates the struggles farmers are facing every day. He also recognizes the important role that businesses play to address these global challenges.

'I think the biggest lessons I've learnt through the local olive grower community with whom I work is the real impact on small farmers, and just how important the environment and climate are to a small farmer. Most of our farmers are irrigating, but the drought has had significant impact on small farmers in California. And it's something that they're wrestling with every day. Climate change is affecting many people's livelihoods, and so we need to do what we can to get ourselves on the right trajectory around carbon emissions.'

## Decarbonizing business on the path to net zero

In a dire attempt to change the trajectory of climate change, the United Nations has called on nations globally to act and invest in initiatives aimed at decarbonizing the planet. During the United Nations Climate Change

Conference (COP21) held in Paris, France, in December 2015, 196 countries came together and endorsed the Paris Agreement, a legally binding international treaty on climate change. The overarching goal of the Agreement is to hold 'the increase in the global average temperature to well below 2-degrees Celsius above pre-industrial levels' and pursue efforts 'to limit the temperature increase to 1.5-degrees Celsius above pre-industrial levels.'[9] Despite commitments on the part of nations to support the agreement, in the form of investments and action plans, many are still falling short of meeting their goals. According to a 2023 report from UN Climate Change, national climate-action plans are not on track to meet the goals set out in the Paris Agreement.[10]

In addition to calling on nations and world leaders to do their part to halt climate change, the UN is also looking to corporations and business leaders to help accelerate sustainable transformation across their industries. Heeding the call for action from the business sector, in 2019, Amazon and Global Optimism co-founded The Climate Pledge, an initiative developed to stimulate corporate investments and actions towards decarbonizing businesses, products and services globally. Central to the pledge is a commitment to reach net-zero carbon emissions by 2040 by agreeing to three areas of action, including regular reporting, carbon elimination and credible offsets. The pledge also promotes joint action and cross-sector collaboration. As of April 2024, 479 companies have signed on.[11]

The Glasgow Financial Alliance for Net Zero (GFANZ) is another notable initiative that was formalized in the occasion of COP26 in Glasgow. It is the world's largest coalition of financial institutions committed to transitioning the global economy to net-zero greenhouse gas emissions. GFANZ was founded for two equally important purposes: to expand the number of net-zero-committed financial institutions and to establish a forum for addressing sector-wide challenges associated with the net-zero transition, helping to ensure high levels of ambition are met with credible action. GFANZ brings together independent, sector-specific alliances to tackle net-zero transition challenges and connects the financial community to the Race to Zero campaign, climate scientists and experts, and civil society.

However, making ambitious commitments to achieve net zero is just the beginning. It is also the easy part. The real test, of course, lies in the implementation and fulfilment of those commitments – and this is where businesses need to get serious about meeting their sustainability targets and objectives.

## A new risk for business: climate litigations

With the rise of climate-related risks threatening humanity and the planet comes an escalation in climate litigation aimed at tackling the biggest GHG emitters. Amid the rising regulations, companies face legal and financial risks if they do not adapt to the changing legal landscape.

Underscoring the need for corporations to adapt to the escalating legal risks associated with climate change, Paolo Taticchi, co-author of this book, shared his perspective on this topic in an article published by the *Financial Times* Sustainable Views in May 2024. In the article, Paolo referred to the UN Environment Programme's 2023 Report, which stated that climate-related legal cases doubled in the span of just five years, between 2017 and 2022.[12] Given the escalation in climate legal actions in recent years, Paolo emphasized the need for organizations to act to mitigate the climate-related legal and financial risks they face. Fortunately, there are several actions companies can take to help them adapt and mitigate the risks. One step companies can take is to engage more with local communities and stakeholders to gain a better understanding of the issues and threats they are facing, and to understand the impacts the company may be having in the community, and to work together to address those issues and reduce the threats. Businesses that choose to not engage with the communities where they operate risk facing legal and financial challenges.

Paolo pointed to the example of a climate-action lawsuit that was led by Peruvian farmer Saul Luciano Lliuya. With the support of the local community and Germanwatch, a German environmental NGO, in 2015, Mr Luciano Lliuya sued RWE, Germany's largest power company and Europe's second-largest emitter. Between 1854 and 2010, RWE emitted nearly 7 billion tonnes of GHG into the atmosphere. At the centre of the lawsuit was the claim that RWE's activities have accelerated the melting of glaciers above Palcacocha, causing Lake Palcacocha to overflow to dangerous levels. Mr Luciano Lliuya's legal team argued that due to the swelling of Lake Palcacocha – which is a picturesque turquoise lake located in Peru's Cordillera Blanca mountain range – surrounding communities face imminent risks of avalanches or landslides that will destroy entire communities, including Mr Luciano Lliuya's home.[13] Nearly a decade later, the outcome of the case is yet to be determined, with the next legal proceeding slated to take place in 2024. The case has inspired other cases to spring up around the globe, bringing hope to people in communities facing similar struggles as Mr Luciano Lliyua and his neighbouring farmers and villagers.[14]

In addition to engaging communities to understand the risks related to climate change, companies need to avoid greenwashing or face reputational, financial and legal risks, especially amid tightening sustainability disclosure regulations and requirements. Additionally, looking at risks through an investor's lens, investors need to apply rigorous standards to ensure their investments align with sustainable and ethical outcomes. To support investors with this endeavour, we suggest leveraging frameworks such as UCL's IMmPACT Framework, Harvard's Impacted Weighted Accounts, and Esade's 'Governance of Impact' report. These frameworks provide valuable guidelines for risk assessment and stakeholder engagement, guiding corporations and investors towards more sustainable practices and decision-making processes.

When it comes to ensuring companies are ready for the inevitable rise of climate litigation, companies need to proactively assess and address legal risks related to climate change. By integrating environmental considerations into their core business strategies and engaging stakeholders along the way, organizations can be better positioned to navigate the complex and rapidly changing climate litigation landscape, thereby setting themselves up for long-term success.[15]

## Measuring and tracking an organization's carbon footprint

In a business context – be it finance, manufacturing or other – we often hear that to improve something, you first need to measure it. This approach holds true when it comes to an organization's efforts to reduce its carbon emissions and improve its sustainability performance.

A company's carbon footprint refers to the total amount of greenhouse gases (GHGs) emitted directly or indirectly by its operations, expressed in terms of carbon dioxide equivalents ($CO_2e$). This footprint encompasses all activities across the value chain, including production, transportation, energy use and waste management. Key concepts in measuring a company's carbon footprint involve categorizing emissions into three scopes: Scope 1 covers direct emissions from owned or controlled sources; Scope 2 accounts for indirect emissions from the generation of purchased electricity, steam, heating and cooling consumed by the company; and Scope 3 includes all other indirect emissions that occur in the company's value chain, such as those from purchased goods and services, business travel and waste disposal. Methods for calculating these emissions typically involve data collection on energy consumption and other relevant activities, applying emission factors and utilizing standardized reporting frameworks like the Greenhouse Gas Protocol. Accurate measurement and reporting of a carbon footprint are critical for businesses aiming to implement effective decarbonization strategies, set reduction targets and monitor progress towards achieving a lower environmental impact.

## Setting carbon-emissions targets

Once a company has a solid understanding of its carbon emissions and impact, it can then turn its attention to developing a decarbonization strategy.

To help organizations with their decarbonization strategies and plans, there are several frameworks, currently recognized globally, that aim to provide guidance and standards in decarbonization projects. One of the most commonly used frameworks is the Science-Based Targets Initiative (SBTi). The SBTi provides companies with a clearly defined path towards reducing their emissions in line with the Paris Agreement target of limiting global warming to 1.5-degrees Celsius above pre-industrial levels. In an effort to remove the complexity that is often associated with carbon calculations and accounting, the SBTi offers the following five-step process that is designed to simplify and support organizations on this journey:[16]

1 Commit: submit a letter establishing your intent to set a science-based target.

2 Develop: work on an emissions reduction target in line with the SBTi's criteria.

3 Submit: present your target to the SBTi for official validation.

4 Communicate: announce your target and inform your stakeholders.

5 Disclose: report company-wide emissions and track target progress annually.

While on the surface, this appears to be a simple and clear process, it is important to note that step two, which asks companies to develop their decarbonization strategy and targets, requires some heavy lifting and deep diving into the company's carbon footprint and most carbon-intensive activities. As is the case with any process – the output is only as good as the input. The more comprehensive and accurate the data that goes into assessing a company's carbon footprint, the better informed the company will be about their emissions, and about the areas they need to focus on improving. Well-organized and high-quality carbon data at the corporate level and supply chain level are key to best channel the company's efforts, investments and resources.

## The road to net zero: three main levers

Businesses have three primary levers to decarbonize their activities: mitigation, neutralization and offsetting.

- Mitigation – involves taking direct actions to reduce greenhouse gas emissions at their source. Strategies include increasing energy efficiency, transitioning to renewable energy sources, improving process efficiencies and adopting sustainable practices throughout the supply chain. Mitigation efforts focus on preventing emissions from being generated in the first place.

- Neutralization – refers to actions taken to remove an equivalent amount of greenhouse gases from the atmosphere to balance out unavoidable emissions. Examples include investing in carbon capture and storage (CCS) technologies or enhancing natural carbon sinks such as reforestation and soil carbon sequestration. Neutralization aims to counterbalance emissions by ensuring an equivalent amount is absorbed or captured.

- Offsetting – this involves compensating for emissions by investing in external projects that reduce or remove greenhouse gases from the atmosphere. These projects can include renewable energy installations, methane capture initiatives, or afforestation programmes. Offsetting allows businesses to support global emission reduction efforts outside their direct operations.

Utilizing these three levers enables businesses to strategically manage their carbon footprint, achieve emission-reduction targets and contribute to broader climate-action goals. A popular tool to assess scenarios and strategic options are marginal abatement cost (MAC) curves that represent the cost associated with reducing an additional unit of pollution, such as carbon dioxide. They illustrate the costs and potential of various abatement options, showing how much it would cost to reduce emissions by each method and the total possible reduction for each.

## The mitigation lever

Mitigation is a critical lever for businesses aiming to decarbonize their activities, focusing on directly reducing greenhouse gas emissions at their source. This involves a comprehensive approach to enhancing energy efficiency, transitioning to renewable energy sources and adopting sustainable practices throughout the supply chain. For instance, companies can upgrade to energy-efficient machinery, improve building insulation and optimize logistics to reduce fuel consumption. Retail giant Walmart, for example, has implemented LED lighting and advanced HVAC systems across its stores to cut energy use, while automotive manufacturers like Tesla are leading the charge in electric vehicle production to reduce emissions from transportation.

One initiative that Smurfit Westrock (formerly Smurfit Kappa) has been exploring as part of the company's decarbonization and mitigation efforts is retrofitting a gas boiler at its mill in France. As Garrett Quinn, Group Chief Sustainability Officer at Smurfit Westrock explained, the plant's existing gas boiler is being retrofitted to process green hydrogen. He credits the advancement of technological solutions as being key to the company's future decarbonization efforts.

'I think our understanding of delivering on net zero has dramatically changed in a very short space of time. There are technologies that are relatively within reach, and there are other technologies which are a little bit further away. But what's quite encouraging is that in some instances the capital required is not astronomical to resolve these issues. The project in France is a broad collaborative project, including energy, machinery and academic partners, and while still a concept project it demonstrates how you can retrofit our existing machinery to use green energy rather than having to buy brand new equipment. I think that is fantastic because it proves a concept now that is much more practical and economically feasible, and we can consider as part of our net-zero mapping. That's fantastic, and that is something that wouldn't have been an option just a few years ago. Now, to be clear, it's still not an option today (widespread availability of cost-effective green hydrogen) but it shows how far we've come.'

Shifting to renewable energy such as solar, wind or hydropower significantly cuts down emissions associated with electricity and heating. Google, for instance, has invested heavily in renewable energy projects to match its entire energy consumption with renewable energy purchases.

Economic considerations are also crucial in the mitigation strategy. While the initial investment in energy-efficient technologies and renewable energy infrastructure can be substantial, the long-term benefits often outweigh the costs. Businesses can achieve significant cost savings through reduced energy bills, lower maintenance expenses and enhanced operational efficiency.

Financial markets are also beginning to reward companies with strong environmental performance, providing better access to capital and favourable lending terms. By prioritizing these actions, businesses not only lower their carbon footprint but also often realize cost savings, improve operational efficiency and enhance their overall sustainability performance.

## The neutralization lever

To limit global temperature increase to 1.5-degrees Celsius as per the Paris Agreement and avoid the most severe effects of climate change, the world must achieve net-zero carbon emissions by mid-century. This means balancing the amount of carbon dioxide released into the atmosphere with the amount removed and stored from the air. Reaching climate goals requires, therefore, strategies that actively remove $CO_2$ from the atmosphere. There are both natural and technological methods to remove carbon dioxide from the atmosphere and store it in various ways, including in trees and plants, soils, underground reservoirs, rocks, the ocean, and even products like concrete.[17]

Microsoft, for example, has committed to becoming carbon-negative by 2030, partly through investments in CCS projects that capture emissions from industrial processes and store them underground. Similarly, companies like Patagonia support reforestation and afforestation projects, which absorb $CO_2$ as trees grow, contributing to the natural sequestration of carbon.

The benefits of nature-based solutions are many, not least of all their contribution to addressing global challenges such as climate change, human health, and food and water scarcity. Protecting the planet's ecosystem and preventing biodiversity loss was the focus of the UN's Biodiversity Conference, also referred to as COP15, which took place in Montreal, Canada, in December 2022. During the summit, Inger Anderson, the UN Under-Secretary-General and UNEP Executive Director, urged world leaders to act swiftly to strengthen the web of life – which arguably is in a fragile state at this moment in time.

'We cannot live without nature and biodiversity. Nature provides the very essence of life. Technology cannot replace the trees, the soil, the water, and the species that teem in them. We have no other world to flee to. When the web of life falls, we fall with it. In the coming days, you have a unique responsibility to deliver: to agree on the plan to make peace with nature. This responsibility is not a choice between something or nothing. It is a choice between everything or nothing.'[18]

Coming out of COP15 was a landmark biodiversity agreement that aims to guide global action on nature through this decade. The meeting resulted in the adoption of the Kunming-Montreal Global Biodiversity Framework (GBF). Central to the GBF's objectives are the mandate for nations to put concrete measures in place that will address biodiversity loss, restore ecosystems and protect indigenous rights. Part of the plan includes putting 30 per cent of the planet and 30 per cent of degraded ecosystems under protection by 2030.[19] The goals are ambitious, and require ambitious actions and collaboration on the part of governments and industries. To achieve these goals, corporations must do their part.

It is important to emphasize that nature-based solutions are not a side project or nice-to-do initiative for companies to consider alongside their decarbonization efforts. Rather, they are an integral part that can significantly propel a company's efforts to reduce their carbon footprint. According to a 2019 study by the Intergovernmental Science-Policy Platform on Biodiversity and Ecosystem Services (IPBES), nature-based solutions are estimated to provide 37 per cent of the mitigation needed by 2030 to achieve the targets that have been set within the Paris Agreement. Planting trees is just one example of a nature-based solution that removes carbon from the atmosphere. Climate-smart agriculture, which refers to a set of practices and technologies farmers can leverage to store carbon in their fields while boosting productivity of their crops, is another example of a nature-based solution that is gaining traction in the agricultural sector.[20]

An alternative to nature-based solutions are carbon-reduction technologies. These are still nascent, and it is uncertain when they will become available, and when they will become scalable and viable from an economic perspective for companies to use them as part of their strategies. One example of an emerging carbon reduction technology is direct air capture. This method, which utilizes chemical reactions to capture $CO_2$ from the atmosphere, is attracting investments as it is showing promise of being an effective decarbonization tool for industries to adopt.[21] Other examples include carbon mineralization, biomass with carbon removal and sequestration, and ocean-based carbon removal.

Implementation costs, energy requirements and volume limitations of new materials are some of the concerns industries are grappling with at this nascent stage of carbon capture technology. To address these issues, research and development efforts in this field are ongoing and evolving.[22] The Carbon Capture and Sequestration Technologies initiative developed by MIT is mapping all projects being developed around the world.[23]

### The offsetting lever

*To include carbon offsets as part of a company's decarbonization strategy, or not to include them?* That is the question weighing on the minds of many business leaders who are focused on achieving their net-zero targets in the coming years. With more and more companies pledging to achieve net-zero emissions within the next decade, there is a plethora of initiatives business leaders can choose from to advance their decarbonization efforts. And while companies have a multitude of products and services to choose from, knowing which initiatives will have the biggest impact can be a challenge.

As we discussed in Chapter 9, carbon offsetting refers to a way companies can compensate for their $CO_2$ emissions by funding solutions that will remove the equivalent $CO_2$ emissions elsewhere.[24] As more companies vie to achieve their decarbonization targets, the topic of carbon offsetting has gained traction. It is also somewhat of a controversial topic. Although carbon offsets are a viable option for companies to leverage in theory, there are valid concerns that must be considered in practice. To begin with, regulators are placing greater scrutiny on carbon-offsetting practices due to the fact that some carbon credits are not credible. A key challenge for organizations is discerning which carbon-offsetting options are viable and credible.

The more significant concern raised by critics, perhaps, is the argument that carbon offsets are hindering rather than advancing efforts to curb global warming. Supporting the viewpoint that carbon offsetting undermines climate targets, more than 80 civil society organizations advocating for greater accountability and action on the part of nations and organizations to address climate change have put forward a joint statement urging climate target-setting governing bodies, including the SBTi, not to allow companies to include offsetting in their carbon accounting and corporate climate target-setting plans. In the statement, the group voices their opinions about why offsetting impedes rather than aids decarbonization efforts, stating that offsetting could actually delay climate action. The group points to the fact that offsets provide a social licence for high-emitting activities to continue. Furthermore, the group argues that offsets, at best, do not reduce the concentration of GHGs in the earth's atmosphere, they simply move emissions from one place to another. In other words, according to the statement, emissions are not being removed or offset – instead they are simply being moved around, much like in a shell game.

We agree that in an ideal world companies wouldn't need to rely on carbon credits to offset their emissions. In an ideal scenario, companies would engage in a timely transition towards net zero, without the need or use of carbon offsets. And while this scenario is indeed aspirational, we recognize that for many businesses achieving net zero without carbon credits is not realistic, at least not within the urgent time frame in which we need this transition to occur.

We can also see why the topic of carbon offsets is a debatable one. On the flip side of the argument that offsets are undermining climate targets is the argument that – for the world to achieve net zero – carbon offsets need to be part of the solution.

Michelle Davies, Global Head of Sustainability at EY Law, underscored the point that carbon credits are essential for the world to achieve the targets that have been set. When discussing the viability of carbon offsets or carbon credits, it is important to first understand the difference in terminology. While carbon offsetting refers to when a company funds an external project that removes GHG emissions to compensate for its own emissions, carbon credits are what a company purchases to offset its unavoided emissions. In the context of a voluntary carbon market, where businesses choose to fund carbon reduction projects, one carbon credit represents one tonne of $CO_2$ being avoided or sequestered from the atmosphere.[25] In some regions, there are compliance markets where governments impose programmes that cap emissions. In this scenario, businesses must act in accordance with the regulations, and in some cases the regulations allow for emissions to be offset with carbon credits.[26] It is this acceptance that critics of carbon offsets fundamentally oppose.

As a sustainability leader working at the intersection of corporate sustainability and law, Michelle understands and appreciates the debate and concerns around carbon offsetting. Leaning on her years of experience working with companies to navigate these challenges, Michelle believes sustainability leaders must remain steadfastly focused on helping organizations transition in a valuable and sensible way that will enable them to grow and be sustainable.

'On the topic of carbon credits, my personal view is that I wish we did not have to use carbon credits. But I think, if we want to get to net zero, we're going to have to leverage carbon credits, especially in these hard to abate sectors. We need them to transition in a way that, firstly, enables their business to be viable and to continue, and secondly – and this is really important – in a way that enables their people to be part of the transition. Because for this transition to be successful, you want your people to transition into the sustainable environment that your organization is moving towards. But this outcome can only be achieved if it is done in an orderly, thoughtful and carefully crafted way. As I look forward to where we need to get to on the path to net zero, I ardently believe that if used not as a licence to misbehave but as part of a considered and accountable transition plan, carbon credits have the potential to enable the transition at pace, both within organizations and at a macro level. I hear and appreciate the criticisms, but I do not see how some organizations, sectors and nations can accelerate efforts and fund their transition without some kind of carbon price. If used carefully and transparently, carbon markets can be an important part of the transition – but never instead of it.'

Klaus Kunz, Founder and Managing Director at Ephrin, shares Michelle's viewpoint that carbon offsetting is an essential tool for companies to leverage as part of their decarbonization strategies. Sharing his perspective on carbon offsets and the important role they play, Klaus firmly believes that for the world to reach net zero, offsets need to be part of the solution.

'With carbon offsets, companies pay another party to remove the carbon they emit so that they can achieve their net-zero targets. I think offsetting is a very good mechanism – planting trees is one example of this approach. However, currently this is so massively criticized, and I think that has become more problematic than helpful. Offsetting is criticized for being used as a greenwashing tool, or for not being credible. I agree that there is a lot to improve, but it is one of the most powerful mechanisms to make money from the private sector available for doing the right things. And I would not allow companies to use the argument that they have reputational concerns, stating they don't want to risk having a reputational disadvantage if they buy offsets. The reality is that they just want to save money. We need to all make sure that offsetting becomes standardized and credible – it is one of the most powerful tools that can be used to do good stuff.'

As Klaus explains, dollars that are invested into carbon offsets go directly towards funding initiatives that remove carbon from the atmosphere. And while the practice may draw some criticism – we agree it is necessary. Companies are right to be wary, but rather than moving away from the practice altogether, organizations need to dedicate resources to ensure the carbon offsets they are investing in are indeed credible. An article from *The Economist* underscores the point that carbon offsets are needed to meet global targets, stating: 'if the world is to achieve net-zero emissions, then offsets are part of the plan.'

For carbon offsetting to be leveraged responsibly, companies need to be diligent about their decisions and investments. It is imperative that organizations, guided by the knowledge and expertise of their CSO, assess the viability and credibility of carbon-offsetting services or products to ensure the money invested is, indeed, going towards funding projects that remove carbon from the earth's atmosphere – in line with the company's decarbonization goals and objectives.

> 'I would not allow companies to use the argument that we have reputational concerns, stating they don't want to risk having a reputational disadvantage if they buy offsets. The reality is they just want to save money. We need to all make sure that offsetting becomes standardized and credible – it is one of the most powerful tools that can be used to do good stuff.'
>
> **Klaus Kunz, Founder and Managing Director at Ephrin**

## Engaging and decarbonizing the supply chain

Companies that are leading in the area of sustainability in their industries are moving beyond transforming their own organizations and are focused on engaging their partners and suppliers to bring them along on this journey. Regardless of how much sustainability is embedded into a company's processes and culture, fulfilling the commitments and promises they have made requires the support and contribution of their partners and suppliers.

As former Head of Sustainability at Enel, a key part of Giulia Genuardi's role was to engage the company's supply chain on this journey. Enel is a leading multinational energy utility company with its headquarters based in

Rome, Italy. Listed as a top 100 sustainable company by *Sustainability Magazine* in 2023, Enel is an industry leader that has been engaging with sustainability for some time. Over the past decade Enel has made immense strides in decarbonizing the business. As an industry-leading company working at the forefront of the energy transition era, in addition to decarbonizing its own operations, Enel is focused on reducing carbon emissions across its supply chain.

'We are in the middle of the energy transition, and we are completely changing our approach. During the last 10 years, we have changed the way we produce energy and have defined an ambitious target in terms of reduction of our $CO_2$ emissions. What this means is that over the past decade we have worked so hard to know our value chain, because we have to work with all of our partners and suppliers to reach our target. And decarbonizing our business is a big challenge because we have different companies with different dimensions. We have different customers with different levels of awareness of this topic. We also need to ensure we make a just transition by involving all stakeholders in this process. If we change our business model, this impacts our suppliers as their business models also need to change. And they need the right skills to do that, which means they have to train and upskill their people. It is not an easy task, but it is important to engage all our stakeholders on this journey.'

As Giulia highlights, for companies to achieve their net-zero targets, engaging partners and suppliers to change their business models and practices in line with a net-zero strategy is imperative. Underscoring this point is the UN's sustainable development goal 17, partnerships for the goals, which the UN describes as 'strengthening the means of implementation and revitalizing the Global Partnership for Sustainable Development.'[27]

While there are many options for companies to leverage on the path to net zero, it is clear there isn't one magic answer or solution to addressing the global challenge that is climate change. Just as sustainable transformation requires organizations to adopt a holistic approach that considers a company's impact across environmental, social and economic spheres, a company's approach to decarbonization also requires acting on, and investing in, multiple solutions on this journey. Equally important is that companies develop a commercial mindset to explore market opportunities associated to decarbonization (e.g. the development of new products, services or business models), as noted by decarbonization expert Riccardo Angelini Rota:

'Last year (2023) was the warmest year ever recorded globally, with average temperatures exceeding pre-industrial levels by 1.5°C, and projections indicate a dramatic increase by the end of the century. Human activities have significantly contributed to this historical change, directly impacting the climate crisis. In this context, companies need to be committed to decarbonization and climate action, which can simultaneously serve as fundamental levers to boost competitiveness, particularly through new sustainable business value propositions.'

---

KEY TAKEAWAYS

- **Importance of decarbonization**: Reducing business emissions is crucial to addressing climate change and achieving net-zero targets, making businesses pivotal in mitigating climate-related risks.

- **Impact of climate change on industries**: Climate change, particularly extreme weather, significantly impacts industries like agriculture, highlighting the need for businesses to act and support sustainability.

- **Effective decarbonization strategies**: Companies should use a mix of reducing emissions, carbon neutralization and offsetting, supported by frameworks like the Science-Based Targets Initiative (SBTi) for structured and steady progress.

- **Climate litigation and regulatory compliance**: Businesses face rising legal and financial risks from climate litigation and tightening regulations, necessitating integration of environmental considerations into core strategies.

- **Collaborative supply chain engagement**: Leading companies engage partners and suppliers in sustainability efforts, ensuring decarbonization extends throughout the value chain for broader impact.

- **Economic and reputational benefits**: Investments in mitigation, neutralization and compliance not only reduce emissions but also enhance brand reputation, operational efficiency and access to capital.

---

## Notes

1  IPCC (2024) IPCC Chair Jim Skea speaking at the opening of the Copenhagen Climate Ministerial, 21 March, www.ipcc.ch/2024/03/21/ (archived at https://perma.cc/K3MR-4GP8)
2  United Nations (2024) Secretary-General's special address on climate action 'A Moment of Truth', 5 June, www.un.org/sg/en/content/sg/statement/

2024-06-05/secretary-generals-special-address-climate-action-moment-of-truth-delivered (archived at https://perma.cc/WSH5-7RCN)

**3** Carbon Majors (2024) https://carbonmajors.org/briefing/The-Carbon-Majors-Database-26913 (archived at https://perma.cc/3NUF-FYNQ)

**4** Waugh, C (2022) Corporations vs consumers: Who is really to blame for climate change? The University of Manchester, Global Social Challenges, 7 July, https://sites.manchester.ac.uk/global-social-challenges/2022/07/07/corporations-vs-consumers-who-is-really-to-blame-for-climate-change (archived at https://perma.cc/7QWS-9SCD)

**5** Seabrook, V (2022) Europe's drought on course to be worst for 500 years, European Union agency warns, Skynews, 9 August, news.sky.com/story/europes-drought-on-course-to-be-worst-for-500-years-european-commission-researcher-warns-12669153 (archived at https://perma.cc/PYG5-W69P)

**6** Oliver, C (2022) It's hot and dry out there, but it ain't as bad as 1540 (yet), Politico, 17 August, politico.eu/article/hot-dry-aint-bad-1540-yet/ (archived at https://perma.cc/CQ86-XEMX)

**7** Galindo, G (2022) Climate change threatens the EU's lucrative culinary treasures, Politico, 29 August, politico.eu/article/climate-change-puts-the-heat-on-the-eus-culinary-treasures/ (archived at https://perma.cc/V8L3-QUKH)

**8** Galindo, G (2022) Climate change threatens the EU's lucrative culinary treasures, Politico, 29 August, politico.eu/article/climate-change-puts-the-heat-on-the-eus-culinary-treasures/ (archived at https://perma.cc/V8L3-QUKH)

**9** United Nations Climate Change, The Paris Agreement, https://unfccc.int/process-and-meetings/the-paris-agreement (archived at https://perma.cc/P2FQ-2MLD)

**10** United Nations Climate Change (2023) New analysis of national climate plans: Insufficient progress made, COP28 must set stage for immediate action, 14 November, https://unfccc.int/news/new-analysis-of-national-climate-plans-insufficient-progress-made-cop28-must-set-stage-for-immediate (archived at https://perma.cc/LR26-WVX5)

**11** The Climate Pledge (2019) About the Climate Pledge, www.theclimatepledge.com/us/en/the-pledge/About (archived at https://perma.cc/8T2F-6PND)

**12** UCL School of Management (2024) UCL Professor Paolo Taticchi spoke to Financial Times About Climate Legal Risks, May 8, 2024, www.mgmt.ucl.ac.uk/news/ucl-prof-paolo-taticchis-op-ed-climate-legal-risks-ft-sustainable-views (archived at https://perma.cc/46DA-FRV4)

**13** Huaraz (2022) A Peruvian farmer takes on Germany's largest electricity firm, *The Economist*, 2 June, www.economist.com/the-americas/2022/06/02/a-peruvian-farmer-takes-on-germanys-largest-electricity-firm (archived at https://perma.cc/4QM6-3G58)

**14** UCL News (2023) Opinion: A Peruvian farmer is trying to hold energy giant RWE responsible for climate change, UCL News, 28 November, www.ucl.ac.uk/

news/2023/nov/opinion-peruvian-farmer-trying-hold-energy-giant-rwe-responsible-climate-change (archived at https://perma.cc/KA2S-KKYH)

**15** UCL School of Management (2024) UCL Professor Paolo Taticchi spoke to Financial Times about climate legal risks, 8 May 8, www.mgmt.ucl.ac.uk/news/ucl-prof-paolo-taticchis-op-ed-climate-legal-risks-ft-sustainable-views (archived at https://perma.cc/46DA-FRV4)

**16** Science Based Targets, https://sciencebasedtargets.org/how-it-works (archived at https://perma.cc/C2WL-VG3X), accessed July 2024

**17** World Resources Institute, Carbon removal: Assessing carbon removal pathways, their potential, barriers and policy options to accelerate development as part of a suite of climate actions, www.wri.org/initiatives/carbon-removal (archived at https://perma.cc/Y3AY-HBZR)

**18** United Nations Environment Programme (2022) COP15 Opening remarks by Inger Anderson at the UN Biodiversity Conference, 7 December, www.unep.org/news-and-stories/speech/framework-all-life-earth (archived at https://perma.cc/QJZ4-2XFF)

**19** United Nations Environment Programme (2022) COP15 ends with landmark biodiversity agreement, 20 December, www.unep.org/news-and-stories/story/cop15-ends-landmark-biodiversity-agreement (archived at https://perma.cc/MH4U-U6FE)

**20** World Bank Group (2024) Climate-smart agriculture, www.worldbank.org/en/topic/climate-smart-agriculture (archived at https://perma.cc/BK8N-JEPN), accessed July 2024

**21** World Resources Institute, Carbon removal: Assessing carbon removal pathways, their potential, barriers and policy options to accelerate development as part of a suite of climate actions, www.wri.org/initiatives/carbon-removal (archived at https://perma.cc/Y3AY-HBZR)

**22** Davies, B (2023) 5 key carbon capture technology trends for 2023 (with examples) Elsevier, www.elsevier.com/en-gb/connect/5-key-carbon-capture-technology-trends-for-2023 (archived at https://perma.cc/JWN5-75YM)

**23** Carbon Capture and Sequestratian Technologies Program at MIT, https://sequestration.mit.edu/index.html (archived at https://perma.cc/ENA9-DAG3)

**24** Carbon Footprint, Carbon Offsetting, www.carbonfootprint.com/carbonoffset.html (archived at https://perma.cc/3D2C-TLNA)

**25** Climate Impact Partners (2024) www.climateimpact.com/services-projects/carbon-credits-explained-what-they-are-and-how-they-work/ (archived at https://perma.cc/A6FJ-9QU3), accessed July 2024

**26** Climate Impact Partners (2024) www.climateimpact.com/services-projects/carbon-credits-explained-what-they-are-and-how-they-work/ (archived at https://perma.cc/A6FJ-9QU3), accessed July 2024

**27** The Global Goals, 17 Partnerships for the Goals, www.globalgoals.org/goals/17-partnerships-for-the-goals/ (archived at https://perma.cc/6RHD-E5SB)

# 11

# The CSOs' crystal ball and inspiring words of wisdom

## Inspiring words of wisdom for aspiring CSOs

As we discussed in Chapter 4 of this book, there is no single path to becoming a CSO. For a grad student or a professional who is looking to pursue a career in sustainability, knowing which path to take can seem daunting.

To support aspiring sustainability leaders on this journey, and to help them choose the path that's best for them, we asked each of the CSOs we met with to share what advice they have for anyone looking to build a career in sustainability. In this chapter we share their insightful and inspiring advice for aspiring sustainability leaders.

### Charlotte Wolff-Bye, Chief Sustainability Officer at Petronas

'I think it's a very pertinent question because a lot of people feel very passionate about sustainability and want to work in sustainability. But, of course, they can probably make even more of an impact by working where they are. So, if you are a lawyer or you work in marketing, both functional areas also need to embed sustainability into their day-to-day work. So, if you're a professional in your own domain and passionate about sustainability, I would rather you remain in your position because that is where you can create most impact. But it is also worth asking, how do you get involved and engaged? I think there are many opportunities for where to engage in a corporate environment around sustainability being shared, and there are also more opportunities to raise concerns. You can contact the sustainability team and ask, what more I can do? As a CSO, you want to have empowered and mobilized employees, and the task at hand should be to harness all the energy around. That's a good place and space to be in. I would also say that now with the workforce being predominantly millennials and younger generations coming in, the context is changing. It's no longer that you have a small team somewhere doing sustainability; it really permeates everything. Because that's what the younger workforce really expects and demands from their employer.'

'If you're a professional in your own domain and passionate about sustainability, I would rather you remain in your position because that is where you can create most impact.'

**Charlotte Wolff-Bye, Chief Sustainability Officer at Petronas**

## Sean Jones, Chief Sustainability Officer at Microsoft Germany

'Don't study to be a CSO. Sustainability needs to be an embedded part of any curriculum. So, still study to be an electrical engineer, a chemical or a mechanical engineer, or a business leader or a philosopher. I don't know. But add sustainability in there. How does sustainability, how does our impact on our planet Earth, from an environmental, social governance perspective, how is that part of what you're doing in the future? And especially investment bankers, they definitely need to study sustainability.'

## David Costa, Chief Sustainability Business Officer at NTT Data

'I strongly believe that this profession will allow us to make an impact, and it's for the medium to long term. You learn a lot because you get to work with people who are very unique, as most of them have been in this before it became trendy or sexy or whatever. But my advice would be "choose in which area you want to start". And this is something that we hear now when we talk with employees. Some people are more interested in the personal part, so their personal impact; other people want to develop our services to become more sustainable, others want to engage with everything related to the planet, natural regeneration, net zero and zero waste. And other people are more interested in the human rights, equality, diversity side. So, my advice is, focus on an area where you can have the biggest impact.

As I said, for me, it's a dream job. And it's very interesting because I think it's a job that will see many more opportunities in the future. But if we do it right, it will not be needed. So, at some point, if all the executives and people across the organization do their job, we are redundant. I think this work requires people who are brave, and who can change behaviours with a lot of self-confidence. People with a lot of energy, and people who are genuinely generous – people who do things without expecting anything in return. People who like freedom – and if you add passion to this, then I think you have everything you need to be successful.'

## Elisa Moscolin, Executive Vice President of Sustainability and Foundation at Sage

'My plea is – if you want to work in sustainability, don't fake it until you make it. Build your technical knowledge and expertise. We really need solid, robust, reliable subject matter experts in the field. So if you are passionate about climate, human rights, supply chain – gain deep subject matter expertise on the subject. Also, don't get discouraged if progress feels slow. Be prepared that it's not going to be a straight and linear path. Sometimes working in sustainability feels like dancing the tango: you're going to go a bit forward and suddenly a bit backwards, you're going be a bit on the right and then left. That's fine, as long as you keep trying to be the master of that choreography. My last thought on this is the importance of being resilient. As I stated before, working in sustainability is not about painting fences and hugging trees. It's a tough gig. You'll have to influence and drive big organizational change that not many are ready for. It requires business acumen because sustainability is about business. I think the credibility and success of our practice comes down to being able to link sustainability to a business strategy successfully. If there are trades-offs that need to be considered, you need to really understand what the trade-offs are for the planet, the people and the bottom line – and then you need to be able to eloquently and credibly discuss those trade-offs and support the executive teams and boards to make informed decisions.'

## Garrett Quinn, Group Chief Sustainability Officer at Smurfit Westrock

'My advice is to stick to an industry that you understand, because that comes back to the business rationale, and making sustainability relevant. So, if you come from financial services and you have a PhD in being a Chief

Sustainability Officer, I would say the worst thing you could do is go into industry, because it's a very different approach and it has a different set of challenges. I think having technical capabilities in sustainability is important, but understanding the company you work for, ideally at an operational level, is essential. You don't necessarily have to have worked for the company, but you need to ask yourself, do you understand the industry of the company you're going to work for? And if you do, then I think you stand a much better chance of being an effective Chief Sustainability Officer rather than someone who has a very strong formal education in sustainability, but maybe has no practical experience of the industry they're looking to join. In my view, I prefer that it is the other way around – that you have strong industry experience, and then you add sustainability to that – because you run the risk of losing your audience potentially if you do not have a deep understanding of the industry.'

*Giulia Genuardi, Managing Director at Enel Foundation, former Head of Sustainability at Enel*

'I think that this kind of work is the work of the future – and it will always be the work of the future because we are always looking forward. So, if you work in sustainability, you will always be working on the next frontier. I think there are a lot of opportunities in this kind of work. I suggest, one of the key things to succeed in this role, is you will need to have humility to work with other people. Sometimes you are not the leader – sometimes you are a service for other departments. And secondly, you need courage to sometimes change the business model. And so, I think it is wonderful and rewarding work – but at the same time you need humility, and you need courage to do this work and succeed in your role.'

*Jeffrey Whitford, Vice President of Sustainability and Social Business Innovation at Merck Life Science*

'We need a lot more people to be interested in this topic, and to take these decisions into how they live everyday life. And to make an impact and be in a role like mine – you can work to influence your senior leaders, the organizations you work for, and even the big multinational global institutions. We need that. But we also need people who are changing their buying behaviours – so it all comes together. So be focused on impact. That is probably my biggest piece of advice.

'And dream big. We need people who are willing to dream big, and who are resilient. I say to my team, "we are going to run into the brick wall, slide down, have to pick ourselves up and keep rinsing and repeating that a lot of times. Because what we're doing is not easy. It is tough work."'

### Klaus Kunz, Founder and Managing Director at Ephrin

'For me, the most important advice I would have for any career you want to do is don't focus on career all the time. Focus on doing the right things. That's much more satisfying than taking a career step or getting a higher salary grade. Do the right things and surround yourself with the right microcosm of people who are like-minded. And be super courageous because we need this for the next generation. And now I'm making a very open and honest reflection, but I think our generation is praising the next generation a lot for all their amazing insights and drive – but I want to see the proof points still. I think too much praise too early is also not helpful. When you think of Greta Thunberg, I think she was instrumental in starting a movement – but we need the next generation to show that they do what they have been claiming, which will mean to a certain extent to step back from all the nice things that they were used to. It's easy to make demonstrations on a Friday, relative to stepping back from having a car. And for anyone interested in working in sustainability, as I mentioned earlier my advice is to dream big. And I would also say, go for it.'

> 'For me, the most important advice I would have for any career you want to do is don't focus on career all the time. Focus on doing the right things. That's much more satisfying than taking a career step or getting a higher salary grade. Do the right things and surround yourself with the right microcosm of people who are like-minded. And be super-courageous because we need this for the next generation.'
>
> **Klaus Kunz, Founder and Manging Director at Ephrin**

### Magali Anderson, Chief Sustainability and Innovation Officer

'There are still today quite a lot of young people in the whole scene who are having some key roles because they are very smart, very well-educated. Just go for it, basically. Don't hesitate to challenge the older people. Don't hesitate to push people. In terms of education, I recall having a discussion with my daughter, who has been passionate about environment since a very young age. And when she was picking her topic for becoming an engineer, she was asking for my advice because while she was interested in the environment, she didn't like much the topics part of those studies. So, I advised her to become a mechanical engineer because she likes mechanics. And actually, in sectors like hard to abate sectors, the industrial sector, I think the mechanical engineers, electrical engineers, could actually have more impact to decarbonize in terms of innovation, technology, than perhaps environmental engineers who are more looking more at the overall system. The reason I'm giving that story is to say every single skill is important because no matter where you are in the company, no matter what you do, you can have an impact, you just need to believe in it. I would also suggest following some great thought leaders like Clover Hogan. I'm a super fan of her Force of Nature, where she's getting young people to fight their eco-anxiety by finding a way to influence companies from the inside. So just continue believing in it and never doubt how much impact you can have as an individual, no matter where you are in the organization.'

## Michelle Davies, Global Head of Sustainability at EY Law

'I think in the field of sustainability you need to obviously be driven, be focused, network with as many people as you can, do all those things, which is true for any job. In sustainability, though, it's really important to take a step back and think about where you can be most impactful and valuable, because that's where you're going to really enjoy your role. My goddaughter did a master's degree in sustainability at UCL, which I was so pleased about, and now she is an ESG officer for one of the big renewables' funds. And that was her approach. She constantly thinks about "where am I going to be the most valuable and impactful?" And because this sector is so dynamic, it can be very distracting. And if you're not careful, you can get distracted by it and end up somewhere where you one day think, "hang on a minute, this isn't what I wanted to do". And so, you have to constantly think about where you can be the most impactful and valuable and keep positioning your career. Reflecting on this will also help you determine the kind of organization that you want to work with – is it an NGO, or an organization like EY, or an investment bank? You really need to think about this. I had said to my god-daughter that going into a fund is a fantastic place to be because they are deploying the capital into this sector, and this sector cannot achieve what it needs to without capital. So, you've got to really think it through, and be very refined in your approach. And that is difficult when there is so much noise in this space – so my advice is to try to keep focused and refined and work out where you're going to be most impactful and valuable.'

## Montse Montaner, former Chief Sustainability Officer at Novartis

'First of all, my advice is that this is not a fashionable role, so it is not a role that will disappear in a few years. Rather, it is a role that will be very much ingrained in organizations for years and years. It is my dream that maybe in 70 years from now, we don't need to have CSOs, but it's not the case today. So, there is a lot of work to be done, and we need a lot of people with the right mindset, spirit and with that super commitment to be the steward for sustainability and for the planet. And so, my advice for anyone aspiring to work in sustainability is to nurture their hard skills and soft skills as much as possible, because it's a fascinating opportunity to use both of these skill sets. I will also say that they will grow a lot as a human being, and they will learn a lot. Definitely this role will require individuals to have a lot of resilience because it's not an easy job – but it is a very rewarding job! So, I would definitely encourage people to go on that journey.'

## Peter Bragg, EMEA Sustainability and Government Affairs Director at Canon

'Well, my first piece of advice is, it's a great role to have – and it's definitely something worth doing. There aren't many roles where you can have such influence in an organization and influence such positive change as well. And knowing that you're doing it for a very important reason as well, underlies everything. So, if you want to get to the level of a CSO there are some hard skills you need to know, but you also need the soft skills, such as building your influencing skills, your communication skills, and building your network as well. Recognizing who within an organization has a lot of influence is key, and being able to connect and be aligned with them is important, because you need those people to be your advocates. But you also need to understand the business and have the confidence to articulate through a business lens why sustainability is important. You have to recognize that sustainability is 100 per cent part of your job, so you have to be passionate, positive and embody it all the time. Now, it's actually unrealistic to expect that of everyone else in the organization. It can't be everyone. People might still be personally passionate, but they have their own jobs to do and you have to acknowledge that as well. So, it requires being patient, being pragmatic. Celebrate the wins when you get them. You also need to build that capacity for change, because when that change does happen, sometimes it can be really fundamental and substantial, and it is those times that keep you going. So yes, building those networks is probably the number one thing I would advise to succeed in this role'.

## Sam Israelit, Partner and Chief Sustainability Officer at Bain & Company

'There are a couple pieces of advice I would give. One is start where you are. If you are in a line role somewhere, whether it is in operations, in finance, procurement, or another part of the organization, start to look for opportunities to implement these types of sustainability-focused initiatives in your function. Start at the ground level. And as you start to have success in those initiatives, you can build on them and expand them. That type of experience is actually what you need to get things done in big companies. That's invaluable for people to prove they can make progress and achieve results, and that is going to be really important to you later on. Second, I would also say that to be effective as a Chief Sustainability Officer, you have to understand how the business runs. There are a lot of people with aspirations for doing the right thing and they really do hope for better performance – but if you don't understand how the business runs, you're not going to be successful. So, make sure that you're spending time to not only look at sustainability, but also take time to look at the strategy and operations of the organization you're in, and then integrate those together. This is critical because there are both risks and opportunities you need to take advantage of in this role, and if you're the person who brings those up and drives them forward, you will gain credibility and be successful.'

Based on the wise advice shared by the CSOs we interviewed for this book, it's evident that working in the field of sustainability, though demanding and requiring significant resilience, is also highly rewarding.

What also came to light is that, regardless of one's role, title or career interests, we can all engage with sustainability and make a positive impact through our everyday decisions and actions, at work and at home. Charlotte Wolff-Bye put this best during our discussion, stating: 'In a way, it is through your own actions that you can become your own sustainability manager.

And if you follow your interests and passions, good things tend to happen to you.'

## The CSOs' crystal ball: a look at what the future holds for corporate sustainability

According to the UN's Sustainable Development Report 2024, which provides a comprehensive overview of how the world is tracking against the SDGs that have been set for 2030, on average only 16 per cent of the SDG targets are on track to be met globally, while the remaining 84 per cent are showing little progress or even a reversal of progress in some cases.[1] While the report focuses on progress – or lack thereof – at a country level, it also emphasizes the need for systematic transformation to food and land systems globally. Here, no doubt, the private sector plays a vital role in working with governments to shape and transform global food and land systems, for better or worse.

As the report states, in 2030 approximately 600 million people will continue to suffer from hunger, obesity will continue to rise, and agriculture, forestry and other land use (AFOLU) will account for nearly 25 per cent of total GHG emissions. In an attempt to curb these trends, FABLE (The Food, Agriculture, Biodiversity, Land-Use and Energy) Consortium assessed the SDG targets related to food scarcity, climate mitigation, biodiversity conservation and water quality and offered a list of 'global sustainability' recommendations for the way forward. The list of recommendations included the following: 1) avoid overconsumption and limit animal-based protein consumptions, 2) invest to foster productivity, especially for products and areas with high demand growth, and 3) implement inclusive and transparent monitoring systems to halt deforestation and reduce $CO_2$ emissions globally. Additional measures were provided to address and prevent water pollution.[2] Altogether the recommendations serve as a guide for nations, industries and organizations to collaborate and work together to address the SDGs globally, in line with SDG 17 partnerships for the goals.

And while it's clear from the UN's report that more urgent action is needed to meet the SDGs set for 2030, what is also clear is that over the last decade organizations have come a long way on shifting mindsets and advancing efforts to elevate their sustainability performances. More companies are embracing technological innovations to help resolve some of the world's greatest challenges, not least of all climate change. Take the example of NTT Data and the work they are doing around artificial photosynthesis to reduce $CO_2$ from the atmosphere; or the example shared by Magali Anderson about the progress the cement sector is making to reduce its impact, with the likes of the Global Cement and Concrete Association, whose members committed altogether to being net zero by 2050. These represent 80 per cent of the cement made outside China. Each of these are promising examples of the positive impact organizations can make to help drive sustainable transformation globally.

As we look forward, we asked CSOs how they are feeling about the future – and more specifically about the future role that businesses will play on this journey towards creating a more sustainable world.

## Cautious optimism for the way forward

One common theme that arose from our discussions was a feeling of cautious optimism. While every CSO we met with acknowledged there is still a lot of work to be done and that more pressing action and leadership is needed on the part of many corporations and governments, they generally maintained and shared an optimistic outlook for the future. Rather than being discouraged by the lack of progress or slow pace of change globally, they were all encouraged by the opportunities for businesses to innovate and accelerate efforts and to do more.

When asked what keeps them motivated, many responded that it's the wins, big and small, along the way that keep them going. They draw inspiration from the innovative solutions that are born out of collaboration and a desire to genuinely contribute to global sustainable development efforts. Giulia Genuardi underscored the need for collaboration on this journey, stating it is imperative we all need to work together towards the common goals.

'I think that it is a challenging journey for sure, but I am optimistic that we will reach the long-term target we set at Enel for 2040. It's absolutely necessary that in the next years, we accelerate with all our stakeholders together to achieve that goal. So, I think that the most important and telling years will be 2030 and 2035, because these will be the milestone years where we will see – on a global scale – exactly what kind of fossil fuel or energy will be maintained or not maintained; and it will be the moment where we will see if electrification is feasible in terms of infrastructure, but also in terms of cost and in terms of economics. But, yes, in this moment,

I am optimistic. But I also have to be realistic. For this reason, every year I consider and reconsider the different actions that we need to put in place, while always bearing in mind the target that we have set. Most likely we will change the actions that we take along the way – but our target for the future will remain. What is also important to keep in mind is that we need to be open to change. Change is an essential part of this journey.'

As Giulia aptly points out, change is an essential part of this journey. As the UN's latest Sustainable Development Report shows, unfortunately change is not happening fast enough. And when we think about the challenges alongside the urgent response that is needed – no doubt there is reason to be concerned.

When asked about his thoughts on the future, Sam Israelit, Chief Sustainability Officer and Partner at Bain & Company, who is generally an optimist by nature, expressed concern about the slow pace of progress towards the Sustainable Development Goals (SDGs) set for this decade.

'I wouldn't necessarily say I'm optimistic. I am actually a little worried. For sure there are a set of companies that are leading the way. You can see and read about companies that are really investing their resources to have an impact and they're taking this very seriously. I think this is primarily because the leading companies are viewing their sustainability efforts not just as a risk or a cost of doing business to them, it's actually an opportunity. They're seeing opportunities for new products and services, and they are seeing how incorporating sustainability is actually driving new business and growth. And those are the companies that I think are really leading and pushing their industries to have an impact. And then there are a lot of companies that are still wrestling and trying to understand what this means to them. And they haven't invested in the education to understand what it means to set a target and what they need to do to actually achieve it.

'I think part of the challenge is the bodies that create standards, such as SBTi or GHG accounting protocols, are pushing companies to do the right thing. Yet, as companies become more sophisticated, we're learning quickly those organizations are not able to keep up with the pace of change. If you look at the Greenhouse Gas accounting standards, for instance, it has been years since it's been updated. And there are a lot of questions coming from companies who are trying to measure and reduce their footprint accurately that can't be answered because the standards bodies didn't anticipate some of the challenges that would be faced when the standards were widely adopted.'

Sam points to the GHG accounting standards as an example of a framework that has not kept pace with the needs of corporate users. As a result, there are many questions from organizations that go unanswered for the simple reason that the standards have not been updated to take into consideration evolving issues and impacts. Working from home is one example Sam pointed to that shows just how much the world has evolved, yet measuring the nuances of the impacts of this trend is not part of current standards. For example, understanding how companies should account for electricity consumed when working from home is an area that is not consistent with current capabilities. The same can be said for other impact areas, such as measuring the impact of waste and recycling practices while working from home. Going back to the topic of energy, one of the things Sam is proud of in relation to Bain's progress is that the company has been operating on 100 per cent renewable energy for a few years now. In line with the company's efforts to reduce its impact, a key initiative Sam was keen to implement was the purchasing of renewable energy credits to offset the electricity Bain's employees use when working from home. Yet, when Sam discussed this initiative with the company's auditors, they advised that he could certainly purchase the credits, but they wouldn't count towards his carbon footprint. Sam was surprised to learn this, considering the standards did allow for individual solar purchases to be counted as a reduction in the company's footprint. This was just one example Sam pointed to that illustrates how the current standards are not keeping up to the latest innovations and solutions companies could employ as they strive to reduce their impact.

Another cause for concern that came to light and that is contributing to the lack of progress being made by many organizations is the recession that started in 2023. As Sam pointed out, the recession began right around the same time as more companies were starting to come forward with not only their commitments, but also putting resources and investments behind those commitments. As financial pressures grew, however, many of those organizations put their plans on pause. In turn, rather than accelerating efforts, which is what the world needs, in many cases efforts are slowing down or have come to a halt. Getting those companies back on board will take time – and arguably time is the one resource that collectively the world cannot afford to waste.

Speaking of time – time is perhaps one of the biggest challenges the world faces on this journey of sustainable transformation. The time it will take to drive systemic transformation across hard to abate industries, such as airlines, concrete manufacturing and agriculture, to name a few, is considerable. As Sam puts it, transforming these industries will take time to implement and – considering the slow pace at which governments and industries are moving – Sam questions whether we are going to be able to achieve the goals that have been set within the time frame that is needed.

All of the challenges Sam has raised are indeed valid reasons for concern. Demand for improved and more streamlined standards for measuring, calculating and reporting sustainability performance metrics, not least of all metrics that calculate a company's carbon footprint, has been growing for some time. This is becoming increasingly important amid the tightening regulations that require organizations to transparently track and disclose their impact in various regions. Add to this the increase in financial pressures organizations are facing, keeping sustainability at the top of the corporate agenda will continue to be a challenge for CSOs and executive teams in the coming years. Finally, as Sam points out, helping the hard to abate sectors to transform at a pace needed to meet the global challenges is nothing short of a herculean task. Amid the uncertainty, one thing is clear: herculean challenges need to be met with a herculean response. To meet these global challenges, the world needs bold and unwavering leadership, global collaboration, a pooling together of resources, a commitment to innovation and creativity, and the harnessing of human ingenuity. No doubt the road ahead will be bumpy but – with the right focus, determination and collaboration – it is not impossible to achieve our goals and reach and create a more sustainable future.

When we asked Klaus Kunz how he was feeling about the future and the role that corporations play to drive sustainable transformation, his response was both pragmatic and personal, stating he has no choice but to be optimistic about what the future holds for the next generation.

'I have three kids and a grandchild. I must be optimistic. The last five years for me have been a mixture of optimism, but also frustration, of course. Because on the one hand I see awareness that is increasing. You can even see that in the US there is such a heated and critical debate around ESG, for example – and I would say this is just a sign that this topic has become serious now, while before it wasn't even considered to be serious enough to have a critical conversation. So, I think we are on the right track – but we are not fast enough. We need to move faster.'

Not going fast enough was a sentiment shared by Sean Jones, Chief Sustainability Officer at Microsoft Germany. Reflecting on his experience at COP 28, the UN Climate Change Conference which took place in Dubai in late 2023, Sean came away from the meeting feeling cautiously optimistic. He was optimistic about the growing awareness of sustainability among corporations, with more companies attending the summit than ever before.

At the same time, he recognized the need for the private sector and govern-ments to collectively intensify their efforts to accelerate global progress, particularly to achieve a net-zero future.

'Yes, I'm feeling positive. I'm generally an optimistic person. On the one hand, though, I recognize we are not going fast enough to meet the objec-tives we have set ourselves for 2030 and 2050. On the other hand, I think there is a large and growing awareness. At COP in Dubai, we had more companies attend than ever before. And that was a statement. It is no longer just governments saying this is where we need to be, it is companies that were there and saying this as well. As Microsoft, we had a big presence there and we had a lot of very fruitful meetings that we are following up with and continuing. I understand some of the criticism from some companies that say, "you can't let an oil-rich country decide on these things in the future." I think that is absolutely wrong. I think that these are exactly the countries to convince. Europe is already working on the way forward. Whether Germany does nuclear or not is small by comparison, so I don't get too worried about that because I know we are all motivated. But getting these countries agree-ing to these things is significant, and pushing that message and being present is crucial. Now, of course, I'm highly dissatisfied because it is true that major oil companies need to do much more. And if you consider the IMF report that indicates 700 billion in renewable investments, but 7 trillion in fossil fuels investments – those are not the numbers we want. Those need to change. But I think the best way to change that is to go to places like Dubai and have those discussions. So, the mere fact that we were present in Dubai, I thought was significant.'

As Sean pointed out, the strong presence of corporations in Dubai showcased that businesses are starting to take sustainability seriously, and in many cases are taking the lead and pushing for more industry-wide regu-lation aimed at accelerating the global sustainable development agenda. Reflecting on the progress being made towards the global targets that have been set, Sean Jones concedes the world is not on track to meet those goals. He remains optimistic, however, about the potential for the world to get back on track, noting that in the corporate world missing targets along the way is not unusual. What is important, though, is that targets are set – even if aspirational – so that all stakeholders are clear on the long-term direction, vision and focus of the organization. And when problems arise, everyone can work together to address the challenges and keep moving forward – one collective step at a time.

Elisa Moscolin shares the viewpoint that we have no choice but to be optimistic on this journey. She believes to achieve a net-zero future, adopting a play to win attitude similar to that of an Olympic athlete going for the gold is exactly the approach that needs to be taken to achieve the targets that have been set for the coming years.

'I don't think we have an option but to be optimistic. This is a defining moment of human history. We have no choice but to give it our best despite the many challenges along the way. We want to get to net zero, but the methodologies to calculate emissions and deliver on net zero are still being developed. We need to be cognizant of the challenges, but we do need to play to win. If I can use a sports analogy, when you hear athletes talking about the Olympics, I never hear an athlete say, "I train for bronze" or "I train but it's hard, so I am never going to win". They all train for the gold. And that is what I tell my team and my company. I know it's hard, but we have to play to win. We need to go for the gold here because humanity is at stake. If that's not enough of a motivation, then I'm not sure what is.'

While it is easy to get discouraged by the daunting news and headlines quoting the latest scientific evidence or trajectory of climate change, or the lack of progress on many of the SDGs, for Jeffrey Whitford what keeps him going is the opportunities and possibilities that lie ahead. Focusing on what is possible, rather than on the bumps on the road, is a powerful source for motivation.

'It is true that if you read the things coming out of COP, you can get depressed easily – but I am an optimist. I'm always going to look at what the possibility is in front of us, and I may not be fully digesting the importance of some of these things. I understand it, but I think we also have to be realistic. Did we really think going into this work that we were going to have countries whose economic futures are related to the production of non-renewable resources say, all of a sudden, "We don't need those revenues, let's stop"? Probably not. But when you think about the opportunity sustainability brings to business – it is 100 per cent happening. I see it happening every day within our organization – there has been a significant cultural shift where not that long ago people used to laugh at me, saying that ideal will never materialize. And that has changed. I ran into somebody at the airport recently, and they said to me, "you know when you were talking about that greener solvent, and we thought that was never going to happen, guess what – it is happening." So, things are evolving. Sustainability has become central to our new approach to business across the organization. It reinforces our need to be resilient and not be discouraged. When faced with challenges, I choose to focus on the opportunities and look at what we could do differently – and that comes with persistence. As we look to the future, we need people who are resilient and who are actively advocating to get things done.

But we also have to recognize they may not be the people who are going to deliver the action. They could advocate for massive change, but then there are those who are working in the middle and trying to figure out how you operationalize and action the change.

'And that's where I find myself – with my sleeves rolled up, trying to figure out how do we make these things happen? Every day I think about how can that be done differently? And how can I change my own buying behaviours? Because it is a combination of all the things – it's not going to be just one answer. And when there are setbacks along the way, we have to keep pushing to bring about meaningful change. The one thing we've learnt on this journey is that science continues to evolve, and we get new data. As new information and data becomes available, it is important to keep in mind that the solution could be right around the corner – and we just don't know it yet. But if we don't keep trying, we're not going to find out.'

By focusing on the impact rather than the challenges, Jeffrey remains motivated to keep going and not get distracted or dragged down by the depressing headlines that tend to circulate day-to-day. It is sound advice for anyone keen to pursue a career in this field.

As Michelle Davies, Head of Global Sustainability at EY Law, contemplates the future role of corporate sustainability, she also believes it is imperative that organizations focus on the opportunities that lie ahead. Reflecting on the takeaways from her experience at COP 28, despite the criticism directed at oil- and gas-producing nations, she left the event feeling encouraged about the direction of travel on the part of governments' and organizations' efforts to advance the global SDGs. Whether governments and organizations are moving fast enough remains a concern, but the fact that conversations are happening, at least, shows promise.

'Coming out of COP 28, I suppose the statements around oil and gas weren't quite what everybody was hoping for, but I personally believe the statements that were made were hugely significant. I am very grateful for that because I believe it sets the direction of travel. I appreciate it's not what it could have been, but it sets the direction of travel. And I think if you are in an oil- and/or gas-producing nation, or you are an organization that is heavily involved in oil and gas – I don't think you can come to any conclusion other than knowing the demand for your product is going to dramatically change within a period of time. Now, what that period of time is, we don't know, but we do know it is not something that can just go on and on. So, in 10 years' time, I think they know it is going to be dramatically different, and they are gearing up for that transition.

'The other thing that came out of the summit this time, that stood out to me, was there seemed to be a much greater emphasis on financial institutions and how the energy transition in particular is going to be financed with financial institutions. I think they are waking up to the fact that sustainability offers real opportunities for them to monetize. I believe there is far more innovation around that, and I think that GCMU is a really good example of how financial institutions could come together to create something that is innovative and that can really drive the transition forward by creating a financial instrument that can be traded, and also be used to finance transition projects. The third observation was that there was a lot of business being done at COP around sustainability. And somebody made the comment that this COP was as much a business meeting as it was a meeting around policy. That could be taken as a negative thing, but I don't see it as negative at all. I see it as hugely positive. You've got organizations, real economy clients, financial institutions, governments, all coming together to find ways in which they can make this happen. And if they can make it happen on the sidelines, by actually agreeing to deals, I personally think that's a fantastic thing. And while we absolutely need policy, governments can't do this alone, they need the private sector to fully engage.'

As Michelle pointed out, three key themes emerged from COP 28 that are setting the direction of travel for nations and organizations working towards the SDGs. Firstly, there is a need for greater innovation from financial institutions to invest in (and gain profits from) sustainability. Secondly, the oil and gas statement should not be viewed as being entirely negative. Thirdly, the elevated presence of businesses at these global summits is a sign of the important role that businesses can play to collaborate and advance global sustainable development efforts, globally.

Magali Anderson, Chief Sustainability and Innovation Officer, shares the view that for the world to achieve its goals, we need to be optimistic about the future. She also concedes, however, that there is cause for concern, stressing the world is not going fast enough to meet the goals.

'I have to be optimistic. But I am also worried. Are we going fast enough? Definitely not. We see what happened coming out of COP 28, and how after seeing great growth more companies are starting to backtrack their targets and are greenhushing. So yes, all of these things are worrisome. But then I look and see what's happening in nature – and it is quite encouraging. We are finding a way to measure nature, and more and more companies are making commitments in this area. For example, we saw coming out of COP 15 in Montreal (the global summit that centres around nature) that companies will now have to disclose their impact on nature. And so, when I think about the future, I have really mixed feelings. I have mixed feelings because I think the world is taking the topic more and more seriously. Legislation is moving the right way – but I just don't think it's fast enough. And I think some key players are not playing the game. And I'm not sure we can do it without them. We need everyone in the game to achieve our goals.'

## The road ahead is bumpy

Mixed feelings perfectly describe the sentiments we have heard about the future. While there is a general feeling of optimism about the future, in the context of corporate sustainability, there is a justifiable feeling of uneasiness and apprehension at the same time. The CSOs we spoke with all shared the common view that sustainability leaders need to walk the fine balance of focusing on the opportunities that lie ahead, while continuing to advocate for massive transformation at every step of the way. No doubt the road ahead is bumpy, and the speed in which the world is moving is slow but – as Michelle Davies wisely pointed out – given the significance of the progress we are seeing, we can be confident that the direction of travel is right.

---

KEY TAKEAWAYS

- **Embrace the journey**: Becoming a Chief Sustainability Officer is not about following a set path but about carving your own way. Pursue your passions, integrate sustainability into your current role, and seize every opportunity to make a difference. Your unique journey will shape your impact.

- **Harness the power of collaboration**: Building a sustainable future requires strong networks and collaborative efforts. Engage with colleagues, industry peers and external stakeholders. Together, we can innovate and drive transformative change.

- **Lead with optimism and courage**: Despite the challenges, maintain an optimistic outlook and lead with courage. Bold leadership is essential for driving sustainability initiatives and inspiring others to join the mission.

- **Focus on impact and adaptability**: Aim to make a significant impact in your chosen area of sustainability. Stay adaptable, as the field is constantly evolving. Embrace change and be ready to pivot strategies to achieve long-term goals.

- **Invest in continuous learning**: Sustainability is a dynamic field that requires ongoing education and skill development. Stay informed about emerging trends, technologies and industry-leading practices to remain at the forefront of sustainability leadership.

- **Champion innovation and financial ingenuity**: Leverage innovative technologies and financial levers to advance sustainability goals. Lead the way towards finding creative solutions that drive both environmental and economic benefits.

- **Foster a culture of sustainability**: Embed sustainability into the core values and culture of your organization. Inspire your team and stakeholders to prioritize sustainability in every decision, creating a lasting positive impact.

## Notes

**1** Sachs, J D, Lafortune, G and Fuller, G (2024) Sustainable Development Report 2024: The SDGs and the UN Summit of the Future, Dublin University Press, Dublin, Ireland, https://dashboards.sdgindex.org/chapters/executive-summary (archived at https://perma.cc/QEK4-YS97)

**2** Sachs, J D, Lafortune, G and Fuller, G (2024) Sustainable Development Report 2024: The SDGs and the UN Summit of the Future, Dublin University Press, Dublin, Ireland, https://dashboards.sdgindex.org/chapters/executive-summary (archived at https://perma.cc/QEK4-YS97)

# Conclusion

## *Not all heroes wear capes*

As we draw this exploration of sustainability leadership to a close, it is evident that the role of the Chief Sustainability Officer (CSO) is transformative and essential. What is also evident is that given the courage, resilience and perseverance needed to do this work – not all heroes wear capes. The narratives and insights captured in this book underscore the profound impact of effective sustainability leadership on business, society and the planet.

Throughout the book, we have delved into the varied and sometimes complex responsibilities of CSOs. These leaders are tasked with not only integrating sustainability into the core operations of their organizations but also with driving innovation and fostering a culture of continuous improvement. They navigate the intricate balance between economic growth and sustainability-driven stewardship, proving that profitability and sustainability can coexist and even thrive together.

Several compelling themes and questions emerged from our discussions, such as whether the CSO should report to the CFO or CEO. Or the debate about whether companies should include carbon offsetting as a viable lever in their decarbonization strategy. All of these are valid questions – and just as sustainability is multidimensional and complex, so are the answers to these questions. A key takeaway for us, and possibly for our readers, is that there isn't a one-size-fits-all solution to many of the challenges facing businesses today. Regardless of where companies are positioned on this journey, by committing to assessing, measuring and improving their performance they will undoubtedly be moving in the right direction.

Another key theme that emerged was the necessity of adopting a data-driven approach to sustainability. CSOs employ rigorous data analytics to make informed decisions, manage risks and measure progress. This approach ensures that sustainability initiatives and commitments are not just aspirational but grounded in measurable and actionable goals. By harnessing the power of data, companies can effectively track their impact and adapt as needed to stay on course.

Collaboration has also been highlighted as a critical element of success. The partnerships that CSOs build, both within their organizations and across industries, are instrumental in achieving sustainability goals. Just as the UN's SDG 17 (partnerships for the goals) promotes, these collaborative efforts enable the sharing of best practices, the exchange of knowledge, the pooling of resources and the amplification of impact.

We also learnt about how education and community engagement are vital components of a company's sustainability strategy. Engaging stakeholders, especially employees and communities, is crucial for making a positive impact and nurturing the next generation of sustainability leaders. These initiatives also demonstrate the importance of inclusivity and the far-reaching benefits of empowering diverse voices in the sustainability conversation.

Purpose-driven leadership also emerged as a powerful force in sustainability. The CSOs featured in this book are motivated by a deep sense of purpose that aligns their personal values with their professional goals. This alignment not only fuels their dedication but also inspires those around them, creating a ripple effect that extends beyond their immediate sphere of influence.

Looking ahead, the role of the CSO will undoubtedly continue to evolve. As global challenges become more complex and stakeholder expectations rise, CSOs will need to remain resilient, agile and forward-thinking. The insights and lessons shared in this book will serve as a valuable resource for both current and aspiring sustainability leaders, providing guidance and inspiration as they navigate this dynamic field.

In conclusion, the journey of sustainability leadership has proven both challenging and rewarding. The insights and strategies presented here are a testament to the profound impact that dedicated and purpose-driven CSOs can have on their organizations and beyond. Their work underscores the importance of integrating sustainability into the very fabric of business operations, driving positive change that benefits both society and the planet.

This book aims to be more than just a collection of insights and industry-leading examples; it is a call to action. For those who are already approaching their work with sustainability in mind, it offers a reaffirmation of the importance of their work and new strategies to consider. For those who aspire to lead sustainable transformation in business, it provides a roadmap and inspiration to embark on this vital journey. And for all our readers, it underscores the imperative that sustainability is not peripheral to a modern business strategy – it is central.

In the previous chapter, we shared inspiring words of wisdom for those aspiring to pursue a career in sustainability. As we consider the path forward, and the work that remains to be done, we draw inspiration from another visionary leader, Leonardo da Vinci, who said, 'I have been impressed with the urgency of doing. Knowing is not enough; we must apply. Being willing is not enough; we must do.'

May the insights from these pages inspire and empower you to apply the knowledge gained and contribute to creating a more sustainable world for future generations. As we've learnt through our discussions with those doing this work today, the path can be challenging, but it is also rich with opportunities for growth, innovation and lasting impact. Let us continue this vital work, building a brighter future for generations to come.

As you continue on this journey – embrace the challenges, celebrate the victories, and never lose sight of the profound impact that committed, passionate leadership can have on the world. Together, we can build a future where sustainability is at the heart of every decision – driving progress and prosperity for all.

# PODCAST LINKS

Follow our conversations with each of the sustainability leaders we interviewed for this book and for our *Chief Sustainability Heroes* podcast series, which you can find on Paolo Taticchi's *#InLoveWithBusiness* podcast channel on Spotify and YouTube:

## Episode 1: Michelle Davies, Global Head of Sustainability at EY Law

Spotify: https://open.spotify.com/episode/4KiVkq1fMFULgJrzYjaaEJ?si=d2
b8d159c8db4106

YouTube: https://youtu.be/yxSHJWZnFSo?feature=shared

## Episode 2: Charlotte Wolff-Bye, Chief Sustainability Officer at Petronas

Spotify: https://open.spotify.com/episode/0i7qcsT7O5fzUJmi4kbCm4?si=6
0485265d93e4d7e

YouTube: https://youtu.be/9tcRYoeYoyQ?feature=shared

## Episode 3: Klaus Kunz, Head of Development at PI Industries, and Founder and Managing Director at Ephrin

Spotify: https://open.spotify.com/episode/4MbrcUhW9CdLkaxIwNuYlS?si
=7a6bb7a345854e79

YouTube: https://youtu.be/fMie7F6CQj4?feature=shared

## Episode 4: Jeffrey Whitford, Vice President of Sustainability and Social Business Innovation at Merck Life Science

Spotify: https://open.spotify.com/episode/5ah3OM2s7QFB4ldHlV1pLP?si=
835d242565be49e6

YouTube: https://youtu.be/1ukCsQxcqA0?feature=shared

## Episode 5: Sean Jones, Chief Sustainability Officer at Microsoft Germany

Spotify: https://open.spotify.com/episode/4n6ABEu0FqBhFXEAMA2Unf?si
=ed8f072ec9dc4f4c

YouTube: https://youtu.be/IQng7RjyESE?feature=shared

**Episode 6: Montse Montaner, former Chief Sustainability Officer at Novartis**

Spotify: https://open.spotify.com/episode/4WJZrLe9KrKMk6U1j9aQAw?si
=8867f5b97ddf4287

YouTube: https://youtu.be/CcPcOCrpeDE?feature=shared

**Episode 7: Elisa Moscolin, Executive Vice President of Sustainability and Foundation at Sage**

Spotify: https://open.spotify.com/episode/3W3wLACbCYfK7aSWs9UiVi?si
=0b8cbe40ac404e66

YouTube: https://youtu.be/-E-pauKW-zs?feature=shared

**Episode 8: Peter Bragg, EMEA Sustainability & Government Affairs Director at Canon**

Spotify: https://open.spotify.com/episode/4VXdimuvJRS9THaCsLvNlG?si=
4cba7ddaf5934c95

YouTube: https://youtu.be/SwcRNL2-0Qk?feature=shared

**Episode 9: David Costa, Chief Sustainability Business Officer at NTT DATA Inc Group**

Spotify: https://open.spotify.com/episode/6jvfoPK6HqjbEUOOFP3Ypl?si=7
89f37e589294fe6

YouTube: YouTube: https://youtu.be/GuJUoO-1oGU?feature=shared

**Episode 10: Sam Israelit, Partner and Chief Sustainability Officer at Bain & Company**

Spotify: https://open.spotify.com/episode/5MGkxe2LSSf2qOu2UVEi23?si=
077997db5c90457e

YouTube: https://youtu.be/0QRfY_M8LNY?feature=shared

**Episode 11: Garrett Quinn, Global Chief Sustainability Officer at Smurfit Westrock**

Spotify: https://open.spotify.com/episode/6EaXb1hEigALxA1mBSI98u?si=
7184887bd7704a45

YouTube: https://youtu.be/2NLXzoc7FH8?feature=shared

**Episode 12: Magali Anderson, Board Member, Chief Sustainability and Innovation Officer**

Spotify: https://open.spotify.com/episode/5feeT95wnk7xRxjdVWjOtZ?si=
  PoKMd-vEQaSeOtgYIkWItg

YouTube: https://www.youtube.com/watch?v=nN8a0hHQBxw

**Episode 13: Giulia Genuardi, Managing Director at Enel Foundation, former Head of Sustainability at Enel Group**

Spotify: https://open.spotify.com/episode/61Dv8573eZbZeliKbzwxGX?si=
  Wk89hxWlS0C3rABljnQHfw

YouTube: https://www.youtube.com/watch?v=KkeBIEY1jlY

# INDEX

The index is filed in alphabetical, word-by-word order. Numbers within main headings are filed as spelt out, excepting COP meetings and GHG Scope emissions, which are filed chronologically. Acronyms are filed as presented.

# Looking for another book?

Explore our award-winning
books from global business
experts in Responsible
Business

Scan the code to browse